Rethinking W ntre

Series Editor: Profess

In an age of increased academic specialization where more and more book smaller and smaller topics are becoming the norm, this major new series is designed to provide a forum and stimulus for leading scholars to address big issues in world politics in an accessible but original manner. A key aim is to transcend the intellectual and disciplinary boundaries which have so often served to limit rather than enhance our understanding of the modern world. In the best tradition of engaged scholarship, it aims to provide clear new perspectives to help make sense of a world in flux.

Each book addresses a major issue or event that has had a formative influence on the twentieth-century or the twenty-first-century world which is now emerging. Each makes its own distinctive contribution as well as providing an original but accessible guide to competing lines of interpretation.

Taken as a whole, the series will rethink contemporary international politics in ways that are lively, informed and – above all – provocative.

*Published*

Mark T. Berger and Heloise Weber
**Rethinking the Third World**
Nick Bisley
**Rethinking Globalization**
John Dumbrell
**Rethinking the Vietnam War**
Martin Griffiths
**Rethinking International Relations Theory**
Adrian Guelke
**Rethinking the Rise and Fall of Apartheid**
Ray Kiely
**Rethinking Imperialism**
Richard Stubbs
**Rethinking Asia's Economic Miracle**

*Forthcoming*

David H. Dunn
**Rethinking Transatlanticism**

Peter Shearman
**Rethinking Soviet Communism**
Fredrik Söderbaum
**Rethinking Regionalism**

*In preparation*

**Rethinking Europen Integration**
**Rethinking Global Governance**
**Rethinking the Cold War**
**Rethinking the Emergence of a Global Economy**
**Rethinking the First World War**
**Rethinking the Post-Cold War World Order**
**Rethinking the Rise of Islam**
**Rethinking the Second World War**
**Rethinking the Twentieth Century**
**Rethinking the Twenty Years Crisis: 1919–39**
**Rethinking US Hegemony**

**RETHINKING THE THIRD WORLD**
Series Standing Order
ISBN 978–1–403-99522-3 hardback
ISBN 978–1–403-99523-0 paperback

*(outside North America only)*

You can receive future titles in this series as they are published by a placing a standing order. Please contact your bookseller or, in the case of difficulty, write to us at the address below with your name and address, the title of the series and one of the ISBNs quoted above.

Customer Services Department, Palgrave Macmillan Ltd,
Houndmills, Basingstoke, Hampshire RG21 6XS, England, UK

# Rethinking the Third World

## International Development and World Politics

Mark T. Berger

and

Heloise Weber

First published 2014 by
PALGRAVE MACMILLAN

Palgrave Macmillan in the UK is an imprint of Macmillan Publishers Limited, registered in England, company number 785998, of Houndmills, Basingstoke, Hampshire RG21 6XS.

Palgrave Macmillan in the US is a division of St Martin's Press LLC, 175 Fifth Avenue, New York, NY 10010.

Palgrave Macmillan is the global academic imprint of the above companies and has companies and representatives throughout the world.

Palgrave® and Macmillan® are registered trademarks in the United States, the United Kingdom, Europe and other countries

ISBN 978-1-4039-9588-9 hardback
ISBN 978-1-4039-9589-6 paperback

This book is printed on paper suitable for recycling and made from fully managed and sustained forest sources. Logging, pulping and manufacturing processes are expected to conform to the environmental regulations of the country of origin.

A catalogue record for this book is available from the British Library.

A catalog record for this book is available from the Library of Congress.

Typeset by Cambrian Typesetters, Camberley, Surrey, England, UK

Printed in China

This book is dedicated to
Margery and Theo, for absolutely everything (*Marcos*)

and to Sacha Rudolph and Carra De Fry, 'The Belles'
(*Heloise*)

# Contents

# Acknowledgements

Like all books, this book has its own particular history: a somewhat long history given the distance between when we signed the contract down to when we delivered the manuscript. At the risk of leaving someone out, we would like to acknowledge friends and colleagues who have influenced our work in various ways (large, small, direct or indirect) over the years. On the part of one or the other, or both of the co-authors we would like to say thank you to: Jan Aart Scholte, Marcela Alvarez Perez, Jonathan Adams, John Arquilla, Jennifer Bair, Roger Bell, Mark Beeson, David Blaney, Morten Boas, Doug Borer, Shaun Breslin, Toby Carroll, Claire Cutler, Dia Da Costa, Walter Christman, Bruce Cumings, Matt Davis, Jade DePalacios, Radhika Desai, Jennifer Duncan, Michael Freeman, Jasper Goss, Devleena Ghosh, Stephen Gill, Emma Hutchison, Kanishka Jayasuria, Sebastian Job, Dilwar Khan, Dave Lopez, Kama Maclean, Rianne Mahon, Gordon McCormick, Phil McMichael, Andrew Mitchell, Armando Malof, David Moore, Diana Palaversich, Sherry Pennell, Nuno Pires, Dieter Plehwe, Vijay Prashad, Shahid Qadir, Justin Reese, Tim Shaw, Susanne Soederberg, Diane Stone, Marcus Taylor, Kees van der Pijl, Humberto Ventura, Martin Weber, Marc Williams and Yao Souchou. That said there is no suggestion on our part that this group of people agrees with us, or bears any responsibility for the contents of this book. We also want to particularly thank our publisher, Steven Kennedy, for his energy and encouragement throughout a process that, while not intended, became a veritable 'Long March'. We also thank the series editor, Mick Cox, for his enthusiasm and support from start to finish.

Heloise, meanwhile, would like to acknowledge the support of her family, especially her Mum Zoe, her sister Barathi, her brother-in-law Gaspar, her niece Sacha, and her cousin, Carra, as well as the De Frys. Working with an outstanding cohort of PhD candidates has meant great intellectual companionship and lasting friendships. In particular, she would like to thank Kamil Shah, Samid Suliman, Kazi Rahman, Nikki Reeves, Michael Spann and Leah Aylward for their critical insights and inspiring conversations. Kamil also took the time to read

xii    *Acknowledgements*

and comment on previous drafts of this volume. Heloise also extends her sincere thanks to some very special people who have, in various ways, supported her with their friendship, advice and friendly criticism where and when it was needed: Her heartfelt thanks go out to Caroline Thomas, Julian Saurin, Philip McMichael, Cristina Rojas, Mustapha Kamal Pasha, Sandra Halperin, Richard Higgott, Siba Grovogui, Robbie Shilliam, Ritu Vij and Naeem Inayatullah. Meanwhile, many other close friends have helped in various ways over the past years, among them Uli, Ayuska, Kirana and Bennett, Ai, Rebecca and Jasna. The School of Political Science and International Studies, at the University of Queensland, where the work on this book was done has been and continues to be a fantastic place to work, and she extends her thanks to her colleagues. In particular, she gratefully acknowledges the support of Gillian Whitehouse, Roland Bleiker, Richard Devetak and Tim Dunne. She especially thanks Roland Bleiker and Tim Dunne for their excellent support during her time there: Thanks to Roland for always taking time to read and comment on my work! Thanks to Tim for being generally supportive, and for taking time to offer detailed advice and encouragement when it was most needed. Last but not least, I thank Martin Weber for always being there for me and for believing in me! Thanks also for taking time to read and offer valuable feedback on the semi-final and final drafts of this book.

For Marcos, the Department of Defense Analysis at the Naval Postgraduate School provided the setting for the writing and the completion of the book. The administrative staff and the interdisciplinary collection of colleagues and faculty members are what has made and continues to make the department a great place to work. Marcos also wants to acknowledge the support of his parents Theodore and Margery, who have always been there for him for over 55 years. Marcos's sister, Heather, has been a source of great support, as has his brother Bruce and sister-in-law, Fiona. Meanwhile, his nieces, Brooke and Paige and nephews, Bailey and Carter have provided intermittent doses of youthful enthusiasm that continue to be much appreciated. He also needs to single out his aunt, Beverly Berger, and his uncle, Tom Berger. Finally, Marcos wants to thank Laura for loving him and providing wise counsel: *Te quiero hasta siempre y tu sabes no importa donde yo estoy, tu estas siempre a mi lado.*

MARCOS (MARK T.) BERGER
HELOISE WEBER

# Foreword

For those of us fortunate or unfortunate enough to grow up in those 'interesting times' known as the Cold War, perhaps no single issue seemed to be as important as the fate of those living in what is now rather tamely termed the 'global south'. No doubt suffering as many of us were at the time from our own fair share of post-colonial guilt, and excited as we also seemed to be by the sound of revolutionary gunfire coming from afar, there was little doubting on whose side many of us knew we ought to be standing in the great struggles then unfolding in countries as far apart as Algeria, Angola, Cuba, Mozambique, Nicaragua and Vietnam. Neutrality was not an option in the Cold War. Nor were traditional ideas of much use either – and no new idea was to do as much heavy lifting from the 1950s onwards as the idea that there existed a besieged 'Third World' wedged somewhat uneasily between the first capitalist world and the then second communist world. If nothing else, this notion helped us all make sense of what looked like an immensely complex international order. It also denoted something more than just a mere number. A sense of possibility to be sure, but also a belief that countries on the 'periphery' were united in a progressive project that would not only make them 'modern' but over time would turn the world upside down, and, as a result, make it a more equitable and hence more humane place for the first time in centuries.

But the challenge to old ways of thinking did not end there. Radical theorists in the West from Paul Baran to Andre Gunder Frank also provided critical thinkers and political activists with their very own theory of underdevelopment. This rejected the now near universal view that the only path to prosperity lay in joining the world market and playing by its rules. Instead, it argued for a radical break with the market and the West. Indeed, only by adopting 'socialism' in one form or another could the newly liberated countries defend their national sovereignty; and they would only be able do this – Baran and Frank maintained – by rejecting foreign investment, refusing to become part of the world division of labour, and making the state the key stakeholder in the economy. Any other path, they concluded, would only lead to continued dependence on the more powerful West.

In this challenging and engaging volume the two authors critically address the idea of the 'Third World'. As they reveal it, the idea itself was without question an understandable response to a profoundly unequal world. Still, long before the Cold War had come to an end in the late 1980s, it was clear that  the radical rejection of the West and the western model had not delivered on its promise of modernity and development. But they go on to show something else as well: that modern globalization in its neo-liberal form is no panacea either. Indeed, for all its promise, the economic project espoused through the 1990s and after now faces its own kind of 'crisis'. A new way forward has to be found, therefore, based less on the sovereign nation-state and more, according to Berger and Weber, on regions and what they term a 'regional development-security framework for progress'. In fact, what they propose is no less than a forceful downgrading of the role of the sovereign nation-state and the creation of powerful new regional forms: a new agenda in short for a huge percentage of the world's population who hitherto have experienced the dark and exploitative side of global modernity. Combining shrewd analysis with a vision for a new world order, Berger and Weber have done more than just interpret a very significant part of the world: they have rethought it, and it is to be hoped, as a result their book will help change it as well.

MICHAEL COX
*IDEAS, London School of Economics*

# Introduction: International Development, World Politics and Global Modernity

The idea of the Third World emerged against the backdrop of the end of the Second World War, the dramatic post-1945 spread of moderate anti-colonial nationalism, increasingly radical national liberation movements, the corresponding acceleration of the pace of decolonization and the onset of the Cold War. The characteristics that were increasingly seen to define the Third World changed over time, but the most important was, and continues to be, the way in which the Third World was directly associated with the question – and the problem – of development. The central task of this book is to rethink the implications of the history and political struggles of the Third World particularly as they relate to development. The overall concern is to look critically at the history and political economy of the Third World in relation to international development, world politics and global modernity. We are doing this at a time when it is still widespread and routine to implicitly or explicitly view the nation-states in the erstwhile Third World as being in need of modernity (or more accurately the more desirable aspects of what has become global modernity) and international development in order to catch up to the 'developed' nation-states of Europe, North America and parts of Asia. Such assumptions have had and continue to have the effect of generating a misleading narrative about development as a quasi-natural process, one that is organized nationally and one that can primarily be both equated with and measured in terms of national economic growth.

1

As we show, our task entails a critical examination of the concept and legacies of the Third World, its multiple uses and implications, and its continuing association with 'a condition of underdevelopment', albeit under changing and divergent circumstances. We argue that the reframing of the problem of development is not resolved by replacing the term Third World (or the wider imaginary of Three Worlds distinguished by 'stages of development') by the use of related terms such as 'less developed countries' (LDCs), 'developing countries' or even 'the Global South'. While we look at the history of the Third World by accounting for both nation-state-centred analysis (a practice that is widespread) as well as political struggles oriented towards nations and/or states (expressed, for example, in terms of 'emancipatory nationalism'), a central concern of this book is to elucidate the limitations of continuing to take the nation-state as the primary unit of development. In this sense, the book calls into question the assumed pre-eminence of the universalization of the system of sovereign nation-states after 1945, and its association with the process of global modernization processes in general. Before briefly outlining the chapters that make up the book, this introduction provides some background on those issues that set the scene for the rethinking of the idea of the Third World.

## The Idea of the Third World: Decolonization, the Cold War and Third Worldism

The idea of the Third World increasingly anchored the momentous anti-colonial/nationalist responses to the remaking of the global politico-economic and social order after the Second World War. By the 1950s Third Worldism was widely conceived as a source of political identification in the context of nationalist resistance to colonialism, struggles for decolonization and the onset of the Cold War. For example, anti-colonial struggles that led to decolonization were increasingly and explicitly linked to Third Worldism; both were underpinned by the collective experiences of – as well as resistance against – racism and myriad forms of social and psycho-logical denigration, dispossession and exploitation that had been integral to colonialism. In this regard, most of the anti-colonial nationalist struggles directly and indirectly related to Third Worldism sought (at least in theory), at a minimum, to establish a post-colonial international world order premised upon the recognition of universal individual and collective rights in political and economic as well as social and cultural terms, premised significantly on egalitarian principles. Third Worldism as a political initiative was thus directly related to anti-colonial nationalism, national liberation, decolonization, the universalization of the sovereign nation-state system, the pursuit of international development and non-alignment in the Cold War.

In order to understand how and why the idea of the Third World influenced actual political struggles in ways that reinforced conceptions about 'what it was', 'what it wanted' and 'who it represented' (Murphy 1983: 55–76), it is useful to reflect further on the context (painted in broad strokes above) out of which it derived its meaning. As we will discuss in more detail below, the actual coining of 'the Third World' as a term associated with specific geographical and socio-political locations is often associated with an article written by the French demographer Alfred Sauvy in 1952. In this article, Sauvy used the French concept of *tiers monde* to describe the social, economic and political condition of those nation-states not formally aligned with the capitalist bloc ('First World' centred on the US) or the socialist bloc ('Second World' centred on the USSR) during the Cold War. The Second World, of course, disappeared in the late 1980s and early 1990s with the collapse of the Soviet Union and the more general systemic demise of state socialism. Meanwhile, in the 1950s, the nation-states concerned were primarily the newly independent post-colonial nation-states, but the Third World also implicitly referred to the unfinished struggle for national independence and decolonization worldwide. Sauvy's use of the concept also had normative connotations, in the sense that his scheme assigned politico-economic and social status and aspirations to a growing number of mainly new post-colonial or soon to be post-colonial nation-states in the 1950s and 1960s, and that the relative status thus assigned implied in turn a set of prescriptive assumptions about the changes and transformation each of these societies was to embark upon (Wolf-Phillips 1987:105–15).

Specifically, Sauvy used the term to draw parallels between the Third Estate before the French Revolution and the newly independent post-colonial nation-states. Sauvy was likening the Third World to the marginalization and dispossession that had characterized the Third Estate. But at the same time he was also recognizing the potential power that was increasingly manifested within the Third World. The concept captured the significance of the changes in world politics: the emergence of a 'third force' and what came to be characterized as a coherent political project of Third Worldism. In this context, in addition to the rivalry between capitalism and socialism, which was played out from the late 1940s to the late 1980s in terms of the international politics of the Cold War and competition between the First World and Second World of development, there was a new and distinctively different political force, oriented and shaped by shared experiences of colonial rule. Third Worldism articulated an ostensibly independent identity and political presence, reflected not least in terms of organizations such as the Non-Aligned Movement (NAM) and the growing number of representatives from post-colonial nation-states in the General Assembly of the United Nations (UN). Proponents of Third Worldism expressed their desire to position themselves as a third bloc with a distinctive social, political and economic outlook that sought a collective path between the political and economic alternatives presented by Washington on the one hand and Moscow on the other. Despite the challenges faced by the NAM, not least the notable fact that virtually all members were aligned in some fashion or other with either the First World or the Second World, it was an astute collective political movement in the context of the Cold War, affecting the pursuit of global modernity and international development from the 1950s through to the 1980s.

In this context, some commentators were, in fact, more inclined to see the Third World as associated with the NAM, and not, in the first instance, with the question of (global) modernity and (international) development. For example, as Peter Worsley has noted, 'What the Third World originally was, then, is clear; it was the non-aligned world. It was also a world of poor countries. Their poverty was the outcome of a more fundamental identity: that they had all been colonised. This was my basic sense of what the Third World meant by the 1970s' (Worsley 1979: 102). Only later, argues Worsley, was 'an increasing emphasis' 'placed upon the economic sense of the term "Third World"' (103). This was a direct consequence of the failure of the vast majority of the nation-states of the Third World to achieve the 'development' goals set out between the 1940s and the 1970s (Worsley 1979: 103).

Worsley's stance associates the NAM with a particular geo-political position in the first instance. In contrast, we argue that the NAM, even in taking the geo-political positions it did, emerged out of its central engagement with the question of development, and what it meant for the Third World: this connection emerged in the early years of the Cold War and has continued in many quarters down to the dawn of the twenty-first century, even if sometimes in a contradictory manner (Prashad 2007: 10–15).

Alongside the commitment to modernization and development, the Third World, as an emerging international political force (through cases such as the NAM and the UN) gave significant momentum to collective nationalist efforts to both end colonialism and transform the post-colonial international political order in the Cold War era: in short, it was both a movement and project which meant that the Third World was a voice at the international political level and also a movement aimed at inflecting the direction of social and political change. While their impact may not have led to the fundamental transformations envisaged or, in some cases, anticipated, alliances among representatives of the newly independent post-colonial nation-states, as well as between others (such as some Latin American nation-states) did significantly alter power relations in international politics. For example, through their rising collective representation in the UN (at least in the General Assembly), radical demands were put forward in the late 1970s for a restructuring of the international economic order. The call for a New International Economic Order (NIEO), which will be discussed in more detail in Chapter 3, sought to redress the structural inequalities inherited as the legacies of the post-colonial order of international development (and the division of labour that went with it). They also asserted the right to more substantive sovereign national development pathways, which included the right to define and articulate strategies of 'national development', including the right to nationalize industries and corporations, including foreign-owned corporations (Thomas 1985). The NIEO, which never got off the ground as an institutional framework, is still a good example of the political content of what might be called the mainstream policy orientations of Third Worldism down to the 1980s and beyond.

The NIEO constituted the pinnacle of how Third Worldism as a political project sought to develop and institutionalize the capacities to resolve major contradictions that were the legacy of the colonial era, together with the lasting impact the latter had on the populations of the Third World. Third Worldism as a political project was a powerful force in the aftermath of decolonization and the onset of the Cold War that attempted to radically alter the profound inequalities which were the legacy of colonialism. In particular, it was a project explicitly targeted at the levels of international relations and world politics, aiming to inaugurate a fundamental shift in power-relations associated with the previous era. Vijay Prashad makes this point nicely in the opening passage of *The Darker Nations*:

> The Third World was not a place. It was a project. During the seemingly interminable battles against colonialism, the peoples of Africa, Asia and Latin America dreamed of a new world. They longed for dignity above all else, but also the basic necessities of life (land, peace and freedom). They assembled their grievances and aspirations into various kinds of organizations, where their leadership then formulated a platform of demands ... The 'Third World' comprised these hopes and the institutions produced to carry them forward. (Prashad 2007: xv)

Similarly, others, such as Marc Williams, in an analysis of the ways in which relations between Third World nation-states (or their representatives) have interacted with international economic institutions, have argued that if the Third World is 'anything', it 'is a political and ideological concept' (Williams 1994: 4). While we share the analyses put forward by both Prashad and Williams, our concern is to add a somewhat different perspective. As we have emphasized, central to the ideologies that underwrote the Third World political project (Third Worldism) was the quest for more equitable economic development as well as social and cultural recognition. Yet, the dynamic political project articulated by those representing the Third World (especially in its early days) was a project that arguably could never be completed as envisaged. This is, to a large extent, because international development and the system of sovereign nation-states as they were consolidated between the 1940s and the 1980s ultimately rested on the institutional foundations of the contradictory global political reality that assumed that the modern sovereign nation-state was both the symbol of global modernity and the natural unit by which to pursue modernization, and national (economic) development (for critical examinations of this, see Chatterjee 1993: esp. 202–19; Mitchell 2002: esp. 209–43; Walker 2002; Saurin 1995).

## The Idea of National Development: The Cold War, Third Worldism and International Development

The inability to negotiate this contradiction successfully, as we have seen, meant that with the onset and consolidation of the Cold War by the late 1940s the explicitly political demands of Third World nationalism(s), and Third Worldism more generally, led to a refocussing of struggles about development and independence in more explicitly nationalist terms. Although the project of Third Worldism thus joined in reproducing the institutional framework for 'international development' and the universalized order of sovereign statehood, it still retained a degree of collective transnational solidarity projecting a shared political identity, underpinned by common goals and aspirations. The contradictions of attempts to pursue the national development project without profoundly altering the unequal integration of respective national political economies in the post-colonial world were inherent from the very beginning. On the one hand, struggles for political recognition in the form of independent sovereign nation-states became increasingly associated with the idea of national (economic) development. On the other, there was a growing concern about unequal economic inter-dependence as well as relations of economic dependency between the post-colonial nation-states and the erstwhile colonial states (primarily due to the legacy of the colonial division of labour). However, there was and has continued to be a powerful optimistic view articulated by nationalist leaders assuming that sovereign national political independence could provide the foundation on which the economic problems of the colonial past could be overcome quickly, and a new era of modernity ushered in swiftly and effectively. Third Worldism as a political project aspired to achieve significant aspects of the latter through collective political solidarity. It is in this context that national development and economic nationalism became the dominant terms of reference in relation to international development, world politics and global modernity. The idea of national development enabled the implementation of economic plans that were expected to meet the social, economic and political aspirations of the majority of those people who were living, primarily, in the newly independent nation-states of the Third World.

As already implied in the previous section of this introduction, by the 1970s it had become increasingly clear that (international) development generally failed more than it succeeded to deliver on its early promises. Furthermore, in many instances the developmental gains that were achieved were often reached by inflicting chronic and/or profound levels of displacement and repression on sometimes very large sections of the citizens and residents of the new nation-states. It is important to clarify that our point here is not to discount national development *per se*. There were *some* obvious 'success' stories such as the economically dynamic albeit politically authoritarian post-colonial nation-states of East Asia, such as South Korea, or even the somewhat later economic rise of the People's Republic of China in the late Cold War era, a process that has nevertheless also entailed major social and environmental costs. Nor are we dismissing the obvious historical significance of national liberation in the context of decolonization and the Cold War. Rather, we are concerned that to better understand the limits of international development and the contradictions of global modernity we need to move beyond the national frame of reference, and in turn we also need to move beyond continuing to invest analytically and politically in Third Worldism and the idea of the Third World. Or, to put it another way, it is paramount to problematize the assumption that the sovereign nation-state, embedded in the nation-state system, remains the main unit of development within a worldwide system of sovereign nation-states that both symbolizes and provides the means by which to achieve (global) modernity and (international) development. In so doing, our purpose is to stress that all nation-states are the product of processes of world-historical transformation and our analysis should accordingly adopt a critical historical perspective in relation to the nation-state system as it emerged and was universalized. If history tells us anything about the reasons for the failure of the project of Third Worldism, it is that a growing number of exercises in state-led national development served to naturalize the sovereign nation-state as both the unit and the agent of development (Bose 1997:153). Further, the framing of the Third World (and Third World States) as the referent of development in world politics had the effect of reinforcing state-centred analyses of development, thereby disconnecting development from the broader history of unequal global social relations. The latter, however, were precisely the critical target of the political project of Third Worldism.

   The framing of development in relation to the Third World has played out on at least two levels that are of significance here. On the one hand, the Third World as a broad category became, and to a considerable extent remains, a key territorially circumscribed designation within which the respective units and citizens have been conceived primarily as referents of underdevelopment. Thus, heterogeneity and rich cultural histories have been relegated to a simplistic condition of 'underdeveloped areas' (for a good critique see, for example, Escobar 1995).

On the other hand, the association of development with the Third World was from the start conceived through the categorization of individual nation-states (primarily post-colonial nation-states), based on how they measured up in relation to the main (often economic) indicators of development. All nation-states have been categorized in these terms, with the stage of development of Third World nation-states being determined based on their position in comparison to other, usually deemed 'more advanced' nation-states. Development itself has since been measured primarily by aggregated statistical data, focused on nation-states and representing economic growth and development in terms of changes in the gross national product (GNP), the gross domestic product (GDP), or a host of other 'performance indicators' around health, productivity or policy capacity. The abstractions that underpin state-centred analysis of development are a central concern to our project (for a good critique, see Saurin 1996); many aspects of our analytical approach and the scrutiny of dominant conceptions of development therefore resonate with the methodological concerns of, for instance, critical feminist studies that challenge the validity of 'unit-based' analysis of political relations (for example, Enloe 2000; Bedford 2007; Elias 2008).

The question of development, therefore, was in the past, and still is, firmly grounded in relation to the idea of a Third World in perpetual need of catching up to the developed world. Through the lens of a growing array of nation-state-centred indices of development, the Third World has been identified as underdeveloped or poor in comparison to those states categorized as the developed world. These state-centred indicators conceal both global inequalities shaping and influencing the experienced conditions, and important constitutive relational dynamics expressing and underpinning the contradictory pressures lived out in the contexts where the 'imperatives' of global development have to be processed by local actors. However, the dominant view continues to emphasize that the application of the right economic policies (for instance, the prescriptions of neo-liberalism) will eventually lead to a benevolent version of global modernity, subject only to some 'further adjustments'. In both cases, the nation-state remains in focus as the central unit and agent of development.

Given the renewed (and/or continuing) interest in development and poverty, especially at the level of institutions of global governance, rethinking the Third World is both timely and imperative. In the second decade of the twenty-first century, destitution and inequality, both of which have been integral to global modernity, are increasing worldwide. These contradictions are most starkly evident in the organization and governance of what Mike Davis (2006) has called a *Planet of Slums*, and what Patel (2007) has identified as a crisis of a global food and health, which affects the life prospects of the poor and underprivileged across the world, whether in 'developing' or 'developed' countries. At the same time, contemporary discourses on development, inequality and poverty (as well as security and stability) continue to focus on particular nation-states, which are now identified as 'developing states' or 'underdeveloped states' (not to mention 'failing' or 'failed' states). Once again, the frame of reference is the 'national economy' and/or the 'national polity' of particular nation-states, rather than the global relations through which (international) development is pursued and institutionalized. Equally, the way in which development is conceived and measured continues to be premised upon a 'stages-of-growth' temporal logic, thereby naturalizing the idea of a standardized, orderly and predictable process of 'catch-up' (see, for example, Sachs 2005; Rostow 1960). This occurs in two ways. The first involves the notion, often implicitly if not explicitly expressed, of a development ladder comprising fixed steps to be taken by the nation-states of the Third World relative to the 'developed' high-mass-consumption nation-states of the First World that are seen to be already at the top of the ladder. The second (related to the first) comprises the way in which national units of development placed on this ladder are conceived as discrete, enclosed and internally comprehensive formations that can be compared with one another up and down the ladder. It is beyond the scope of this book to address the detailed *methodological* implications of this framing of the problem of development, but it can be argued that a reorientation of the overall focus in the direction of social relations (and actual experiences) constitutive of development would help to make visible the wide array of sources and sites of social conflict and inequalities within, between and across nation-states. Consequently, to rethink the Third World means calling into question the contemporary relevance of the Third World and related terms, despite recognizing the former's political significance and the promises held out by the project of Third Worldism (see for example Pasha 2013; Prashad 2007; 2012).

The problem associated with viewing the Third World and national development as primarily involving moving up the ladder of development also becomes apparent if we look briefly at the implications of ongoing practices of categorization and classification of the nation-states in the erstwhile Third World. For instance, it is incumbent to ask whether concepts such as 'the developing world', 'low-income countries', 'failing states', 'failed states' or even 'the Global South' are simply instances of insignificant category shifts that continue to reproduce the problems associated with the use of the term the Third World. We argue that the usage and the purposes of deploying such categories matter, and that the practice of categorizing and classifying the erstwhile Third World has considerable national and international political significance. Below, we therefore continuously point out that (and in what ways) categorizing has significant implications for the theory and practices of development, both historically and currently. This is reflected not least in the continued salience, for many observers, of the idea of the Third World, despite the fact that the term has now lost much of the descriptive and prescriptive value that was once associated with it in relation to the pursuit of global modernity.

The limitations of state-centred analysis more generally, and its particular framing of the problem of development in terms of Third World nation-states in particular, is partly a consequence of taking the nation-state as a natural unit of development in the first place. This practice of categorization, which in turn also produces the more specific practice of associating the 'problem of underdevelopment' with the Third World, situates particular (individual) states and/or the Third World generally in a hierarchical order. What this means analytically is that the Third World and its ascribed condition, 'underdevelopment', is separated out from any account of the wider (global) power relations (of the colonial and Cold War era) from which it originated. We thus end up with a fragmented understanding of the erstwhile Third World, turning on the bifurcation of (national) developed versus underdeveloped 'units as positions' (this, of course, makes clear the severe limitations of conventional comparative analysis in relation to the Third World). Most approaches to development do not reflect on this assumption, which we argue has been a crucial limiting factor in a range of attempts to understand the problem of development. Overcoming such an analytical limitation is more pertinent than ever given growing levels of inequality worldwide and the renewed focus on what is identified as the 'fragility' of a growing number of nation-states within the overall system of sovereign nation-states (for a critical account of these practices, see Saurin 1995; Grovogui 2002). Our attempt to rethink the Third World ideologically, politico-economically and historically is thus grounded in a fundamental critical examination of core categorical assumptions, particularly the preoccupation with the sovereign nation-state as the focus of development within a formally established conception of international development.

## Rethinking the Third World: Third Worldism, International Development and Beyond

The Third World, at a general level, has thus been increasingly framed in terms of a collection of nation-states mired in poverty, economic backwardness and powerlessness, even though such framings obscure the fact that the project of Third Worldism itself constituted a powerful form of political self-authorization, which significantly challenged the colonial and the subsequently prevailing post-colonial order. This observation notwithstanding, the framing of the problems of the Third World was prescriptive from the outset in the sense that the development lens through which societies and states were 'measured' articulated with the logics of comparison and the development ladder metaphor. For example, numerous studies of the Third World have, in one way or another employed this framework of comparison to both define and measure the 'stage' of development of (Third World) states on the road to global modernity. The standard of comparison has thus been routinely employed to both describe and prescribe 'development' in terms of a particular, modernization-driven logic (usually the logic of catching up to the developed nation-states), and to a large extent by conceiving of destitution (and poverty) as an 'original condition' (cf. McMichael 2008: 206) rather than as the outcome of uneven development and the contradictory dynamics of global capitalist (and socialist) modernity. Because such analyses have taken the unit of development to be the nation-state in an unproblematic way, implicit or explicit comparisons became firmly established as comprehensive accounts of independent units. This has had the effect of enabling narratives about 'degrees of statehood' (Clapham 1998: 143–57) as well as conceiving of development (or characterizing the nation-state in question) through the metaphor of the 'development ladder' (the full implications of this are often missed even in critical accounts of neoliberal developments; indicatively, Chang 2002).

The vision of development thus engendered (if not the terms of the project itself) was embraced and aspired to by representatives of the 'new' nation-states. The post-1945 development project was thus organized and promoted through a range of targeted policies by international development institutions, such as, for example, the World Bank as well as through a range of UN agencies, such as the United Nations Conference on Trade and Development (UNCTAD). Yet, after over 60 years of pursuing the 'development project' (McMichael 2012:46) there is an emerging recognition of a 'crisis of global poverty' (or, more comprehensively, a crisis of global modernity centred on the contemporary system of sovereign nation-states); debates ensue about the relationship between ecological degradation, social inequalities and development (for example, Shiva 2009); and questions are raised continuously about how to manage the development challenges posed by those seen to belong to the 'reserve army' of global capitalism right across the world (see Standing 2011). With regard to the latter, one response has been to attempt to turn crisis into opportunity by extending micro-loans to poor (unemployed) men and women, on the ostensible premise of fostering self-sustaining micro-entrepreneurship (for a critique of this, see H. Weber 2002; 2004; 2010; see also Soederberg 2014). Micro-loans are advanced (a) to enable financial sector liberalization; (b) to further opportunities for profiteering; and (c) to extend new disciplinary measures in the context of managing the crisis of development in a range of different contexts. They are now part of development strategies for slum dwellers, measures for 'empowering' poor women, provisions for absorbing the under- and unemployed more generally, and the creation of a conducive environment for collecting user fees for public goods and services (whether related to utilities or health care). Accompanying such or similar 'micro-level' initiatives have been more macro-level strategies such as the World Bank's and International Monetary Fund's (IMF) Poverty Reduction Strategy Paper (PRSP) initiatives for low-income countries (H. Weber 2006; Cammack 2002). Such country-level strategies in turn are conceived to articulate with global governance objectives, of which a key example is the facilitation of economic growth through investment and liberalization policies advanced under the World Trade Organization (WTO). The WTO and the Doha Development Round are thus part of a 'global development architecture' constructed and consolidated across the global, regional and national, as well as micro-levels (see Higgott and Weber 2005; H. Weber 2002). Initiatives such as the Millennium Development Goals are part of this push towards the comprehensive neo-liberal governance of development (Amin 2006).

Two aspects deserve some further attention here. First, to reiterate, for a very large number of people worldwide the promise of global modernity and international development have not materialized after more than 60 years of pursuing national development within the dominant international development framework. That is to say, even if we take the orthodox measurement of development, and even if we do it in cases where economic growth rates have increased, this does not necessarily translate into improvements in the day-to-day lived experiences of very large numbers of people across the planet, especially, but far from exclusively, in the erstwhile Third World. On the contrary, inequalities have increased, in some cases dramatically, and new challenges (for instance in health, nutrition and environmental safety) have arisen, which further accentuate the gap between the rich and the poor. Rarely have such growth patterns been sustainable in the medium to long term, whether economically, ecologically or socially, and successes in integrating these concerns have been few.

Second, the framing of the question of development by the official representatives of nation-states and international development agencies still continues to be associated with (or confined to) the capacities of ostensibly sovereign nation-states, even if these nation-states are now formally categorized as low-income countries, middle-income countries, 'emerging markets', 'failing states' or 'failed states', rather than the Third World. *Thus, while the language of representation has changed in some cases, the standard of comparison has not, and neither has the unit of comparison (the sovereign nation-state).* It is worth noting that at both the policy and popular level the term 'Third World' is still widely used primarily to suggest an absence of modernity, when in fact the experienced inequalities and suffering are an integral aspect of the negative or dark side of global modernity itself. This, however, has to be distinguished from the politics of Third Worldism, which projected collective agency,

resistance, and sustained challenges back on to that very constellation.

Thus, the idea of the Third World has had and continues to have
significant resonance for development and inequality. This, however,
inadvertently also had implications for the ways in which references
to the Third World became quickly associated with concerns for
economic development and modernization. In particular, the idea of
the Third World provided a way of thinking about poverty. That is to
say, poverty came to be associated *with,* and reduced *to* a problem that
afflicted the nation-states that made up the Third World, a problem
that would be solved by modernization and development (for a good
critical discussion of this, see Nandy 2002).

As we have outlined above, the conceptual framing of the problem
of poverty as a constitutive feature of the Third World has been
accompanied by a perspective that has foregrounded the nation-state
as the natural unit of development. This has continued to be the case
down to the present. However, at the same time, it needs to be emphasized that the project of Third Worldism served a powerful purpose
during a particular historical moment achieving one form of 'emancipation' (decolonization and sovereign national independence).
However, as we have argued, the political form and economic character of that emancipation rested from the outset on profound contradictions. The argument we advance about rethinking the Third World
with particular emphasis on the developmental limits of the nation-
state and the shortcomings inherent in the comparison of nation-states
to each other is not simply one that aims to establish a technical point
with regard to analytical clarity. Rather, it calls for an alternative
understanding of international development, world politics, and
global modernity, one not premised on 'assumptions (…) that either
state or society (meaning 'national' society) are the points of analytical departure and return' (Saurin 1995: 245).

## Conclusion: International Development, World Politics and Global Modernity

In order to build our critical reconstruction of the Third World, Third
Worldism and the contradictions of development, we proceed in the
following order. Chapter 1 explores the origins of the Third World in
the late colonial era, while Chapter 2 examines in detail the complex

dynamics driving national liberation and decolonization in the early post-colonial and Cold War eras. Chapter 3 looks at what we (and others) have referred to as the 'golden age' of Third Worldism during which the idea of the Third World was in the ascendant against the backdrop of the Cold War and the increasingly obvious limits of international development centred on the system of sovereign nation-states that had been universalized by the 1970s. Chapter 4 charts the relative retreat of Third Worldism and the crisis of international development that became increasingly apparent with the rise of uneven globalization and the end of the Cold War. Chapter 5 looks at the revival of the theory and practice of nation-building in the erstwhile Third World in the post-Cold War era, particularly in the wake of the tightening of the link between development and security after 9/11. The link between development and security in the Third World had clearly been important if not explicit during the Cold War, but had, at least briefly, been given less emphasis in the 1990s. The renewed emphasis on development and security is reflected in Chapter 6, which attempts to sketch a possible path for a revised global modernization project centred on the idea of a regional development-security framework for progress; we argue that the outlines of this are implicit (and sometimes explicit) in some parts of the world, and could potentially offer a serious attempt to resolve some of the contradictions that beset the idea of the Third World in an era of global modernity. The regional development-security framework is represented here as an incipient, open-ended and potentially systemic alternative to the contradictions of international development and the crisis of global modernity centred on the contemporary system of sovereign nation-states. The Conclusion acknowledges the growing depth and breadth of the development debate, while emphasizing that it is time to move beyond the Third World as a collection of nation-states in need of development. We briefly look at some recent efforts to recast Third Worldism in relation to what some observers and proponents have called the Beijing Consensus. We also discuss recent Third Worldist efforts by leaders not only from China but from India and Brazil, not to mention other efforts by nation-states from Venezuela to Iran, and even Russia, to excavate and redirect an earlier Third Worldism in ways that have garnered support in some quarters, but do not stand up to critical scrutiny as serious efforts to expand and deepen the contemporary pursuit of progress. The Conclusion also briefly restates the rise and relative decline of the idea of the Third World and of Third

Worldism, along with the contradictions and crisis of international development and their implications for world politics. Finally, the Conclusion reiterates the new or revised approach outlined in Chapter 6: an open-ended regional development-security framework for progress that would see political authority dispersed to democratically accountable regional institutional arrangements (something that has occurred in an ad hoc fashion in a wide range of benevolent and malevolent forms). This agenda for reconfiguring global modernity moves beyond the nation-state and the Third World, particularly on the question of political authority. Finally, it is important to emphasize that even as our rethinking draws repeated attention to the shortcomings of the idea of the Third World, Third Worldism was premised on the realization that global modernity and development could not be pursued by individual sovereign nation-states despite the predominant focus on national development. It had to be done in some sort of collective fashion, even as the proponents of Third Worldism continued to embrace and routinize the sovereign nation-state as the key unit through which to organize the collective pursuit of international development. Until the idea of the Third World as a collection of nation-states that lack development and modernity is more thoroughly rethought, the limits of international development will continue to frame contemporary world politics, to the detriment of any effort to realize a more genuinely inclusive form of global relations of development.

# 1

# Global Modernity and International Development: The Origins of the Third World

In the Introduction we emphasized that the consolidation of the idea of the Third World after the Second World War was directly connected to both decolonization and the universalization of the nation-state system between the 1940s and the 1970s. It was also made clear that the immediate origins of the Third World are not only to be found in the social and political struggles surrounding decolonization and national liberation. The onset of the Cold War, in the context of which the US and its allies/clients were positioned as the First World and the Soviet Union and its allies/clients as the Second World was also of crucial significance. As we have seen, the Third World emerged during the Cold War as part of an effort by primarily new post-colonial nation-states to find a path to modernity between the First and Second Worlds. It was in this context that nation-states (often the new post-colonial nation-states) became the main objects of an elaborate set of overlapping international institutions, whilst at the same time they sought to re-shape the unequally structured conditions through which their respective national development projects were to be pursued.

Meanwhile, in order to thoroughly understand the political and ideological aspirations, the diverse and shared characteristics, as well as the territorial designation of what became the Third World it is crucial that we look in detail at the historical background. To this end, this chapter looks briefly at the overall history of the dominant idea of progress and modernity that preceded and then coincided with the rise of the Third World. We then turn more specifically to the history of imperialism and colonial expansion and the emergence of the idea of the 'civilizing mission' in the late nineteenth and early twentieth centuries. This is followed by an examination of the critical challenges to colonialism in the 1930s and 1940s, which, against the backdrop of the Second World War and the subsequent onset of decolonization and the Cold War, provided the crucible for the emergence of the Third World and the systemization and universalization of the idea and practice of national development within a wider framework of international development. This leads to a discussion of the way in which the nation-state was increasingly constituted and universalized as the naturalized unit of modern national and international development marked by 'sovereignty', at the same time as the idea of the Third World rose to prominence. Between the 1940s and the 1970s there was a broad consensus that the nation-state was, could, or should be the primary vehicle for achieving modernization even as there was considerable debate about the actual content of national development, or, for that matter, 'modernity' (Cooper 2005: esp. 59–152). At the same time, there was considerable disagreement about the dominant explanations of underdevelopment of the Third World. From the perspective of the Third World, explanations of development and underdevelopment needed to account for unequal structural conditions constituted during colonialism but 'naturalized' at the point of decolonization. To this end, in this chapter we also foreshadow the limitations of the overwhelming focus on the question of development as a question of and for the Third World, refracted through the political architecture of sovereign nation-states.

## 'The Idea of Progress': From the Enlightenment to the Civilizing Mission

Given the centrality of conceptions of progress and modernity to the Third World it is, as already emphasized, essential that we begin any rethinking of the latter with at least a brief examination of the history of the idea and practice of progress and modernity prior to 1945. In the context of their diverse and long-standing usage, a partial sense of how terms such as 'progress' and 'modernity' have been used historically is required, given that they became essential to the uses and appropriations of the idea of the Third World.

For some observers, progress is an historical constant that preceded the onset of the modern era and has remained more or less unchanged down to the present. This kind of approach is apparent in Robert Nisbet's *History of the Idea of Progress,* which charted what he regarded as the profound continuity of the idea of progress over thousands of years. Nisbet argued that from the time of the ancient Greeks to the present two distinct but connected trends were evident. First, there has been a 'slow, gradual, and cumulative improvement' in scientific knowledge and artistic endeavour. Second, he discerns an important 'strand of thought' over this entire period that has been preoccupied with 'man's moral or spiritual condition on earth, his happiness, his freedom from torments of nature and society, and above all his serenity or tranquillity'. This tradition of thinking is, for Nisbet, evidence of the continuity in the pursuit of the 'goal of progress' (Nisbet 1980: x, 4–5, 9, 317–18). Ultimately, Nisbet constructs a genealogy of progress that separates the idea of progress from the historical shifts and profound changes of the past two millennia generally, and from the details of ongoing social struggles, revolutionary processes, and practices of dispossession, colonial expansion, imperial conflict and dramatic economic transformation associated with modern history more specifically.

Much more common than Nisbet's approach (which is a reiteration of the common-sense 'Western' view of the idea of progress as beginning with the Greeks) is the tendency to trace the origins of the contemporary notion of progress and development (and the two terms continue to be used interchangeably) to the Enlightenment in Western Europe in the seventeenth and eighteenth centuries. This kind of approach is apparent, for example, in J. B. Bury's influential study of the idea of progress. Bury traced the roots of the modern conception of progress (which, in his view, was grounded in a notion of human history as a slow but continuous advance) to the end of the Renaissance, particularly the first two or three decades of the seventeenth century. More broadly he connected the emergence of the idea of progress in Western Europe to the emergence of modern science, the rise of rationalism and the growing demands for religious and political freedoms that characterized the Enlightenment (Bury 1955: 5, 9, 29, 35–6, 348). This kind of approach to the emergence of the idea of progress is consistent with a number of standard textbook histories of 'Western Civilization' (Hollister *et al.* 2000: 660). However, this narrative is clearly grounded in a linear approach to history that uncritically celebrates the rise of the West.

A more historically nuanced approach to both the relationship between the idea of progress and the scientific advances of the Enlightenment can be found in Peter Gay's classic two-volume study of the Enlightenment. Gay emphasizes that the major figures of the Enlightenment saw progress as dependent on the adoption of 'a program of action – their program' and they viewed progress 'even at its best, as a highly ambiguous blessing'. For the *philosophes* of the Enlightenment, 'everything could be abused, even science'. At the same time, they were supremely confident that science was the key to progress and 'if there was any real hope for man, it was science that would realize it' (Gay 1970: 99–100, 101, 105, 124; Gay 1967).

Jürgen Habermas also stresses the nuances that characterized the history of the Enlightenment, although he does this somewhat differently than Gay. Habermas argues that the Enlightenment produced a conception of progress and global modernity grounded in a sharp distinction between the present and the traditions of the past. In the eighteenth century the philosophers of the Enlightenment embarked on what Habermas calls 'the project of modernity', which rested on 'extravagant expectations' about the ability of the 'arts and sciences' to control nature and promote the 'understanding of the world of the self, moral progress, the justice of institutions and even the happiness of human beings'. The twentieth century 'has shattered this optimism', but according to Habermas, 'instead of giving up modernity and its project as a lost cause, we should learn from the mistakes of those extravagant programs which have tried to negate modernity'. Writing shortly before the end of the Cold War, Habermas concluded that the revitalization of the project of global modernity could only occur if 'societal modernization' is 'steered in a different direction' (Habermas 1985: 3–4, 8–10, 12, 13–14; Harvey 1989: 12–14).

From this angle, however, the Enlightenment is still viewed as the taproot of global modernity. Furthermore, Habermas and others promote a narrow conception of the Enlightenment which fails to capture the complex character of the linkages between the rise and transformation of capitalism, colonialism and imperialism on the one hand and the unfinished, and arguably unfinishable, project of global modernity on the other hand. The concrete practices that characterize modern national and international development, according to which the nation-states of the Third World were to pursue modernization, have not been considered in the requisite critical depth by these approaches.

A more persuasive account of the making of global modernity and the rise of the idea of progress needs to place as much emphasis on the material changes as on the intellectual shifts, and draw more attention to the social crises, colonial and imperial expansion and revolutionary politics which were central to modern world history (P. Anderson 1998: 37, 39, 44, 81; P. Anderson 1984: 25–55; Therborn 2000:148; Therborn 1995; Seth 2013; Grovogui 1996; Chakrabarty 2000; Shilliam 2008). From one angle it can be argued that the rise of modernity in Europe flowed from the onset of the crisis of authority by the early modern era (post-1500) in the context of the interplay between revolution and reaction (counter-revolution) and the modern state emerged as a means to mediate and/or transcend rival social forces in an effort to resolve the crisis of modernity (Hardt and Negri 2001: 70, 74–78). At the same time, however, colonialism was deeply implicated in state formation (including in the West), beginning with the Irish occupation and continuing to 'high imperialism' via the conquest of the Americas. During the twentieth century, these trajectories build up to a significant shift: whereas prior to 1945 states (virtually all of which were absolutist, monarchical, dynastic and/or imperial) were generally consolidated as a result of ongoing inter-state warfare or colonial expansion, this was no longer possible subsequently.

The centralized-absolutist monarchical states that came into being in Western Europe in the early modern era transcended and mediated rival social forces, providing a partial solution to the social and political crises connected to the rise of capitalism (Ertman 1997). As suggested, the imperatives of inter-state warfare also led to the amplification and centralization of early modern states. More broadly, the growing number of colonies and protectorates (that would much later become the nation-states of the Third World) emerged as an important, but not pre-ordained, part of the rise of capitalism and the imperialism and colonial expansion that followed. Over the course of the shift from monarchical or dynastic sovereignty, to territorial and imperial sovereignty and then to national sovereignty the character of the state changed, but sovereignty remained grounded in the state (Walker 1993; Hall 1999: 6).

Between 1415 and the 1770s European conquerors, traders, missionaries and settlers expanded overseas, aided by the growing political, naval and military power of the rising states of Europe. This period encompassed major territorial as well as commercial expansion in the Americas, but prior to the nineteenth century most of Asia and Africa were much less directly affected by the changes that were remaking the Americas. With the industrial revolution, facilitated in part by commercial and colonial expansion, the triangular trade and the labour of those enslaved (see, for instance, Mintz 1986; Shilliam 2008), the character of states in Europe changed dramatically, accelerating the pace and extent of subsequent European expansion (Inikori 2002: 89–155). During the late eighteenth century, and over the course of the nineteenth century, many of the modern states in Western Europe emerged, or were consolidated, as industrializing national-imperial states acquiring both the impetus and the capability to embark on a process of worldwide economic integration (Abernethy 2002: pp. 45–63, 81–103).

By the end of this period, Germany and France (as well as the United States and Japan) began to successfully challenge Britain's earlier primacy. After 1870 these increasingly powerful industrialized and imperial states sought to expand markets and access to raw materials through the annexation of territory. The so-called 'New Imperialism' involved an unprecedented scramble for empire in Africa, Asia and the Pacific between 1870 and 1914. During this period about one-quarter of the surface of the globe was expropriated and 'redistributed' as colonies by half a dozen imperial powers amongst themselves. Britain increased its colonial holdings by some 4 million square miles, France by 3.5 million square miles, while Germany acquired a little more than 1 million square miles, and Belgium and Italy took over just under 1 million each. The US acquired some 100,000 square miles, mainly from Spain, while Japan acquired something like the same amount from China, Russia and Korea. Portugal expanded its colonies by about 300,000 square miles. Of the major colonial empires, the Dutch were the only ones who failed to, or refused to acquire new territory, although they did consolidate control over those parts of the Netherlands East Indies that they had long controlled in a more indirect way (Hobsbawm 1994: 61–2).This immense geographical, territorial and cultural expropriation by the colonizers must be understood in terms of the full range of relations and experiences it engendered; it brought with it human suffering – at times to the point of genocide – social conflict, ecological transformation, and ultimately political deprivation. At the same time, as Said (1995) reminds us, the vast territorial expansion of European colonialism coincided with the consolidation of orientalist discourses according to which rule and coercive force were justified. The experiences of colonialism are crucial to the formation of the Third World, and without appreciating this point, the political project of Third Worldism cannot be wholly understood (see, for example, Seth 2013).

The 'New Imperialism', having been predated by trusteeship and the governance imaginary of the civilizing mission, reached its apogee on the eve of the First World War. However, within two decades of the end of the 1914–18 conflagration the failure of Imperial Germany to attain a 'place in the sun' was revisited with even more ferocity as a new global battle for empire raged from the end of the 1930s until 1945. Hitler's particularly violent, racist and genocidal effort to create a German colonial empire in Europe in the late 1930s and early 1940s obviously resonated to some degree with earlier attempts, by the Habsburgs (1519–1659) and Revolutionary France (1792–1815), to dominate Europe. However, it was probably more grounded in previous European colonial activities in Asia, Africa and the Americas (Mazower 1998: 184; Kennedy 1989: 39–93, 149–80). The rise of Hitler's colonial project in Europe was connected to the wider crisis of colonialism that afflicted the established European colonial powers as a result of economic depression, rising anti-colonial nationalist movements and the dramatic encroachment in Asia of an expanding Japanese empire (Darby 1987: 106–17, 132–40). This was the wider backdrop for the cataclysm of the Second World War and the effective passing in decades of empires that had, in some cases, been built up over centuries.

While varying conceptions of racially grounded ideas of progress had inflected the civilizing missions (Doty 1996) that emerged to complement the New Imperialism, one strand of the immediate origins of the idea and practice of international development that rose to prominence after 1945 (and was directly connected to the emergent Third World) is to be found in the crisis of colonialism that coincided with the Great Depression and the political and social upheaval of the 1930s that was eventually subsumed into the Second World War. In the late colonial era (from the 1930s to the 1960s), development (or colonial development) was increasingly used to describe a series of policy interventions and financial initiatives, with the declared aim of improving the standard of living in the colonies. The British government in 1940, and the French government in 1946, set out to use this new conception of development to revitalize colonial rule at the very moment when it was under siege from nationalists and trade unionists in a growing world context of anti-colonialism. However, the intrusive character of the new-found developmentalism resulted in increased conflict and anti-colonial activism, as nationalists and trade union leaders in Africa (and Asia) appropriated the language of state-guided national, rather than colonial development, escalating their demands for wages, social services and improved living standards as well as political power and national independence (Cooper and Packard 1997: 7). At the same time, the concept of development that emerged in the late colonial era also provided a way for the colonial powers to retain many of their links to their former colonies and to play a role in managing the direction of the new sovereign nation-states of the Third World (Cooper 1997: 64, 75–6).

## From the 'Civilizing Mission' to Colonial Development

The specific historical origins of the post-1945 idea of development and its linkage to the idea of the Third World can be further clarified via an examination of the shifts in the British approach to their civilizing mission in the non-European world in the nineteenth and early twentieth centuries (Adas 1989: 166–77, 201–3; Stokes 1959; Conklin 2000). Britain represents both a good and an important example because of its position by the late nineteenth century as the largest and most influential colonial and imperial power in a world still made up primarily of imperial states. The origins of the British civilizing mission in Asia and Africa can be traced to the writings and practices of a series of English East India Company (established in 1600) administrators and officials. It was these men who presided over the building of the British Indian Empire in the second half of the eighteenth century and the first half of the nineteenth century on the foundations of the East India Company's increasing involvement in sub-continental politics and the governance systems of the Mughal Empire that was in theory if not in practice the dominant political centre in South Asia down to the early eighteenth century.

For example, James Mill (a long-time employee of the English East India Company based in London, and the father of John Stuart Mill, who also worked for the East India Company between 1823 and 1858) was part of an influential group of British administrators and intellectuals who were inspired by the likes of Jeremy Bentham and were interested in 'civilizing' the sub-continent. Their views were influential in the formulation of policy in India prior to 1857. In the early nineteenth century, James Mill (who had never been to India) wrote a multi-volume history of British India, in which he portrayed the British conquest of the sub-continent as an unqualified blessing for the region's uncivilized inhabitants (Mill 1820, vols 1–6). The notion that the English East India Company and British imperialism carried the benefits of civilization to the world remained a mainstay of British identity, and its projection down to the mid-twentieth century. In some quarters it was also complemented or revised by the emergence of the idea of colonial development at the end of the nineteenth century, while there are, of course, observers who continue to find major benefits in British imperialism of the nineteenth and early twentieth centuries.

Some observers, meanwhile, argue that in the case of Britain, Joseph Chamberlain's assumption of the post of British Colonial Secretary in 1895 marked the start of a formal commitment to colonial development. During and after Chamberlain's stewardship of the Colonial Office a variety of proto-development schemes were pursued, although the presence of a long-term and coherent vision focused on the economic development of the Asian and African colonies was still absent. Nevertheless, in the wake of Chamberlain's time at the Colonial Office, 'development' became a key plank in the British government's colonial operations (Havinden and Meredith 1996: pp. 86–7, 90). In particular, Chamberlain played an important role in formulating a concept of development which drew attention to the role of government and also emphasized community, modelled on experiences of 'nation-building' drawn initially from nineteenth-century Australia and Canada. Both were settler-colonial states, who forged national identities out of diverse immigrant populations *against* indigenous peoples, and embarked on comprehensively linking the creation of a nation with the planning and engineering of economic and social development. In the process of its movement from Australia and North America to Britain the concept of development was mediated through the notion of the 'national economy', a concept that Friedrich List had sought to establish as the basic economic policy in Europe. Out of such intellectual resources, eventually the idea of 'trusteeship' emerged, which recast the unequal and exploitative relations between the colonizers and the colonized in the language of 'responsibility': development thus becomes the 'task' of colonial powers, to be pursued and implemented in colonized societies, and through this feat *justified* the continuity of the colonial project. The trusteeship system hence became the major critical target of the rising Third World, and the project of Third Worldism was in no small part a direct contestation of its legacies. The introduction of the idea of a 'dual mandate' for British Africa consolidated the notion that, in order to function as a people and an economy, the nations of the continent would have to be administered by indirect rule, ostensibly for their own benefit, and also (and always) for the benefit of the colonial power. The racially circumscribed politics of the civilizing mission is explicitly articulated in Lugard's *Dual Mandate* (1922).

By the late nineteenth century the Europeans involved in the process of colonial expansion were deeply imbued with the idea (usually couched in racialized terms) that Europeans were particularly suited to rule and reform the people of Asia and Africa because Europeans were representatives of the most technologically and scientifically advanced civilizations in history. Furthermore, while the European aristocracy had played a role in the technological and scientific activities that underpinned the industrialization of Western Europe and provided the wherewithal for the qualitative and quantitative shift in colonial expansion, it was the middle classes of Western Europe that dominated the bureaucracies, commercial operations and missionary societies central to the dispersion of the values and practices of 'European civilization'. The assumption that administering, trading and preaching were working to spread the skills and norms that were the key to a civilized existence represented a potent justification for colonialism and imperialism regardless of the brutality of the actual process (Adas 1989: 209–10).

Following the First World War, brutal colonial power relations continued to operate in tandem with paternalistic and racist sentiments about trusteeship and a civilizing mission. Both these ideas were strengthened in this period by the formation of the League of Nations. Although it was set up at the encouragement of US president Woodrow Wilson, the League operated without US involvement as a result of Wilson's failure to garner sufficient political support for his vision in the US itself (Knock 1992). The signing of the Treaty of Versailles (28 June 1919), which formally ended what would become known as the First World War, had been preceded by the promulgation of the Covenant of the League of Nations. In particular, Articles 22 and 23 of the Covenant outlined the mandate system and provided some member governments of the League with the legitimation of the administrative control of, and responsibility for, territories formerly controlled by the imperial governments that had lost the war (especially the former Ottoman Empire and erstwhile German colonies in Africa, Asia and the Pacific). At the same time as the victorious colonial powers (especially Britain and France) mutually granted themselves mandates over the colonial territories of their rivals through the League of Nations, they were expected to expose their administrative practices to the scrutiny of a Permanent Mandate Commission (PMC) which would ensure the maintenance of administrative standards in keeping with the Covenant. However, the PMC hardly functioned to uphold the rights it was ostensibly created to protect (Rajajopal 2003: 50–72).

Meanwhile, reinforcing the assumptions that underpinned the operations of the European colonial powers and US foreign policy in this period, the League of Nations justified its members' assumption of responsibility for the mandates, allowing them to see their rule in terms of an explicit obligation of the ostensibly 'civilized' towards those framed as 'in need of civilizing'. Although the mandates system was intended to provide a mechanism for the international supervision of the operations of those powers that had been given responsibility for the various mandates, the mandate system actually operated in a fashion that favoured the interests of the colonial states and reflected a revision of, rather than a sharp break from, the 'civilizing mission'. In the language of the Covenant, Article 22 noted that: 'To those colonies and territories which as a consequence of the late war have ceased to be under the sovereignty of the States which formerly governed them and which are inhabited by peoples not yet able to stand by themselves under the strenuous conditions of the modern world, there should be applied the principle that the well-being and development of such peoples form a sacred trust of civilization and that securities for the performances of this trust should be embodied in this Covenant' (cited in Rist 1996: 47, 58–61). At the same time, as a result of its broader institutional shortcomings the League of Nations, aside from consolidating colonial rule, did not achieve the other objectives in world politics envisioned for it by US president

Woodrow Wilson and his supporters. It fell apart in the 1930s, in the wake of the Sino-Japanese conflict, Mussolini's invasion of Ethiopia, not to mention the frenetic imperial effort of Nazi Germany that was central to the coming of the Second World War (Thorne 1973).

Thus, despite changes to colonial policy in the early twentieth century, European and North American (and Japanese) ideas of progress remained grounded in the highly racialized and civilizing visions of the era (Adas 1989: 403; Peattie 1984; Ichiro 1997). In fact, as already suggested, the League of Nations helped to legitimize rather than undermine a racist European civilizing mission. As already noted, serious efforts to revise the civilizing mission on the part of British colonial officials, for example, only became evident in the late 1930s, by which time any promise the League of Nations had embodied had been extinguished. The 1930s is also regarded as a turning point for the US civilizing mission in Latin America and elsewhere. A central goal articulated by the proponents of the Good Neighbor Policy (1933) was to substitute the outdated policy of 'punishing' the United States' southern neighbours for 'uncivilized behaviour' with a Pan-American policy which emphasized a programme of hemispheric political and economic integration under US leadership which increasingly assumed that Latin Americans could and should follow the road to 'national development' charted by the United States (Berger 1995: 50; Benjamin 1987: 101–2). In the 1930s Latin American economists and political leaders in countries such as Mexico, Brazil, Argentina and Chile in particular also focused with increasing energy on state-directed national development and industrialization strategies (Babb 2001).

In the case of the British Empire, this new awareness of the importance of economic development in its colonies was manifested most significantly by Lord Hailey's confidential report to the Colonial Office that led to the Colonial Development and Welfare Act of 1940 (Fieldhouse 1982: 486). In the view of one commentator, the 1940 Act 'represented' the culmination of a process of 'conversion of the official classes to the doctrines of a managed economy' and the 'development idea' which had been underway since the beginning of the 1930s and flowed from the problems of the Great Depression. The meagre funds which this Act provided to the Colonial Office were to be spent mainly on services, especially housing, water, education and health facilities, for the urban workforce in the colonies; however, the major limits during the war on both shipping and supplies meant that the actual spending earmarked by the Act did not occur until after 1945 (Lee 1967: 39–41).

After 1945 the imperatives of post-war reconstruction in Britain itself (in which there was a range of primary product shortages) also ensured the amplification of wartime efforts to facilitate the economic development of a number of its colonies. The wider backdrop against which Great Britain and France discovered development – the dramatic increase in the need to find justifications for colonialism inflected in terms of the needs of the colonized populations at a time when 'self-determination' was becoming a central notion in international politics – converged with the metropolitan powers' increased economic need for primary exports from their colonies in the immediate post-war era. The African colonies, in particular, were seen as important sources of agricultural and mineral products, at the same time as (in contrast to much of Asia) it was thought colonial rule could still be preserved in the face of a rising tide of decolonization (Cooper 1997: 67, 70; Cooper 1996; von Albertini 1982a: 99–115).

Africa was the main, but not the only focus of Britain's late colonial discovery of development (Kingston 1996; Louis 1984: 50, 1812). The British were also committed to retaining imperial influence and Great Power status in the Middle East in the post-1945 era, but did not necessarily see the Colonial Development and Welfare Act as having any particular relevance to their relations with the region in the absence of formal colonies. After 1945, however, the establishment of the Development Division of the British Middle East Office reflected the wider trend. British India was not part of colonial development planning after 1940 either; however, Hailey's thinking had been influenced by his tenure as the Governor of the Punjab in the late 1920s (Lee 1967: 37–8; Cell 1992). At the same time, in 1938, two years prior to the promulgation of the Colonial Development and Welfare Act, the Indian National Congress (which would lead India to independence by 1947) had already established a National Planning Committee which was charged with drawing up plans for the social and economic reconstruction of India in anticipation of eventual independence. As one author has argued, unlike in the case of African societies, the idealization and institutional manifestation of the concept of 'national development' predated that of 'colonial development' in India (Berger 2004a: 61–80). Nevertheless the post-1947 efforts at development planning carried out by the post-colonial Indian state relied more on the colonial era Planning and

Development Department, which had been set up in 1944, than they did on the work of the National Planning Committee of the late 1930s (Bose 1997: 47, 53).

Meanwhile, in 1942, the colonial government of Burma consulted John S. Furnivall (who had worked in various capacities in the British colonial administration in Burma for over twenty years) as part of an effort to prepare for post-1945 reconstruction of the colony. The colonial authorities were particularly interested in what they perceived as relevant practices of colonial administration in the Netherlands East Indies that could be applied to Burma. Furnivall completed a book-length study in 1945 (although it was not published until 1948, by which time the decolonization of Burma had occurred) that contrasted the British colonial tradition of 'the rule of law and economic freedom' with the Dutch colonial tradition of 'imposing restraints on economic forces by strengthening personal authority and by conserving the influence of custom'. In particular he argued that British colonial officials in Burma 'ought to incorporate in our policy the principle of control over economic forces in the interest of social welfare'. This could be done, he said, 'by adapting certain devices of Dutch administrative machinery' to 'lay the basis of a new and constructive policy' (Furnivall 1948: ix–x; Furnivall 1939; Furnivall 1991: 3–137; Trager 1961).

However, the significance of the so-called 'Ethical Policy' (which sought to replace *laissez-faire* with state intervention in the name of social welfare), initiated by the Dutch at the beginning of the twentieth century, should not be exaggerated. Although it led to some improvements in health care, as well as programmes to improve agricultural output and facilitate industrialization, these efforts had a relatively minimal impact. Furthermore, the programmes that were spawned by the Ethical Policy were effectively abandoned during the Great Depression of the 1930s. Nevertheless it did represent an early attempt by a European colonial administration to deal with issues that would later be central to the question of 'underdevelopment'. Also, the ideas and programmes associated with the Ethical Policy went on to inform the thinking of many Indonesian nationalists (Cribb 1999: 12–14; von Albertini 1982a: 166–7, 188). In British Malaya, meanwhile, an Economic Development Committee was set up in 1946 as a direct result of the Colonial Development and Welfare Act. The development planning that ensued remained fairly basic, however, until a detailed 1955 report (produced by a World Bank Mission) established a framework for the First Malayan Plan (1956–60), which overlapped with the peninsula's achievement of formal independence from Britain in 1957 (Robertson 1984: 239).

## 'The Contradictions of National Liberation': From Colonial Development to National Development

Decolonization in Malaya and elsewhere ensured that in a short period of time colonial boundaries, often built up over decades if not centuries, became national boundaries. Against the backdrop of the Cold War, the international recognition of the new nation-states of the emerging Third World and their incorporation into the United Nations served to quickly confer sovereignty and legitimacy and worked to naturalize the new national boundaries. The crisis of colonialism (and struggles for decolonization) provided the context for the emergence of a powerful international development discourse (and the system-ization and codification of increasingly influential theories and prac-tices of modern capitalist development and nation building) in the Third World. At the same time, during the Cold War, particularly the period up to the 1970s, the Soviet bloc (as well as those state-socialist countries, from Yugoslavia to China, not allied with the USSR) also embodied and promoted alternative state-socialist models of develop-ment; however, these models, like the dominant capitalist discourse on international development, also uncritically took the nation-state as the key unit of analysis. In fact, state-socialist regimes in Russia, China and elsewhere not only embraced the nation-state as the key to global modernity, but also sought from the outset to duplicate the economic results of capitalism, setting goals that capitalism was ulti-mately far more able to realize (Dirlik 1994:44; Jowitt 1993). To be sure, these economic achievements must be considered in relation to the social and ecological costs through which they were realized. This was a discovery the People's Republic of China made by the late 1970s, despite the effort by the Chinese leadership to insist that their major economic reorientation by latter years of the Cold Ward did not reflect a turn to capitalism (Berger 2004a; Halper 2010).

The naturalization of the post-colonial nation-state also meshed with and reinforced the wider organic metaphors which have come to underpin the dominant international development discourse and a great deal of social science work on development in the Third World.

From the outset assumptions about the primordial (and even the organic) integrity of the new nation-states which emerged after the Second World War underpinned the nationalist struggles themselves and remained a powerful force in post-colonial political life. For example, political leaders in Indonesia talked about the three hundred and fifty years of Dutch colonialism endured by Indonesians despite the fact that the idea of Indonesia is a twentieth-century concept and large parts of what is now Indonesia were only incorporated into the Netherlands East Indies at the end of the nineteenth century (Kertzer 1988: 179). Sukarno, independent Indonesia's first president, was well known for his oft-repeated observation that even children looking at a map could not help but notice 'how natural the physical integrity' of the new republic was (Cribb 1999: 3). The New Order of his successor, General Suharto (1965–98), was bolstered by the deployment of a powerful and shifting synthesis of national symbols and ideas drawn from the Javanese and wider archipelagic past, and an eclectic mix of organic ideas which, although they were assigned an indigenous pedigree, were derived from Dutch and German legal and political philosophy (Berger 2000).

At the same time, historians (as well as the humanities and social sciences generally) have long been complicit in primordial conceptions of the nation. The tight linkages between the rise of nation-states and the professionalization of the study of history had a profound influence on the understanding of nationalism in the late nineteenth and first half of the twentieth century. The primordial understanding of nation-state formation persisted into the Cold War era. For example, in the 1970s Hugh Seton-Watson argued that in Europe there had been a 'gradual elaboration' of a 'sense of nationality from the time of the barbarian invasions in late antiquity, if not before in classical antiquity itself' (Seton-Watson 1977: 3). Meanwhile, a historical study of the Korean peninsula argues that the start of the 'long nation building process' began with the establishment of the Gohchosun Kingdom (the 'first national state') almost 2,500 years ago (Jung 1988: v, 2–6). That said, however, from the 1960s onwards primordialist approaches to nation building and nationalism, and the easy assumption that the nation-state is the natural unit of study, were increasingly challenged by a growing number of academic commentators (Eller and Coughlan 1993), though the contestations themselves had never gone away, whether in cases of ethnic minority struggles, or, more importantly perhaps, indigenous resistance (see, for example, Alfred 1999). By the 1980s, the beginnings of a veritable explosion of critical interest in nationalism had begun to occur, which was stimulated by the end of the Cold War (Gershoni and Jankowski 1997). While a considerable amount of historical writing continues to be implicated in elite-led state-building and nation-making efforts and works to naturalize the nation-state, there has been a growing effort by historians and social scientists to insert subaltern groups into the wider sweep of history and to denaturalize the nation-state and put contemporary nation-building projects in historical perspective (Chakrabarty 2000; Duara 1995; Guha 1997; Grovogui 1996; Rojas 2002; Shilliam 2008). Some of the main early academic challenges to the naturalization of the nation came from writers who are often characterized as modernists. While there are profound differences between these writers, they all share the view that the nation is a modern phenomenon and any effort to see it as having existed in timeless fashion down through history is deeply problematic (Deutsch 1953; Gellner 1983; Breuilly 1985; Hutchinson 1994: 3–7; Smith 1993: 6–13).

Benedict Anderson is one of the most influential modernists. In his now standard work (*Imagined Communities*), he argues that nationalism and nationality are 'cultural artefacts' and that in order to understand their potency and power one needs to look at their history and their changing content over time. More specifically, he defined the nation as 'an imagined political community' emphasizing that all nations are 'imagined as both inherently limited and sovereign'. Furthermore, despite the social inequality and various forms of economic exploitation that characterize any given national polity, 'the nation is always conceived as a deep, horizontal comradeship' (Anderson 1992: 3–7; B. Anderson 1998). From the early twentieth century modern nationalism was increasingly embraced in differing political and intellectual contexts and began to shape popular political activities and mobilizations in regions and colonies in Southern and Eastern Europe, the Middle East, Asia and Africa. Despite the very different political and economic contexts the nation was still invariably presented as a constitutive element of capitalist and socialist modernization. At the time of, and immediately after, decolonization the nation-state represented the promise of freedom, modernization and self-determination. However, the progressive aspects of nation-state formation were constrained by, among other things, powerful institutional and structural legacies inherited from the colonial era and by the hierarchical character of the nation-state system. The terms on which the newly sovereign nation-states were both consolidated, and then incorporated into the wider global order, ensured that the 'state', invariably a direct inheritance of the colonial era, was 'the poisoned gift of national liberation' (Hardt and Negri 2001: 96, 105–9, 132–4; Chatterjee 1986: 168). *Pace* the misleading notion of the 'gift' in contexts in which independence was frequently fought for and obtained against great obstacles, the political form of the (nation)-state inaugurated further contradictions. The idea and practice of 'national development' which emerged in this context was already beset with inherent contradictions, given that national development itself was already constituted through global and transnational relations. This observation is not new and has been at the basis of dependency and world systems analyses of global social and political change (cf. Cooper 2005: 54; Grovogui 1996: esp.179–207).

The idea of the nation-state was then projected outwards from North America (along with Latin America) and Western Europe, at the same time as it was consolidated and universalized via the rise of anti-colonial nationalism in Asia and Africa. Between the 1940s and the 1970s the many contradictions and tensions of the various nationalist movements in Asia, Africa and the Middle East were played out in the context of, and given a new unity by, the nation-states that were built squarely on the foundations of colonial power (Chatterjee 1986: 161; Chatterjee 1993; Prakash 1995). In Southeast Asia, for example, where a series of complex and variegated colonial empires had been established by the late nineteenth and early twentieth centuries, the structures of the colonial state, which had increasingly been extended into local societies in the form of education, irrigation, agricultural improvements, hygiene, mineral exploitation and political surveillance, also provided the framework within which anti-colonial nationalism emerged (Berger 1996).

And even in Thailand, which was never formally colonized, the process by which the old agrarian-based tributary-state of Siam became Thailand was still profoundly shaped by British and French colonial expansion in mainland Southeast Asia and by the concept of the nation-state that had emerged in Europe. The rulers of the kingdom of Siam were able to play French imperialists and the expanding British Empire off against each other, while quickly building new institutions and trading relationships that allowed it to emerge as an independent and modernizing nation-state in the late nineteenth and early twentieth centuries (Winichakul 1994). Avoidance of colonial rule in Japan also flowed in part from the successful appropriation and domestication of the technological, bureaucratic, and intellectual frameworks and practices that flowed out of the earlier industrialization and colonial expansion of Western Europe and the United States (Morris-Suzuki 1994:13–157). Thailand and Japan and the new nation-states have all emerged in a fashion that has meant that they remain implicated in various forms of Eurocentrism. Individual and collective efforts to overcome Eurocentrism, like nationalist initiatives against colonialism, are constrained from the outset and can work as much to reinforce neo-traditional power relations as they can help in bringing about a more thoroughgoing liberation from the so-called West (Dirlik 1994: 51–2, 96–7).

In many ways, the main problem is not only a failure to overcome Eurocentrism, but also the way in which it is assumed that there is an easy commensurability between the interests of national elites and the majority of the peoples of the sovereign modern nation-states that have emerged in the second half of the twentieth century. The principle of self-determination, as embodied in the UN charter, serves to legitimate the boundaries and sovereignty of existing states (Latham 1997: 32–3). The distinction between states and nations is particularly relevant to understanding the way in which sovereignty, especially national sovereignty, continued to reside with the state rather than with the people that inhabited the new nation (Hardt and Negri 2001: 69–70; Jackson 1990). The concept of national sovereignty served as a crucial element in the establishment of the Cold War order after 1945, at the same time as the idea of international development also became central to the wider process via which the new nation-states were incorporated into a particular spatial and temporal order in the wake of decolonization and national liberation. In keeping with the temporal assumptions of implicit comparative approaches (see Hindess 2007), the new nation-states of the Third World were positioned 'behind' the First World (and also behind the state socialism of the Second World). Regardless of their actual geographical location, meanwhile, the emergent new nation-states were rapidly drawn into the Cold War.

As already noted in the Introduction, the dominant international development discourse, and its network of treaties, organizations and institutions, facilitated the subordination of the Third World (despite the early Third Worldist efforts at finding a third way to modernity), and enshrined 'underdevelopment' as a key characteristic of the nation-states in the Third World. The sharp distinction between the notion of development and underdevelopment conceived in terms of territorial units enabled and continues to enable the use of the idea of the Third World as an unproblematic analytical and conceptual category in international development and in International Relations. Meanwhile, in relation to the universalization of the nation-state system it needs to be emphasized that the establishment of the United Nations and the onset of the Cold War represented a fundamental shift in the significance of 'national sovereignty' in what became the Third World. For the next thirty years, regardless of which side of the Cold War one was on, decolonization, national liberation and the establishment of sovereign nation-states with membership in the United Nations swept aside those colonial empires that had survived the vagaries of the Second World War. By the 1970s, a process begun during the First World War (if not earlier) saw a world of *de facto* and *de jure* empires give way to a world of *de facto* and *de jure* sovereign nation-states. With regard to the period prior to the Second World War, it is argued that the financial and technological imperatives of war making by increasingly important, primarily European, states, led over an extended period of time to heightened levels of economic extraction, mobilization and repression, and where successful resulted in the formation of strong states and latterly 'nation-states' (Tilly 1975; Tilly 1992: 12). For one observer, the 'power' of full-scale conventional warfare 'channelled through deep grooves of societal cooperation etched by war' must be seen as 'a formidable engine of collective action'. The modern 'state' and then the modern 'nation-state' as it emerged out of centuries of warfare in Europe was by the early decades of the twentieth century 'an offspring of the total warfare of the industrial age' (Porter 1994: 192–3, 240–1).

In the light of this argument the growing momentum for decolonization after 1945 combined with the establishment of the United Nations had profound and unforeseen implications that flowed from the universalization of the nation-state system. In relation to the period prior to 1945, strong states emerged over an extended historical period. This required a rising level of political cohesion that was often played out in Europe over centuries. In the post-1945 era war between nation-states takes place within a nation-state system that is already in place. This means that warfare between nation-states no longer works to create the nation-state or the nation-state system. In other words the juridical (or *de jure*) sovereignty provided by the United Nations does not actually create modern nation-states. This problem is compounded by the continued assumption that failing or failed nation-states can be put back together again (if they were ever actually together in the first place) rather than seeing the problem as a crisis of the nation-state system and of international development and global modernity as a whole.

## Conclusion: The Origins of the Third World

As we have shown, the historical constellations behind the rise of the Third World are complex. Its history lies in understanding the interplay between ideas of progress and development in the wider context of the vicissitudes of the project of global modernity and the colonial form through which it was extended. This in turn must be set in the context of capitalist expansion, colonial expropriation and the projection of imperial power, as well as the multitude of practices of resistance and contestations of the arrangements and experiences it entailed. Colonialism and its ostensible 'civilizing mission' entered a period of crisis in the 1930s and the anti-colonial struggles that grew in strength and number converged on the idea of national development, which was consolidated in terms of the sovereign authority of the territorial nation-state.

It needs to be emphasized here that this placed important limits on how to think about development in accordance with nation-statist presumptions in the so-called Third World in at least two major ways that are of particular significance. First (with some exceptions) it set national boundaries in terms that generally coincided with former colonial boundaries. These boundaries had *sometimes* emerged over a long period, while at other times they were drawn up in haste as in the case of the 'Scramble for Africa' in the late nineteenth century and the partitioning of British India into India and Pakistan in 1947; in either case, there was little or no thought about the consequences that would flow from them becoming the naturalized territorial boundaries for the new nation-states as they pursued development after 1945. Second, taking the nation-state as the key unit via which underdevelopment could be measured and addressed helped to submerge any understanding of development in terms of lived experiences and the social and political contradictions within and across the old colonial and new national borders. This meant that complex political and social struggles, during the Cold War and beyond, were subsumed (in an often brutal fashion) into narratives of national and international development that obscured more than they illuminated (cf. Saurin 1996). New and old nation-states were increasingly legitimated and naturalized in the context of widespread acceptance of the more general and developmentally hierarchical notion of a First World centred on the US, a Second World centred on the USSR and an underdeveloped, but rising Third World. This framing of development was resisted by Third World proponents from the outset, a contestation therefore also of the naturalized assumptions underpinning the racially inflected hierarchy of progress and development. It is this resistance and these struggles of the Third World that came to shape the politics of the post-Second World War era. It is to this latter process that we turn in the next chapter.

# 2
# Third World Rising: Decolonization, the Cold War and Third Worldism

During the 1950s and 1960s the nation-state system was universalized; the Cold War was globalized and the modern idea of development was consolidated as an increasingly technocratic and measurable process, available in principle to implementation by the new states of the rising Third World. It is important to highlight the complexity of the formal end of colonialism and decolonization as well as the growing significance of Third Worldism in the Cold War period. The onset of the Cold War, as the first section of this chapter will clarify, inaugurated the competition between capitalist and socialist models of development, all of which accorded a key role to the nation-state in the achievement of progress, while simultaneously reinforcing international relations as a world-wide system of sovereign states. The way in which the latter were constituted, structured and challenged was already part of our account in the previous chapter. The first part of this chapter sets out the relationship between the rise of the Cold War and the consolidation of international development, drawing particular attention to Latin America where a number of governments played an important pioneering role in promoting state-guided national development. This process actually began in the 1930s, but after 1945 state-guided national development, as we will see, was increasingly propounded as a universal prescription via the United Nations and other international organizations. The second section of this chapter analyses decolonization in relation to the Cold

War, while the third section looks at the growing significance of Third Worldism as a direct result of decolonization and the Cold War.

## The Cold War: The Challenge of State Socialism, Third Worldism and the Nation-State System

After 1945 the United States increasingly moved to preside over a dramatic international development effort that would meet the challenge represented by state-socialist models of development associated with, or thought to be associated with, Washington's only significant rival, the USSR. The growing Cold War rivalry between different models of development (First World versus Second World) was closely associated with the universalization and consolidation of the nation-state system. Both the position of the US in the nation-state system and the foreign policies and practices of the Soviet Union had parallels with the colonialism that had been practised by the European colonial powers and Imperial Japan, as well as by the United States in an earlier era. But, despite continuities the Cold War 'empires' of both the US and the Soviet Union departed in crucial ways from earlier colonial projects. Most significantly, in political and administrative terms both the United States and the Soviet Union presided over empires that were made up almost entirely of formally sovereign nation-states. Even within the Soviet Union itself, as opposed to its dominance over the nation-states of Eastern Europe after the Second World War, Moscow had introduced a form of political arrangement that unwittingly facilitated the break-up of the Soviet Union in the 1990s into new nation-states based on the former socialist republics. This was related to the fact that in the wake of the Russian Revolution in 1917, the Bolsheviks had sought to control the different non-Russian nationalities and contain nationalisms within the Union of Soviet Socialist Republics by promoting accepted forms of national identity and nationhood without offering substantive sovereignty or independence (Martin 2001; 2001b).

At one level, from the time of its establishment down to its demise, the USSR could be said to have represented an alternative, at least equally brutal, and more rigid version of the League of Nations (which rose and fell between the First and Second World Wars), both of which were, in retrospect, transitional institutions in relation to the universalization of the nation-state system. The world after 1945 was one in which formally independent and sovereign nation-states increasingly displaced colonial empires as the key units of global politics. In the Cold War era the relationship between the respective super-powers and their allies was increasingly mediated by systems of military alliances, regional organizations and new international institutions such as the United Nations. Apart from the UN, the International Monetary Fund (IMF) and the International Bank for Reconstruction and Development (the World Bank), which had been established on 27 December 1945, were also central to the generation of the international framework for the promotion of national-capitalist development in the Cold War era (see Thomas 1985). With the start of the Cold War the IMF and the World Bank (which were ostensibly part of the United Nations, but in practice operated beyond UN control) became central to US international economic predominance and the international framework for national development and global modernity.

More broadly, the arrangements laid down at Bretton Woods in 1944 produced an 'informal bargain'. On the one side, the US (with the dollar providing the central currency for the post-war order) accepted the increasingly large balance of payments deficits necessary to pay for its expanding network of military bases and the large quantities of foreign aid it was disbursing. This was parallelled by high levels of foreign investments made by US-based companies. On the other side, the United States' allies (particularly key anti-Communist nation-states, such as West Germany and Japan, which also became its main economic competitors) were allowed to retain high levels of control over their economies in terms of trade protection and restrictions on foreign investment. This was accompanied by the implicit agreement that its allies would not attempt to convert large amounts of their US dollar holdings to gold (which was technically permitted by the gold standard). Meanwhile, Washington opened additional North American markets to its more important Cold War allies (Brenner 1998: 43, 47).

A growing array of specifically US initiatives (such as the Marshall Plan and the Point IV Program in the late 1940s), along with new international organizations, ensured that an international capitalist framework for state-building and national development, under the stewardship of the Truman and Eisenhower administrations (1944–52 and 1953–60) took shape to meet the growing challenge of the state-socialist model sponsored by Moscow in the 1950s. It was, however, during the administration of John F. Kennedy (1961–63) and his immediate successor, Lyndon B. Johnson (1963–68) that the state-guided interventionist approach to international development reached its apex. Following the Cuban revolution in 1959 there was a dramatic increase in US interest in Latin America in the context of a growing concern in the US that the USSR was gaining ground in the Third World.

The Kennedy administration placed considerable emphasis on the need for a more ambitious nation-building and counter-insurgency strategy in the Third World. This involved taking the initiative in Asia and Latin America, as well as the Middle East and Africa, to counter the communist threat with the infusion of increased levels of military and economic aid, advice and support. As part of its emphasis on foreign aid and national development, the Kennedy administration formed the Peace Corps on 1 March 1961 and then set up the US Agency for International Development (USAID) in November 1961 to coordinate and combine government foreign aid efforts. Established as a semi-autonomous body operating in the State Department, USAID was responsible for disbursing and administering aid around the world. Apart from South Vietnam, which was emerging as a major focus of aid, a large percentage of the aid this new body disbursed went initially to the Alliance for Progress, which was set up following a famous speech by Kennedy on 13 March 1961. In the speech he called for all the people and governments of the western hemisphere to participate in an ambitious modernizing initiative and contain the communist threat to the region represented by the emergence of state socialism in Cuba (Latham 1997; Berger 2003).

The Alliance for Progress began as a decade-long programme of land and economic reform that was expected to cost US$100 billion. The US made an initial contribution of US$1 billion and a commitment to raise another US$20 billion overall from both public and private sources, setting an annual economic growth rate for Latin America of at least 2.5 per cent as one of the main goals. Emphasizing the importance of national development planning, the Alliance, under US leadership, sought to achieve greater productivity in the agricultural sector, eradicate illiteracy, stimulate trade diversification and industrialization, generate improvements in housing and bring about improved income distribution in the region. A key contradiction of the Alliance for Progress centred on the fact that successful trade diversification would undermine the monopoly of primary agricultural products and mineral extraction enjoyed by a number of US-based transnationals. At the same time any significant land reform threatened the power of the still largely land-based ruling elites in Latin America. The goal of high economic growth rates had been reached by a number of nation-states in Latin America by the late 1960s. However, high growth rates had served primarily to increase social inequality, while the middle classes moved to side with the ruling elites as politics, instead of becoming more democratic, moved increasingly towards authoritarianism and military dictatorship. By the time of Kennedy's assassination in late 1963, the reformist elements of the Alliance for Progress had been displaced by a more straightforward focus on military and economic aid to any regime, regardless of how draconian, committed to the maintenance of US hegemony in the region (Berger 1995: 87–8).

Decades before the Cuban revolution, Latin America had, as mentioned in the introduction to this chapter, played a role in formalizing state-mediated national development as a means of overcoming the limitations of the primary commodity export-oriented economies that were historically characteristic of the region. It was during the Great Depression of the 1930s that the idea of development as a state-mediated redistributive (although not necessarily politically democratic) process of national mobilization and development was consolidated in parts of Latin America and, of course, Western, Central and Eastern Europe. It is also clear that this coincided with the crisis of colonialism and the growing focus on colonial development (discussed in Chapter 1) in the same period. A significant number of the pioneers of development economics were born in East Central Europe and their early research focused on national development in the region. Paul Rosenstein-Rodan (who played a particularly important role in the establishment of development economics in the 1940s), along with a number of other economists, sought to prescribe ways in which the nation-states of East Central Europe could be developed following the nineteenth- and early twentieth- century German experience. The idea that industrialization was the key to national development, and that government planning was necessary for this to take place, was the central element in the work of virtually all of these economists.

Between the 1930s and the 1960s their views increasingly meshed with the developmental preoccupations of Latin American economists and policymakers. For example, Raúl Prebisch, Under Secretary of Finance in Argentina in the early 1930s, emerged as a key figure in development economics and a major promoter of state-guided national development and international development after the Second World War. In the post-1945 era Prebisch served as Director-General of the UN-sponsored Economic Commission for Latin America (Comisión Económica para América Latina – CEPAL) from 1948 to 1962. He also founded and then headed the United Nations Conference on Trade and Development (UNCTAD) from 1964 to 1969. From his perch at the top of UNCTAD he sought to encourage preferential tariffs for the exports of late-industrializing nation-states in the Third World. Apart from Latin America, it was not until decolonization that nation-states in what increasingly became the Third World embraced various versions of state-guided national development.

### The Ending of Empires: Decolonization, Third Worldism and the Nation-State System

The dynamics of decolonization involved three overlapping trends (Berger 2004b). The rising nationalist movements combined with alterations in the global order after 1945, while also interacting with shifts in the outlook of key groups and interests in the colonial capitals and/or on the ground in the colonies. The relative significance attached to each of these variables depends on the observer and the specific examples of decolonization. More broadly, the Cold War, which increasingly grounded national and international development in relation to the idea of the Third World, provided the key backdrop to the process of decolonization that took on growing impetus with the end of the Second World War.

The defeat of Imperial Japan in 1945, for example, led to the decol-onization of its empire and the emergence of independent polities on the Korean peninsula. Meanwhile its erstwhile colony of Taiwan was quickly enmeshed in the post-1945 struggle for power between the Chinese Communist Party (CCP) and the KMT (Kuomintang), a struggle that was quickly inflected by the emerging Cold War. By the late 1940s South Korea and Taiwan had emerged as truncated nation-states and as key allies/clients of the United States, while their Cold War *doppelgängers*, North Korea and the People's Republic of China, entered into a complex triangle of alliance–client relationships with the USSR.

Meanwhile, in South Asia, the emergence of the independent nation-states of India and Pakistan (and, eventually, Bangladesh) out of the dramatic break-up of British India in 1947 followed on from the emergence by the 1920s and 1930s of mass-based nationalist movements and was an important manifestation of the wider trend towards decolonization. In the case of Southeast Asia, there was considerable variation in the timing and character of decolonization. It is clear that in most cases (except for the Philippines and what would become Malaysia as well as some of the smaller and more anomalous polities such as Brunei and East Timor) a powerful and armed nationalist movement was a major factor in decolonization. These nationalist movements were strengthened by the Japanese occupation of virtually all of Southeast Asia during the Pacific War. The end of the Pacific War helped precipitate the end of US colonialism in the Philippines in 1946, with independence having initially been discussed by Washington thirty years earlier.

The Japanese occupation of the Netherlands East Indies and the former's subsequent surrender in 1945, meanwhile, led directly to Sukarno's declaration of an independent Indonesia. This was quickly challenged by Dutch military efforts to reassert control in the archipelago, a battle that continued until 1949 before the Dutch gave up. Meanwhile, in 1948, the British transferred power to an independent government in Burma, whose politics had been directly affected by its occupation by Imperial Japan. Following three wars of conquest against the Kingdom of Burma in the nineteenth century, the region had been administratively subordinated to British India up to 1935 when the process of gradually devolving power entered a new phase in both India and Burma. Despite this connection, Burma, which unlike Pakistan and India opted not to join the British Commonwealth, has been identified as part of Southeast Asia rather than South Asia since 1948.

By the end of the 1950s, meanwhile, a range of African colonies (beginning in 1957 with Ghana, formerly the Gold Coast) were also moving towards or had already achieved independence. In 1960 sixteen new nation-states in Africa joined the United Nations, including Nigeria and the Republic of the Congo (formerly the Belgian Congo). By 1960 African independence in general, and Congo's independence in particular, highlighted the growing significance of decolonization for the United Nations. In fact, in short order the Congo turned into a major crisis for the United Nations. The UN force

(Opération des Nations Unies au Congo – ONUC) that was deployed in the Congo from July 1960 to June 1964 was the biggest UN operation since the Korean War in the early 1950s. The Congo crisis started with a mutiny in the former Belgian colonial military establishment (the Force Publique) that had become the Armée Nationale Congolaise following independence. When troops attacked and killed a number of European officers, the Belgian administrators and other Europeans who had remained behind after independence fled the country, opening the way for Congolese to replace the European military and administrative elite. Shortly after this Moise Tshombe led a successful secessionist effort to take the wealthy Katanga province out of the new nation.

At the end of 1960 President Kasavubu dismissed the new Prime Minister, Patrice Lumumba, and a week later Colonel Joseph Mobutu seized power, holding it until February 1961 by which time Lumumba had been killed. Meanwhile, Belgian troops intervened to protect Belgian nationals as civil war spread in the former Belgian colony. The assassination of Lumumba precipitated a Security Council resolution on 21 February 1961 that conferred on ONUC the ability to use force to stop the descent into civil war. Prior to this point ONUC had only been allowed to use force in self-defence. During operations in the Congo, Secretary General Dag Hammarskjöld was killed in a plane crash and was awarded the Nobel Peace Prize posthumously. Even with upwards of 20,000 UN-sponsored troops in the Congo, however, a cease-fire was not agreed to and Katanga was not brought back into the Congo until 1964. At the same time, ONUC was recalled in 1964 in part because the UN itself was on the brink of bankruptcy (a result of the French and Soviet governments' refusal to contribute to the costs of ONUC). It was not until the UN operation in Somalia in 1992, almost thirty years later, that the UN again intervened militarily on the scale of its operation in the Congo in the early 1960s.

Decolonization in Africa also led to the formation of the independent nation-states of Angola, Mozambique, Guinea-Bissau, Cape Verde and Sao Tome out of the collapse of the Portuguese Empire in 1974. Part of this process, but also distinct in important ways, were the paths taken in the settler colonies of southern Africa. What was known as Rhodesia under the administration of Ian Smith gained independence from white settler rule in 1980, becoming Zimbabwe, bringing to an end a struggle that had been deeply enmeshed in the wider Cold War in the region (Berger 2003). Meanwhile, the South

African government withdrew from South-West Africa (Namibia) in 1990, and the anti-apartheid struggle inaugurated majority rule in South Africa itself in 1994. More broadly it needs to be emphasized that the dynamics of the Cold War interacted particularly brutally with decolonization and national liberation in Africa, facilitating, as we have seen, for instance, the rise and consolidation after 1965 of the predatory Mobutu dictatorship in the Congo (renamed Zaire in 1971). Meanwhile, even after their violent struggles for national liberation, Angola and Mozambique (for example) continued to be roiled in the 1970s and 1980s by guerrilla insurgencies seeking to topple the nationalist-Marxist leadership of these newly independent nation-states. These conflicts ground on into the early post-Cold War era.

### The Internationalization of National Liberation: The Cold War, Third Worldism and the Nation-State System

The first stirrings of Third Worldism can be traced to the complex milieu of colonialism and anti-colonial nationalism in the early twentieth century. However, as discussed in the Introduction, the actual term 'the Third World' is a product of the Cold War and is often traced to the writing in the early 1950s of the French demographer and economic historian, Alfred Sauvy. In this schema, the First World was the US and its allies/clients. The Second World was the Soviet Union and its allies/clients. The Third World meanwhile comprised all those nation-states that were ostensibly seeking to take a non-aligned position in the Cold War. At the most fundamental level, Third Worldism was an effort by a number of nation-states that in many cases had just been decolonized to chart a third course between the capitalism of the First World and the state socialism of the Second World. The founding event for Third Worldism was the 1955 Bandung Conference in Indonesia, following a range of preceding conferences, which had already foreshadowed central themes (see Pasha 2013). The meeting in Bandung flowed from the growing concern about the slow pace of decolonization, particularly in Africa, and the way in which the United Nations had become enmeshed in the rivalry between the two Cold War super-powers. More specifically, the organization of the Bandung Conference by the governments of newly independent Indonesia, Ceylon, India and Pakistan was a result of their frustration with the political logjam surrounding new membership in the United Nations. As of 1954 no new members had been inducted into the UN since Indonesia had joined in January 1950. The 1955 meeting in Bandung was attended by delegations from 29, primarily new, nation-states. Also included in the proceedings were members of the African National Congress, as well as observers from Greek Cypriot and African American organizations. The key figures at the conference, and the main leaders of the first generation of Third Worldist regimes, were Sukarno, President of Indonesia (1945–65), Jawaharlal Nehru, Prime Minister of India (1947–64), Gamal Abdel Nasser, President of Egypt (1954–70). Ho Chi Minh, the leader of the Democratic Republic of Vietnam (1954–69), Kwame Nkrumah, the future Prime Minister of Ghana (1957–66) and Zhou Enlai the Prime Minister (1949–76) and Foreign Minister (1949–58) of the People's Republic of China were also in attendance.

At the Bandung meeting, these leaders and the other assembled delegates emphasized their opposition to colonialism, singling out French colonialism in North Africa for particular criticism. The French war (1954–62) to prevent Algerian independence was under way at this time and representatives of the Front de Libération Nationale (FLN), which would eventually come to power in the 1960s and occupy an important leadership position in the Third World, were in attendance in Bandung. There was also a major debate at the Bandung Conference as to whether Soviet domination of Eastern Europe was equivalent to Western European colonialism in Asia and Africa. The final communiqué of the conference condemned all 'manifestations' of colonialism and was thus widely viewed as not only an attack on the formal colonialism of the Western European powers, but also the Soviet occupation of Eastern Europe and the informal colonialism, or neo-colonialism, of the United States. The proceedings ended with a call for increased technical and cultural cooperation between the governments of Asia and Africa and the establishment of an economic development fund to be operated by the United Nations. They also stressed the need for increased support for human rights and the 'self-determination of peoples and nations' singling out South Africa and Israel for their failure in this regard, while also calling for negotiations to reduce the building and stockpiling of nuclear weapons.

Although the Bandung Conference did not lead directly to any long-term organizational initiatives (a second Asian-African

Conference planned for Algiers in 1965 never took place because of the politics of the Sino-Soviet split) it did, as already emphasized, provide the inspiration for various Third Worldist organizations. A particularly radical example was the formation of the African-Asian People's Solidarity Organization (AAPSO) at a meeting in Cairo in 1957. In contrast to Bandung, which was primarily a meeting of government leaders, AAPSO was set up as an organization of ruling and non-ruling political parties, including delegates from the USSR and China. Despite a number of meetings in the late 1950s and early 1960s, AAPSO soon lost its significance in the context of the Sino-Soviet split and the formation of the more moderate Movement of Non-Aligned Countries, which would become known as the Non-Aligned Movement (NAM) by the 1970s. In September 1961 the first Conference of Heads of State or Government of Non-Aligned Countries was held in Belgrade, Yugoslavia. Hosted by Josip Broz Tito, President of Yugoslavia (1953–80), it was attended by officials from 25 governments and representatives from 19 different national liberation movements.

A number of governments, such as Pakistan, which had been in attendance in Bandung, were excluded if they were seen to be clearly oriented towards the US or the Soviet Union. A number of former French colonies that were closely tied to Paris were also excluded, but this stipulation did not prevent representatives of Castro's Cuba from attending the meeting even though Havana was already becoming, or would eventually become, an important client-ally of Moscow. The Belgrade Conference was followed by Cairo (Egypt) in 1964, then Lusaka (Zambia) in 1970 and Algiers (Algeria) in 1973. By the time of the non-aligned meeting in Cairo in 1964, if not before, the complicated and conflicting interests of the new nation-states in Asia and Africa were increasingly preventing the creation of a strong coalition of non-aligned governments. Despite Third Worldist attempts at non-alignment, most nationalist movements and Third World regimes had deeper diplomatic, economic and military relations with one or both of the super-powers than 'non-alignment' would suggest. Also, as already noted, Third Worldism was further complicated by the Sino-Soviet split in the early 1960s. After 1949 the People's Republic of China (PRC) had initially aligned itself with Moscow, signing a Treaty of Friendship, Alliance and Mutual Assistance with the USSR in 1950 (Westad 2000).

The vagaries of Beijing's relations with Moscow coincided with the rise and fall of the PRC's commitment to a Soviet-style development model and its increasing efforts in the 1950s to play a leadership role in the emerging Third World. Meanwhile, in more recent years there has been an attempt to conjure up a Third World-style post-Cold War Beijing Consensus to challenge the dominant US-led liberal order (known at one time as the Washington Consensus) – the Beijing Consensus, which will be discussed below, is at best a tepid echo of the Third Worldism of an earlier era (see also Prashad 2012). From 1949 to 1953 Mao and the Chinese leadership followed economic policies that included cooperating with or allowing the continued commercial activities of those members of the bourgeoisie who had not worked with the Japanese. At the same time, in rural areas they focused on land redistribution, the execution and purging of landlords and the consolidation of the power of the Communist Party. In 1954 the Chinese leadership set up a state planning apparatus and began nationalizing industry and commerce, while in 1955 they moved to collective agriculture along Soviet lines. By the second half of the 1950s, however, many members of the Chinese leadership became increasingly critical of the operation of the Soviet model in China. In particular, they were concerned about low levels of agricultural growth and excessive centralization. This was the context for the launch of the Great Leap Forward (1958–61). Although the Great Leap Forward departed from the Soviet model, it retained links to Stalinist conceptions of economic development and it even resonated with Stalinist approaches to agriculture in the 1930s, not least in terms of its human costs. The Great Leap Forward impacted heavily and badly on the peasantry as the diversion of resources to urban industries led to starvation in the countryside. The loss of life from famine between 1958 and 1961 is calculated to run as high as 30 million people.

The Great Leap Forward was closely connected to China's various foreign policy initiatives towards the emerging Third World generally and towards Southeast Asia more specifically. The CCP leadership was seeking to dramatically increase China's economic significance and its international position. At the Bandung Conference, Zhou Enlai had successfully vied with Nehru for a leading role amongst the non-aligned nation-states in Asia. In the wake of Bandung, China's relations with Indonesia increasingly improved, while Zhou Enlai's personal relationship with U Nu of Burma led to the resolution of concerns about their shared border. China's relations with Cambodia, Laos and the Democratic Republic of Vietnam (North Vietnam) were also strengthened in the late 1950s, while only Thailand and the Philippines had joined the US-sponsored Southeast Asia Treaty Organization (SEATO), set up in 1954 to support South Vietnam. The winding back of the policies associated with the Great Leap Forward in the early 1960s coincided with the complete rupture of Beijing's relationship with Moscow, and growing friction with the United States. The USSR and the United States signed a nuclear test ban treaty in 1963, which was roundly criticized by Mao. China successfully tested its own nuclear weapon in 1964. As the Chinese leadership's war of words with Moscow and Washington escalated, Beijing sought to position itself as a key nation-state in, if not the leader of, a wider Third Worldist challenge well beyond Asia. Ultimately, however, the China-led Third Worldist push had limited success – reflected in Beijing's unsuccessful effort to have the USSR excluded from the 'Second Bandung Conference' that, as discussed above, had been scheduled to meet in Algeria in June 1965. Beijing's initiative led to the cancellation of the conference when many of the governments involved, such as Egypt and India saw continued benefits in maintaining their connections to Moscow and thus not supporting Beijing. Prime Minister Jawaharlal Nehru's opposition to China's manoeuvres also flowed from the fact that the relatively good relations between China and India that had characterized the 1950s had been completely ruptured by the Sino-Indian war of 1962 fought along the disputed Himalayan frontier.

India's credentials as a leading Third Worldist state were also in relative decline more generally by the mid-1960s. In the 1950s, Nehru's international profile and his commitment to a combination of parliamentary democracy, economic planning and socialist principles helped to focus considerable world attention on India, while Nehru's diplomacy sought to mobilize a Pan-Asian coalition and a broader grouping of non-aligned Third World regimes. For some observers in the US, meanwhile, India was regarded as an important prize: they conjured with the political and ideological benefits for Washington that an alliance with one of the most influential non-aligned governments in Asia would bring. According to this vision, if the US strengthened ties with Nehru's government, Washington could help ensure that India would serve as an anchor for, and model of, democratic-capitalist development in the Third World to counter the explicitly anti-capitalist and state-socialist alternatives exemplified by China and the Soviet Union. However, for other US strategists

Pakistan was the most important nation-state in the region for military-strategic reasons: they emphasized its proximity to the Soviet Union and its position in relation to the Middle East. By 1954 the emphasis on the relative importance of Pakistan had led to the decision by the US and the government of Pakistan to enter into a mutual security agreement. At the same time, Pakistan also became a founding member of SEATO, formally established in February 1955 (McMahon 1994: 7, 337–8).

During this period the government in New Delhi set about balancing its relationship with Washington by deepening its economic and military links to Moscow, while also seeking to maintain good relations with the Chinese government. Partly as a result of these changes, by the end of the 1950s the US approach to South Asia had shifted away from an emphasis on Pakistan and towards an emphasis on India. Washington was worried that the USSR, in particular, with its generous trade and aid arrangements, was gaining influence in Indian government circles. In this context, the US was concerned that if the Indian government failed to achieve its national development plans the strength of its communist movement would increase. As a result President Eisenhower expanded his administration's economic aid programme to India in his final years in office. By the end of the 1950s the Eisenhower administration also shared the concern, voiced by Senator John F. Kennedy and others, that economic decline in India could enhance the Chinese government's prestige in international affairs. For the US, India continued to be viewed as an important model of national democratic-capitalist development that could counter the state-socialist model of national development represented by China (Berger 2004a).

Jawaharlal Nehru's commitment to Third Worldism (and to 'Nehruvian socialism') reached its peak during the second half of the 1950s. By the time Nehru died in May 1964 the notion that a benevolent technocratic elite could successful guide India to Nehru's distinctive vision of Indian socialism was in decline. Furthermore the idea that India could be part of a broad Third World coalition and serve as a model for other parts of the Third World was in crisis as were the first generation of Third Worldist regimes more generally. Nehru's conception of state-guided national development is often seen as being shaped by the Soviet model; however, his approach was always tempered by a critique of the lack of democracy in the Soviet Union and the human cost of Soviet industrialization. In fact, for some observers 'Nehruvian socialism' by the 1950s had much more in common with social democracy in post-1945 Western Europe than it did with state socialism in the Soviet Union, despite the much publicized Soviet support for national development in India. Nehru certainly rejected key aspects of the Soviet model and his perspective bore similarities to social democratic currents in Western Europe; however, Nehru's government also drew on China's post-1949 approach to national development, especially its approach to agriculture. In fact, 'Nehruvian socialism' exemplifies the way in which Marxism was assimilated to national circumstances in the wider context of decolonization, the Cold War and the emergence of Third Worldism (Berger 2004a).

In 1965, less than two years after Nehru's death, Sukarno, the president of Indonesia since independence and another key exponent of Third Worldism – who sought to synthesize nationalism, Marxism and Islam, a project that was embodied in his famous formulation *Nasionalis-Agama-Komunis* (NASAKOM) – was overthrown by General Suharto in a bloody coup and anti-Communist purge. Nehru had earlier and somewhat patronizingly regarded Sukarno as one of his disciples in Asia and antagonized his host in Bandung in 1955 as a result. However, by the mid-1960s Sukarno had attained a leading position in the Third World that was as transcendent as, although different from, the position that had been occupied by Nehru earlier. During the 1950s parliamentary democracy in Indonesia had increasingly given way to what Sukarno called 'guided democracy'. By the late 1950s Indonesia had embraced an approach to economic development that involved an increasingly high level of state intervention to restructure the economy in the context of the nationalization of Dutch-owned property. The Indonesian state directed earnings from the commodity export sector into the primarily state-owned and operated manufacturing sector. Export earnings were also directed towards public works, health, food production, education and transportation, not to mention as payment on foreign debts. The Indonesian army played an ever more important political and economic role under Sukarno, taking over direct control of large sectors of the economy in the late 1950s (Berger 2004a).

Sukarno's 'guided democracy', which involved full presidential powers and rule by decree, rested, apart from the military, on a complex web of political alliances that revolved around the *Partai Nasional Indonesia* (Nationalist Party of Indonesia – PNI), a major

Muslim political party and the *Partai Komunis Indonesia* (Communist Party of Indonesia – PKI). The latter was the largest non-governing communist party in the world at the time; it also advocated a parliamentary path to power. He played these parties off against each other, at the same time as he pitted the mainly anti-Communist military against the PKI. 'Guided democracy', underpinned by Sukarno's strident anti-Western nationalism and its synthesis with *Nasionalis-Agama-Komunis (*NASAKOM), bolstered by the Third Worldist vision of which he was an important proponent, represented an explicitly state-led attempt at national development. By the early 1960s, however, stagnation and decline in the sugar and rubber sectors, combined with falling commodity prices, had resulted in a shortage of funds and a serious balance of payments problem. By the first half of the 1960s it was increasingly apparent that not only was Indonesia's economy on the brink of collapse, but the political struc-ture centred on Sukarno was also in crisis. This was taking place against the backdrop of a conflict with Malaysia over the setting of their respective post-colonial borders (Jones 2002). The end of Sukarno's regime in Indonesia involved a much sharper break with first-generation Third Worldism than the more gradual waning of 'Nehruvian socialism' in India. Following Sukarno's overthrow in 1965–66, Suharto dramatically reoriented Indonesia's military and economic links, bringing Indonesia into close alignment with the US and Japan, against the backdrop of the elimination of the PKI, which had been an important source of support for Sukarno. At least 500,000 PKI members and supporters were killed in 1965–66. (This number is the official figure and some observers estimate the number to be 1 or 1.5 million.) Suharto presided over a conservative anti-Communist and authoritarian version of national development in Indonesia, erected on the bloodstained foundations of the coup against Sukarno's failed state-guided national development project (Berger 2004a).

Another pivotal first-generation Third Worldist regime was Egypt under Gamal Abdel Nasser. After the Second World War Egypt emerged at the centre of Pan-Arabism and the wider Third Worldist push in the Middle East: of particular geo-strategic importance because of the Suez Canal, Egypt effectively became a protectorate of Britain in the 1880s (a status that was formalized in 1914). After the First World War, the former Ottoman province emerged as a nomi-nally independent monarchy with links to Britain that were increas-ingly perceived by Egyptian nationalists as neo-colonial. But it was not until over 30 years later, on 23 July 1952, that Egyptian national-ists ousted the British-backed King Farouk in a bloodless coup. This initiated a process that led to the departure of all British troops from Egypt and the Egyptian takeover of the Suez Canal in 1956. The Suez crisis (which involved an ultimately unsuccessful Anglo-French-Israeli effort to regain control of the Canal) dramatically undermined British prestige and influence in the region. At the same time, it cata-pulted Nasser to prominence as a major figure not only in Egyptian nationalism, but also in Pan-Arabism and Third Worldism. A radical and secular nationalist, Nasser's ideas became increasingly socialist over the course of his years in office. Shortly after coming to power he published *Egypt's Liberation: The Philosophy of the Revolution*, which held up the Egyptian military as the vanguard of the national struggle against 'feudalism' and 'imperialism'. He conjured with the idea of an independent Egypt as the pivot, not only of an expanding group of united and liberated Arab nation-states, but of Africa and the Islamic world as well (Nasser 1955).

At the same time, like Nehru in India and Sukarno in Indonesia, Nasser was presiding by the late 1950s over the dramatic deepening of the state-led national development project in Egypt. His central goal was state-guided industrialization, but Nasser's vague notion of progress usually conflated industrialization and socialism. The Egyptian leader also linked industrialization to nationalism, which included social (or populist-socialist) goals and could also be connected to the broader Third Worldist agenda. However, by the 1970s the socialism of the first generation of Third Worldist regimes, such as Nasser's Egypt, seemed tepid to many observers and political actors. For example, although the coup in Libya in 1969, led by Muammar Qaddafi, had been directly influenced by Nasser's own trajectory, the regime that emerged in Tripoli was far more radical in its approach.

A key, if not always terribly effective, vehicle for Nasser's influ-ence in the Middle East was the Arab League. The Arab League was formed in the waning days of the Second World War at a conference in Alexandria attended by the governments of Egypt and Iraq, along with Lebanon, Syria, Saudi Arabia, Transjordan and Yemen. It was set up with the ostensible aim of promoting economic, technical and cultural interaction between the governments and people in the Arab world. A representative of the Palestinian Arabs also attended the initial conference. Libya joined the League in 1951. Sudan joined in

1956, followed by Tunisia and Morocco in 1958, Kuwait in 1961, Algeria in 1962, South Yemen (formerly Aden) in 1968, then Bahrain, Qatar and Oman in 1971. A council based in Cairo guided the operations of the League, but there was no significant central governing body and it operated as a relatively decentralized collection of nation-states. Up to the mid-1960s the main foci of activity for the League were supporting the Palestinians against Israel and attempting to check the French presence in Lebanon and North Africa. While Nasser was president of Egypt, he dominated the organization. With his death in 1970 Egyptian influence on the League declined, while that of the Palestine Liberation Organization (PLO) rose. After Anwar Sadat became president of Egypt, the headquarters of the League shifted from Cairo to Tunis. By the 1980s there were major divisions within the Arab League. Out of a membership of 20 governments, 12 supported the UN-sponsored and US-led 'Gulf War' against Iraq in February 1991 after the latter's invasion of Kuwait. At the same time, throughout the 1950s and 1960s Nasser not only sought to link his brand of Egyptian nationalism to Pan-Arabism, going so far as to federate Egypt with Syria to form the United Arab Republic (1958–61), but also to Pan-Islamism and Pan-Africanism. His government provided political and material assistance to national liberation movements in Africa. Egyptian government radio repeatedly irritated London and Paris with its enthusiastic support for the Mau Mau rebellion in Kenya in the early 1950s and the FLN in Algeria during its struggle against French colonialism from 1954 to 1962 (Young 2001: 190–1).

A major proponent of Pan-Africanism and a key Third Worldist in Africa in the 1950s and early 1960s was, of course, Kwame Nkrumah. He was the first Prime Minister of Ghana, which was, in turn, the first colony in southern Africa to gain independence. Formerly the British colony of the Gold Coast, it became an independent nation-state in 1957. At the same time, Pan-Africanism, which had already gained some significance in political and cultural terms in the United States between the First and Second World Wars, took on an increasingly explicit socialist tone by the 1930s and 1940s, emphasizing cooperative agriculture and state-guided industrialization. However, this vision remained linked to the goal of recuperating Africa's pre-colonial cultural heritage and the building of regional unity along cultural as well as political lines. While Pan-Africanism underpinned the push by Nkrumah and others for national self-determination and some form of

post-colonial socialism, attempts to deepen the political structures of
Pan-Africanism in the immediate post-colonial period were relatively
short-lived. For example, Nkrumah (who ruled Ghana until he was
overthrown in a military coup in 1966) and Ahmed Sikoku Tour of
Guinea formed the Ghana-Guinea union in 1958. However, this was a
relatively brief arrangement, as was the Ghana-Guinea-Mali union,
not to mention the Federation of Mali (Senegal and Mali).

The regional vision that informed Pan-Africanism increasingly
lost momentum as more and more independent nation-states emerged.
Nevertheless, Pan-Africanism survived in an attenuated form with the
formation of the Organization of African Unity (OAU) in 1963
(Young 2001: 236, 240–1). In the early twenty-first century it would
rebrand itself as the African Union (AU), acknowledging the importance of and need for a robust regional organization in Africa and
beyond. Meanwhile, as already noted, the importance of African
regionalism has been present from the early years of decolonization.
For example, in 1966, shortly before the Ghanaian military overthrew
his government, Nkrumah published *Neo-Colonialism: The Last
Stage of Imperialism* (Nkrumah 1966). In classic Third Worldist
terms, Nkrumah argued that although the erstwhile colonies had
gained political independence, national liberation could not be
achieved until they attained economic independence via a break with
neo-colonialism, something that could be more effectively carried out
on a region- or Third World-wide basis. In the post-Cold War era,
Nkrumah's concern that post-colonial nation-states in Africa (and the
erstwhile Third World) could only progress as part of a wider
economic and political grouping now appears more farsighted than
ever. The collective political project envisaged by Nkrumah and
others saw the necessary alterations to be achieved by working politically through the nation-state system to effect global change.
Developments of recent decades, have, however, rendered this
outlook and its scope rather less likely than it was even in the days
when it was first proposed.

**Conclusion: Third World Rising**

This chapter has made clear the way in which decolonization in the
1950s and 1960s and beyond facilitated the universalization of the
nation-state system. It was also emphasized that this process was

overlaid by the Cold War. Despite clearly opposing ideas of development all the major actors in the Cold War took the nation-state as the key means by which global modernity could be achieved. This was the context in which a growing number of often former colonies became nation-states and went on to align themselves with Third Worldism as a way (in theory) of avoiding alignment with either Washington or Moscow and of emphasizing the need on the part of nation-states in the Third World to find a path to global modernity that embraced neither First nor Second World. At the same time, Third Worldists, like their First World and the Second World counterparts, all accepted the centrality of the nation-state to progress even if their conception of progress diverged. As this common assumption suggests and as we have seen in this chapter, the consolidation of international development and the Cold War were closely linked. As we have also seen, by the 1930s a number of important nation-states in Latin America pioneered national development at a time when much of the rest of what would become the Third World was still part of one of the major colonial empires. After 1945 decolonization and the Cold War not only led to the dramatic expansion of the number of nation-states in the world, but also filled the ranks of the Third World and provided the context in which Third Worldism as an international movement took on increasing importance. The Golden Age of Third Worldism is the focus of the next chapter.

# 3
# The Golden Age of Third Worldism: International Development, the Cold War and the Contradictions of Global Modernity

During the period up to the late 1970s, Third Worldism generally and national development more specifically were closely connected and remained committed to state-guidance and redistribution, in theory, if not always in practice. In fact, in retrospect the late 1960s to the late 1970s was the golden age of Third Worldism. This period saw a dramatic shift in many parts of the Third World from nationalist reformism to an emphasis on revolution and even a complete break with capitalist international development. In some cases this latter commitment had existed earlier but was reaffirmed in the 1960s and 1970s. At the same time, by the 1970s the first stirrings of neo-liberalism and the early and often inadvertent foundations for uneven globalization were being laid. The less than successful delivery of global modernity on the part of state-guided national development was increasingly being met in this period by revolutionary-minded Third Worldists (on the one hand) who saw capitalism as the problem and by proponents of neo-liberalism who (on the other hand) saw the welfare state (if not 'government' in general) as the problem. In this context the Cold War relationship between security and development was also elaborated in new or revised ways. To illustrate this latter trend this chapter begins with a discussion of US foreign policy towards the Third World in the 1960s and 1970s, but unlike Chapter 2, the focus is on theories of modernization and state-guided capitalist development and the Cold War context within which they were articulated.

We then turn to a discussion of the rise and diversification of dependency theory, which emerged as part of the wider critique of US foreign policy, modernization theory and capitalism more generally, while also operating as a complement to various forms of radical nationalism and revolutionary Third Worldism. This is followed by a closer examination of the changing character of Third Worldism, revolution and the political economy of international development in this period, focusing on Latin America, the Middle East and Africa. We also look at the consolidation and transformation of the United Nations, with a particular emphasis on the failure of the organization's attempt to establish a New International Economic Order (NIEO) in the 1970s. A more detailed examination of Northeast and Southeast Asia in this period will be reserved for Chapter 4. The main justification for this is the fact that, by the latter part of the period under consideration here (the late 1970s and early 1980s to be more specific), a number of nation-states in East Asia were increasingly seen to be developing 'successfully' and even being represented as providing lessons for the rest of the Third World.

## The Pursuit of Global Capitalist Modernity: The Cold War, the Third World and Modernization Theory

As we saw in the previous chapter, US President John F. Kennedy (1961–63) emphasized the need for Washington to take the initiative in the Third World to a much greater degree than his predecessor, Dwight D. Eisenhower (1952–60). As discussed previously, the increasingly elaborate theoretical justification for the promotion of the Cold War-oriented security and international development framework in the late 1950s and early 1960s is often described as classic modernization theory. The latter was committed to a period of tutelage on the part of the nation-states of the Third World and focused on the need for cultural transformation to achieve global modernity (Hoselitz 1952; Rostow 1960). History was regarded as linear and the achievement of development was seen as an evolutionary movement from the traditional to the modern. Classic modernization theory emphasized the totality of change and saw modernization as a process of diffusion, which spread throughout a national society affecting economics, the type of government, social structure, values, religion and family structure. Classic modernization theorists viewed under-development in the Third World as the result of internal shortcomings specific to underdeveloped nation-states and their pre-colonial rather than their colonial or post-colonial history. Classic modernization theory provided intellectual legitimacy for an evolutionary conception of liberal (capitalist) national development. And in this context security, broadly defined, was about ensuring that the nation-state in question retained a commitment to capitalist development as it evolved towards global modernity.

Classic modernization theory in practice was, of course, somewhat messier. For example, in South Vietnam in the early 1960s the Strategic Hamlet Program initially became the pivot of Washington's wider strategy for security and development. The US drew on previous French colonial initiatives, earlier efforts by the Diem regime, as well as British counter-insurgency programmes in Malaya in the 1950s. The result was a development-security framework that emphasized the removal of peasants from widely dispersed villages, placing them in concentrated settlements that could be controlled more directly by the government in Saigon. With this approach the US Military Assistance Command Vietnam (MACV) and the Agency for International Development (USAID) sought to undermine the National Liberation Front's ability to get intelligence, food and other supplies, as well as recruits from the southern population. The National Liberation Front (NLF) quickly responded by promising the peasants that following the revolution they would be allowed to return to their old villages. The NLF also intensified its military attacks on, and its recruitment activities in, the strategic hamlets.

Despite the apparent failure of the Strategic Hamlet Program by the end of 1963, subsequent efforts to resettle and control the rural population did little but rework the basic approach, while excising the term 'strategic hamlet' from the theory and practice of security and development. Meanwhile, following the overthrow and assassination of Diem and his brother Nhu Dinh Diem in a military coup in late 1963, the rural development efforts that succeeded the Strategic Hamlet Program were increasingly overshadowed by full-scale warfare. The US had hoped that the overthrow of the Diem regime would improve the stability of South Vietnam; however, the deterioration in the military situation following the coup paved the way for the escalation of US involvement and direct military intervention by 1964. This led, in turn, to immense human, material and environmental destruction, but failed to solve the fundamental political problems of the Saigon regime and the turning of the 'fragile' nation-state of South Vietnam into a strong sovereign national polity. The pervasive reliance on US aid generated growing possibilities for government and private corruption. With the Tet Offensive in early 1968 any idea that US power could turn South Vietnam into a viable capitalist nation-state and achieve military victory against the North had disappeared.

With the widening of the war in Vietnam, and the increasingly militarized character of the Alliance for Progress, which was discussed in Chapter 2, the creation of institutions and organizations that could provide order became even more important for proponents of capitalist development in the Third World. The assumptions and concerns of the officials who carried the US into the dramatic widening of the war in Vietnam were closely connected to the revised theories of modernization and development that emerged by the late 1960s. For example, the major concern of Samuel Huntington's influential 1968 book, *Political Order in Changing Societies*, was to determine what might or might not be necessary to ensure continued social order and political stability. Widely regarded as the standard revision of classic modernization theory and a key text in the burgeoning literature on military-led modernization, Huntington held up political order as the ultimate goal of any society. He argued that, contrary to earlier expectations, the instability in Asia and the rest of the Third World since the Second World War was primarily the result of dramatic social transformation and the equally dramatic expansion in the number of new politically oriented organizations without the corresponding creation or amplification of political institutions capable of presiding over this process. Furthermore, US foreign policy since 1945 had, in his view, missed this point, because Washington had placed too great an emphasis on the economic gap, while overlooking the political gap. He emphasized that the political gap had been ignored because of the assumption in North America that political stability flowed from social reform stimulated by economic development. However, in his view it was actually the process of modernization that led to political instability. For Huntington order was the key to political power as well as the basis of capitalist development, and thus ultimately security (Huntington 1968).

Huntington's prescriptions held out the possibility that successful nation-building – conceptualized in terms of consolidating the institutional and ultimately social relations in accordance with capitalist modernization – in South Vietnam and elsewhere remained within Washington's reach. However, as suggested above, with the Tet Offensive in early 1968 the elite consensus in America that US power could turn South Vietnam into a stable capitalist nation-state and achieve military victory against North Vietnam had been completely undermined. As the intractability of the US development-security effort in South Vietnam became increasingly apparent the US-led mission to develop the Third World more generally was also increasingly challenged. In fact, nation-building became synonymous with Washington's failure in South Vietnam to the point where the term was removed from the international development discourse until its resurrection in the years immediately after 9/11, a topic we turn to in Chapter 5. Its second coming, which as of the time of writing may well have peaked if not already begun to fade, increasingly used more specific terms such as capacity-building, stability operations and post-conflict reconstruction. By the late 1960s, revolution and economic nationalism were high on the agenda in Asia, Africa and Latin America.

In this context the US reinforced, but did not necessarily provide the main impetus for the post-1959 counter-revolutionary trend in Latin America and elsewhere towards vehemently anti-Communist and bureaucratic-authoritarian military regimes. Increasing US support for anti-Communist dictatorships in Asia, the Middle East, Latin America and Africa reflected the updating of a long-standing practice, exemplified, for example, by support for Rafael Trujillo (1930–61) in the Dominican Republic and Fulgencio Batista (1934–58) in Cuba. In the 1960s and 1970s (and beyond) entrenched, or new, authoritarian governments, such as, the Somoza family in Nicaragua (1933–79), the Shah of Iran (1953–79), Park Chung Hee in South Korea (1961–79), Joseph Désiré Mobutu (Mobutu Sese Seko) in Congo/Zaire (1965–97), Ferdinand Marcos in the Philippines (1965–86) and General Suharto in Indonesia (1965–98), could be relied upon to, by and large, support the US in its effort to maintain a regional and international order of liberal capitalism. The perception of the relative strategic importance of the nation-states concerned from the perspective of the US ensured a greater or lesser degree of tolerance by the US of the illiberal economic and political practices of its client-allies.

The approach to foreign policy articulated by the Nixon administration (1969–73) was a relatively conservative reaction to various challenges to Washington's influence in the Third World. For example, in 1969 Nixon sent Nelson A. Rockefeller to Latin America to meet with heads of state and then give a complete report accompanied by recommendations. Rockefeller expressed some sympathy for the Latin American view that relations with the US were unequal. He also predicted that the region was 'moving rapidly into a period of revolution' and his recommendations to deal with this trend emphasized a military solution rather than even modest changes to the structure of economic and political relations that had been propounded by Washington in an earlier era. Reflecting the shift from the early optimism of the Alliance for Progress to military modernization theory, Rockefeller argued that 'without some framework for order, no progress can be achieved', and in Latin America the military was 'the essential force for constructive social change'. To this end, he advised that Washington should increase its military assistance to the region. More or less the same perspective can be found in the Latin American Report of Nelson Rockefeller's Commission on Critical Choices for Americans, produced while he was serving as Gerald Ford's vice-president in the mid-1970s (LaFeber 1993 on Rockefeller: 201–4).

The Rockefeller Report was central to the shift from the Cold War liberalism of the Kennedy and Johnson era and its apparent emphasis on economic aid, the middle sectors and democratization, to military modernization with its concern with order as the key to development and progress. The Rockefeller Report clearly sanctioned military regimes and contributed to the legitimacy of the authoritarian and technocratic regimes in Brazil and elsewhere in the 1970s. At the end of 1969, Nixon launched his new policy for Latin America, under the title 'Action for Progress in the Americas', which lined up with Rockefeller's recommendations. It also drew on the Consensus of Viña del Mar, which was a result of a meeting in Chile in May 1969 between representatives of most Latin American governments. Apart from some economic concessions the major thrust was the president's emphasis on taking a realistic approach to inter-American relations. This has generally been interpreted to mean that Washington was willing to deal with military governments regardless of how autocratic and repressive they were. Nixon's Latin American policy meshed with the overall concern of the Nixon Doctrine to support particular collaborative (client) regimes as regional policemen.

In the 1970s the armies of Central and South America expanded, along with a number of other military establishments around the world, as arms sales emerged as the backbone of Nixon's policy. Direct US assistance continued, and generous credit was extended to facilitate the purchase of armaments. The Central American armies continued to participate in the civic action programmes that had been set up by the Alliance for Progress. These programmes, which involved the use of troops in the construction of roads and schools, were aimed at improving the army's image, and also further linked the United States with the Central American military establishments at the local level. Under Nixon the US Southern Command also sought to resurrect CONDECA (the Central American Defense group), which had fallen apart after the Soccer War in 1969 between Honduras and El Salvador. However, the generals in Central America were not particularly interested in regional cooperation, and CONDECA folded by the mid-1970s (LaFeber 1993: 202–4). Also, unlike the early years of the Alliance for Progress Nixon's 'Action for Progress' emphasized trade rather than economic aid and contained even fewer reformist initiatives. Nixon's overall approach was clearly apparent when Washington helped ensure that the Allende government in Chile was ousted in 1973 by a military that had been well supplied for many years by the United States. Meanwhile, the military regime in Brazil also shifted closer to the US in the early 1970s, no doubt in part because of lavish US military assistance as radical movements and ideas continued to converge on a radicalized Third Worldist agenda in the Americas and beyond.

### The Pursuit of Global Socialist Modernity: The Cold War, the Third World and Dependency Theory

Radical theories of development emerged in the late 1960s and 1970s to challenge modernization theory and complement the golden age of Third Worldism. At the centre of the new radicalism were dependency theory and the increasingly attractive model of the Cuban Revolution. Between the late 1960s and the late 1980s dependency theory was continually revised in the context of an ongoing debate with liberal capitalist theories of modernization, and also as a result of criticisms from more explicitly Marxist theorists. Dependency theory, as it came to be understood in the 1960s, developed out of Latin American historico-structuralism, which was initially associated with Raul Prebisch and the United Nations' (UN) Economic Commission for Latin America (ECLA: also known by its Spanish-language acronym of CEPAL) which was discussed in Chapter 2 (see Prebisch 1950). Its origins are also often traced to the work of US-based academics, such as Paul Baran (Baran 1957). In the second half of the 1960s, Andre Gunder Frank emerged as one of the main proponents of classic dependency theory (Frank 1966). Walter Rodney was another important figure whose career and work reflected the linkages between the dependency debate in the Caribbean and Latin America and nationalist and radical debates in Africa, at the same time as his dependency model was also popularized in America and Western Europe (Rodney 1972).

The emphasis on external factors that characterized classic dependency theory in this period, which was linked to radical Third Worldism, had the effect of homogenizing the broader understanding of the Third World as modernization theory had done before, albeit on very different theoretical premises. This was readily apparent in Frank's work. In *Capitalism and Underdevelopment in Latin America*, which was published in 1967, Frank outlined the concept of 'the development of underdevelopment', and articulated a model of historical development, which directly linked underdevelopment and economic stagnation to the siphoning off of the economic surplus from the periphery to the industrialized core. Frank made a dramatic break with classical Marxism, asserting 'that it is capitalism, both world and national, which produced underdevelopment in the past and which still generates underdevelopment in the present' (Frank 1967: xi; Frank 1966) Frank's work rose to particular prominence and his ideas were produced and reproduced so widely that they emerged in the late 1960s and early 1970s as the dominant radical version of dependency theory and Third Worldism.

By the second half of the 1970s dependency theory and Third Worldism had peaked, yet both have survived down to the present in attenuated form. For example, the late populist-nationalist President of Venezuela, Hugo Chávez (who came to power in 1999), drew attention to the work of Andre Gunder Frank during his April 2001 speech at the Fourth Hemispheric Conference against the FTAA (Free-Trade

Area of the Americas) in Havana, Cuba. Chávez was a key, although not always persuasive figure in attempting to pursue regionalism, with as many nation-states in the region as he could persuade to join him and his Alternativa Bolivariana de las Americas (ALBA). His vision of extending his 'Bolivarian Revolution' well beyond Venezuela's borders as a counter-weight to Washington has had considerable appeal. However, prior to Chávez's death in 2013 he remained marginal on the global stage while his regional influence has probably been over-rated. In the Americas itself none of the most important leaders explicitly allied themselves with Chávismo in the ways sometimes anticipated, nor did his vision of 'twenty-first-century socialism' involve breaking radically with global capitalism: as a major petroleum-exporter Venezuela, before and after Chávez, was and remains dependent on its access to world capitalism generally and the US market more specifically.

In some ways the more understated character of Chávez's 'Bolivarian Revolution' (owing not least to the changed circumstances under which it advanced) when compared to the Cuban Revolution of 1959 and even the Nicaraguan Revolution of 1979, highlights the relative obscurity to which classic dependency theory had been assigned by the late 1970s. The demise of classic dependency theory, as with the more radical strands of Third Worldism, can be traced to failures in realizing their political promises (linked, of course, significantly to the historical conjunctures and constraints we identify here). Meanwhile, the rise of the Newly Industrializing Countries (NICs) in East Asia and Latin America (Mexico and Brazil) and the rise of the Organization of Petroleum Exporting Countries (OPEC) led to some reappraisal of the structural barriers to development of significant parts of the Third World. At the same time by the late 1970s, an emphasis on the corruption and authoritarianism of many nation-states in the Third World shifted the blame for underdevelopment back on to the Third World (while we acknowledge the role of 'corruption' within the Third World, we must keep in mind here that some forms of Third World corruption are really not that much different from the intense lobbying of the elected members of the US government that involve increasingly large and weakly regulated financial support for political campaigns). This is by no means to disregard the benefits that elites in the Third World enjoy *vis-à-vis* their citizens, but only to suggest that corruption has to be approached in a more nuanced way. An important factor behind the fall of dependency theory and Third Worldism was that by the mid-1970s they had been partially contained by their political and theoretical incorporation into the dominant liberal capitalist narrative on development and security.

The revised approaches to dependency and international development departed from the determinism associated with classic dependency theory while they continued to facilitate the circulation of the idea of a relatively homogeneous Third World. This was part of the wider shift in the 1970s towards greater influence at the UN by Third World governments. In particular, through the UN, a coalition of Third World state representatives launched a call for a New International Economic Order (NIEO) and the recognition in America and Western Europe that the North–South conflict was more important than the East–West (Cold War) conflict (Thomas 1985; 1987). This reformist agenda envisioned improving North–South relations and major structural changes to the international economic order, but also went to some lengths to ensure that it could not be construed as an all-out challenge to capitalism itself. The initiative resulted in the Charter of Economic Duties and Rights of States. The latter, however, arguably served – perhaps inadvertently – to reinforce the idea of national development as a universal path to global modernity, as well as placing responsibility for 'well-being' back on the nation-state.

Some of the gist of these initiatives was partially reflected in the policies adopted by the administration of President Jimmy Carter (1977–80) in his first two years in office. Carter, as well as Zbigniew Brzezinski, who served as his National Security Advisor, and virtually all of the members of the Carter administration concerned with foreign policy, were members of the Trilateral Commission. They saw US relations with Japan and Western Europe as the central pivot of development and security worldwide. The major goal of the Trilateral Commission was to develop a cohesive and semi-permanent alliance that embraced the world's major capitalist nation-states in order to promote stability and order and protect their interests (Gill 2002). Of course, again, we have to keep in mind exactly whose interests were being promoted through the Trilateral Commission. In the case of the Third World, the Trilateral Commission advocated a limited amount of reform in order to maintain long-term stability. By the end of the 1970s the Brandt Commission and its *North–South* report had also emerged. Produced by the Independent Commission and chaired by the former West German Chancellor, Willy Brandt, the Brandt

Commission represented a major initiative that reflected the attempt by a handful of industrial nation-states to manage the demands articulated by Third World representatives via relatively piecemeal reforms to the theory and practice of security and development. For example, in the US various reformist pieces of legislation were passed by Congress and were generally grouped under the heading of 'New Directions'. These initiatives emphasized both the basic needs of the poor and direct grassroots participation in the process of development. At the same time, the Foreign Assistance Act was amended to provide for an increased focus on human rights in the disbursement of foreign aid.

## The Contradictions of Global Modernity: The Cold War and the Zenith and Decline of Third Worldism

As we have seen, a key factor behind Washington's turn to the Third World was the coming to power of Fidel Castro in Cuba in 1959. Meanwhile, the early successes of the Cuban Revolution ensured that it was quickly held up as an important alternative model of development by dependency theorists and socialist revolutionaries across Latin America and beyond. The emergence of state socialism in Cuba took place alongside the emergence of what can be described as a wider wave of second-generation Third Worldist regimes that were more avowedly socialist than those of the first generation (see Chapter 2). These included Ahmed Ben Bella (1962–65) and Houari Boumédiene (1965–78) in Algeria and Tanzania under Julius Nyerere (1965–85). Also included in this list should be Chile under Salvador Allende (1970–73) Jamaica under Michael Manley (1972–, Libya under Muammar Qaddafi after 1969 and the *Derg* (Committee) in Ethiopia (1974–91). Not to mention Guinea-Bissau from 1974, under Amilcar Cabral's successors, the People's Republic of Angola under the Popular Movement for the Liberation of Angola (MPLA) after 1975, Mozambique under Samora Moises Machel (1975–86) and Nicaragua under the Sandinistas (1979–90). This list might also include the rapid rise and fall of Patrice Lumumba in the Republic of the Congo (formerly the Belgian Congo) in the early 1960s. He was the leader of Mouvement National Congolais (MNC) and he emerged as the key figure and Prime Minister of the Congo at the time of independence in June 1960. As we saw in Chapter 2, Lumumba was assassinated by Kataganese rebels into whose hands he was delivered by Joseph Mobutu (who would later rise to monopolize political power in the Congo, renamed Zaire by Mobutu) and the Belgian authorities, and with the complicity of Washington in January 1961.

Like Ché Guevara after him, Lumumba's early death quickly elevated him to a position of major significance in Third Worldism generally and Third World socialism more specifically. The second-generation Third Worldist regimes, which were framed by the Cuban Revolution at the beginning and the Nicaraguan Revolution at the end, and for which figures like Lumumba and Guevara became powerful symbols, increasingly intersected with a major revolutionary wave between 1974 and the early 1980s. If the revolutionary regimes with problematic long-term, if not short-term, progressive credentials that emerged in the second half of the 1970s are counted, the list of revolutionary-socialist Third Worldist regimes in this period mentioned above becomes longer. It would include: Vietnam, Cambodia and Laos in Southeast Asia; Afghanistan (especially 1979–89) in Central Asia; and Zimbabwe (after 1980), along with São Tomé e Príncipe and Cape Verde (which, as noted elsewhere, emerged out of the collapse of the Portuguese Empire) in Africa. Grenada under Maurice Bishop in the Caribbean was also part of this wave. Meanwhile major, albeit unsuccessful, revolutionary movements were gaining ground in El Salvador, Guatemala and the Philippines, as well as elsewhere, in the late 1970s and early 1980s.

Second-generation Third Worldist regimes reflected a more radical, more unambiguously socialist, Third Worldism than the first-generation ones. There were important exceptions such as the People's Republic of China and the Democratic Republic of Vietnam, which were both first-generation Third Worldist regimes led by Communist parties committed to Marxism-Leninism and state socialism. At the same time, Nehru, Sukarno and even Nasser often had a more complicated relationship to 'socialism' and to their own national Communist parties than is apparent when the distinction between first- and second-generation Third Worldist regimes is measured primarily in terms of a formal commitment to state socialism. Second-generation leaders such as Amilcar Cabral, who led the African Party for the Independence of Guinea and Cape Verde (PAIGC) from 1956 until his assassination in 1973 (a year after Cabral's death Guinea-Bissau emerged as an independent state, while Cape Verde was inducted into the United Nations in 1975), may well have been more

radical than Nehru, Sukarno or Nasser. But Cabral's particularly prag-
matic brand of socialism makes him an untypical example of the
second generation. While he was widely regarded as progressive, he
drew on Marxism rather than positioning himself as a Marxist.

The representation of the first generation of Third Worldist regimes
as reformist and the second generation as revolutionary Marxists
committed to state socialism may be somewhat overdrawn, but the
latter group was still generally more radical than the former. For example, if the Bandung Conference was symbolically the most important
meeting for the first generation of Third Worldist regimes, one of the
key events for the second generation was the Tricontinental
Conference of Solidarity of the Peoples of Africa, Asia and Latin
America held in Havana in January 1966. The Bandung Conference
had brought together a relatively small number of leaders from mainly
recently independent nation-states in Asia in order to stake out a non-
aligned position in the Cold War. The 1966 Havana Tricontinental
Conference, by contrast, involved delegates from throughout Asia,
Africa, the Middle East and Latin America. And the overwhelming
majority articulated a far more radical anti-imperial agenda at the same
time as they formally emphasized their independence from the USSR
and Maoist China (Young 2001:213). Second-generation Third
Worldist regimes, directly or indirectly linked to the Tricontinental-
ism of the late 1960s and 1970s, represented the practical complement
to the rise and spread of dependency theory (along with other revitalized Marxist theories of development and social and political change),
discussed in the previous section of this chapter (Frank 1966; Frank
1967; Rodney 1972) In this era second-generation Third Worldist
regimes and their supporters attempted to radicalize state-mediated
national development efforts in various ways in the name of socialism
and national liberation. The example of the Vietnamese revolution had
influenced many of the second-generation Third Worldist regimes. At
the same time, revolutionary regimes were also directly inspired and,
in the case of Algeria, for example, supported by Castro's Cuba.

In Algeria, the escalating military struggle against French colonialism that began in 1954, in the context of the expanding Cold War,
culminated in the departure of the defeated colonial rulers and the
triumphant emergence of an independent Algeria in July 1962. The
triumph of the FLN in Algeria marked an important turning point for
the region and for Third Worldism more generally. Robert Malley
goes so far as to call the FLN's accession to power in 1962 'a defining

moment in the history of Third Worldism'. The Algerian Revolution was pivotal to Third Worldism because the struggle had been so lengthy and violent at the same time as the FLN was 'acutely aware' of the struggle's 'international dimension' (Malley 1996: 81). At the founding meeting of the Organization of African Unity (OAU) in Addis Abba in May 1963, the Algerian leader, Ben Bella, had delivered a particularly stirring address to those in attendance that attracted the attention of the US. Washington viewed with concern both his radical ideas and his links with Cuba (Gleijeses 2002:38–9). In 1965 Ben Bella was ousted in a military coup led by Houari Boumédiene, his defence minister and also his former comrade-in-arms. The latter, a charismatic military officer who enjoyed considerable popular support in Algeria, remained more or less committed to the populist socialism and state-guided economics of his predecessor. Boumédiene emerged in the 1960s and 1970s as a key figure in Third Worldism. As we shall see, he played a central role in the call for a New International Economic Order (NIEO) at the United Nations in the mid-1970s (Thomas 1985: esp. 122–52).

Meanwhile, Moscow's role was changing. In Latin America at the end of the 1950s the USSR had moved to support the Cuban Revolution as Fidel Castro and his followers set about creating a radical socialist state in close proximity to the US. Following the Cuban Missile Crisis in 1962, and the replacement of Nikita Khrushchev (1953–64) by Leonid Brezhnev (1964–82), Moscow increasingly urged the Communist parties in Latin America to adopt a gradual approach to social change in sharp contrast to the Cuban model. This approach had the effect of further encouraging many revolutionaries to break completely with Moscow in the 1960s and try to emulate the Cuban Revolution. While the new regime in Cuba became very dependent on the Soviet Union, members of the Cuban leadership continued to articulate a far more revolutionary stance than their patrons in Moscow in this period. For example, Havana gave considerable encouragement and support to insurgent groups in Nicaragua and Guatemala that had split from the traditional Communist movement (or had never been linked to it in the first place). In fact, the 1960s in particular were characterized by a concerted effort to try and spread the socialism of the Cuban Revolution to the rest of Latin America and beyond. This process was reflected in the execution in 1967 of Ché Guevara, who had headed a small band of revolutionaries trying vainly to bring revolution and socialism to the peasants of Bolivia.

Guevara personified revolutionary idealism and Third Worldism in its second-generation form. In the 1960s Fidel Castro increasingly aligned himself with the Soviet Union and sought to focus on building communism in Cuba. Guevara meanwhile was increasingly influenced by Trotskyism and by the idea that the success of Cuban communism was dependent on the spread of revolution to the rest of the Third World. However, Guevara departed from Trotsky's emphasis on a vanguard party leading workers, and found in 'foco' theory the key to initiating action. With *foquismo* Guevara emphasized that a small nucleus of guerrillas could provide the leadership and revolutionary *élan* required to establish a successful guerrilla insurgency amongst the peasantry across the Third World. In early 1965 Guevara resigned from the Cuban government and led an expedition to the Congo. This effort was a disappointment, however, and he soon shifted his focus back to Latin America, arriving with his small group of *foquistas* in Bolivia. However, his guerrilla group failed to gain the support of the indigenous peasantry in the Bolivian highlands. His efforts to foment revolution were also regarded with suspicion by the Bolivian Communist Party. He was captured and executed in October 1967 by counter-insurgency troops of the Bolivian armed forces. Following Guevara's death, and the virtual elimination of guerrilla groups in Colombia, Venezuela and Guatemala by the end of the 1960s, rural insurgency and Cuban militancy in Latin America were curtailed.

As the 1970s began, Cuban policy in Latin America had come more into line with the USSR. At the same time, the Cuban government had helped to educate and influence an entire generation of revolutionaries in Latin America and beyond. For example, the Frente Sandinista de Liberación Nacional (Sandinista National Liberation Front – FSLN) in Nicaragua, and its leader Carlos Fonseca (who was killed in 1976 in a battle with Somoza's National Guard), was profoundly influenced by the Cuban experience. And, although Cuba had curtailed its direct involvement in Latin America by the 1970s, Africa was a different matter – Cuban troops played an important, even pivotal, role in the revolution in Angola in the 1970s. As mentioned in Chapter 2, the ongoing armed struggles in Portugal's colonies, combined with the overthrow of dictatorship in Portugal itself, led to the independence of Angola, Mozambique, Guinea-Bissau and São Tomé e Príncipe and Cape Verde in 1974–75. Angola and Mozambique, however, continued to be torn by guerrilla insurgencies attempting to bring down the Marxist and Third Worldist leadership. This continued into the post-Cold War era, only apparently winding down in the case of Angola with the onset of the twenty-first century. Angola represents a particularly stark example of the tragedy that came in the wake of national liberation and the ostensible pursuit of Third World socialism.

Meanwhile, Zimbabwe also increasingly emerged as a post-colonial and post-Cold War tragedy in the same league as Angola. In 1965 the white settlers of Southern Rhodesia, under the leadership of Ian Smith, had launched the famous Unilateral Declaration of Independence (UDI). What followed was a protracted war of national liberation led by the Patriotic Front, an uneasy coalition of Joshua Nkomo's Zimbabwe African Political Union (ZAPU) and Robert Mugabe's Zimbabwe African National Union (ZANU). In 1980 Zimbabwe achieved full independence and majority rule under the elected government of former guerrilla leader, and now President, Mugabe. However, Mugabe's increasingly erratic and despotic rule has become something of an example of the exhaustion of national liberation as a political project, and perhaps the more tragic legacies of Third Worldism's responses to colonialism more generally. Third Worldist regimes, such as Mugabe's in Zimbabwe, had come to power with the intention of dramatically transforming what were still profoundly hierarchical and primarily rural societies via land reform and state-directed import-substitution industrialization strategies. However, despite these efforts, which sometimes never went beyond the planning stage, long-standing divisions in these societies, in the context of complex colonial legacies, were reinforced and reconfigured rather than undermined. Most state-capitalist and socialist-oriented national development projects in the Third World were already in crisis before relative latecomers such as Mugabe even came to power (Mamdani 1996). The state-mediated national development projects, which were the key object of international development, as they emerged in Africa and elsewhere rested on a growing range of governmental structures to manage production for domestic and export markets. These elaborate tariff systems and dual exchange rates, and a range of subsidies on food and other items, combined with the expansion of the education system, health care and other social services led to the emergence of overburdened nation-states. By the end of the 1970s state-led national development initiatives were coming under increasing strain with rising foreign debt and the predations of corrupt elites, both civilian and military.

The growing contradictions of international development provided the context for the UN Declaration on the Establishment of a New International Economic Order (NIEO) in the mid-1970s. The formal call for a restructuring of the world economy in favour of the nation-states of the Third World was made at the Sixth Special Session of the General Assembly of the United Nations from 9 April to 2 May 1974, which passed the Declaration and Programme of Action for the Establishment of a New International Economic Order at the end of its deliberations. The call for an NIEO came in the wake of the negative impact of the 1973 oil crisis. Also of significance is the fact that Third World governments had gained a dramatic numerical influence at the UN by the 1970s. The UN's membership rose from 51 in 1945 to 156 in 1980. The vast majority of the new members were from Asia and Africa. At the same time, the idea of an NIEO built on earlier efforts to address the structural inequalities of the international politico-economic order. These previous efforts included the establishment of the Group of 77 at the 1962 Economic Conference of Developing Countries in Cairo and the establishment in 1964 of the United Nations Conference on Trade and Development (UNCTAD). The immediate impetus for the NIEO, meanwhile, was the decision by the Non-Aligned Movement, taken at its meeting in Algiers in September 1973, to ask the UN to hold a special session on what was somewhat blandly described as issues surrounding raw materials and economic development.

A central figure in the promotion and planning of the NIEO Declaration was, as noted above, Houari Boumédiene, President of Algeria. He was responsible for the initial request to the UN to convene a special session on international economic development. The other main sponsors were the unlikely trio of Latin American populists, the presidents of Venezuela and Mexico – Carlos Andres Pérez (1973–78) and Luís Echeverría Álvarez (1970–76) – and the last incarnation of the Persian Emperor, the Shah of Iran, Mohammed Reza Pahlavi (1954–79). The call for an NIEO followed on the heels of the 1973 oil crisis and the demonstration by OPEC of its ability to set the price of oil. While some commentators see OPEC's assertiveness in the 1970s as an example of the wider Third Worldist push in this period, OPEC's growing influence weakened rather than strengthened Third Worldism. The rise of conservative, anti-

Communist, oil-rich nation-states, particularly in the Middle East, and their often strong links to the US, represented a major obstacle to the realization of the NIEO and the wider Third Worldist project. Of course, in an equally contradictory fashion, the new 'petro-states' were also in a position by the 1980s to resist the economic liberalizing thrust of uneven globalization. They were also supported by their allies in maintaining undemocratic governance, even in the face of the end of the Cold War and the focus on 'democratization' elsewhere.

The Declaration and Programme of Action for the Establishment of a New Economic Order effectively pushed for a wholesale reform of the international political-economic system, including redistributive measures and policy resolutions to redress the structural inequalities of the post-colonial world economy. If the period of decolonization from the 1950s to the 1970s had proceeded by and large under the presumption that the 'new' nation-states would be able to achieve their development goals through internal reform and external world market integration, by the 1970s the capitalist core countries themselves experienced significant crises, pointing to a deepening set of contradictions in this international conjuncture (Amin 1997: 16). Implementing the envisaged set of reforms would have required a new global structure of governance that went far beyond the UN-centred international system. This new global structure would have required the power to reorganize global markets and extract taxes at a global level and then redistribute them globally as well. The concrete comprehensive governance vision put forward in the context of the NIEO was, of course, never implemented. Within another decade or so neo-liberalism would be in the ascendant, while proponents of uneven globalization emphasized that state-guided national development and redistribution was the problem rather than the solution. The uneven spread of globalization would be further exacerbated, as we will see in the next chapter, by the end of the Cold War: a world-historical shift that was interpreted as a triumph not just for capitalism, but for liberal or neo-liberal capitalism. At the same time, by the late 1970s radical politico-religious challenges were increasingly being mounted against the secular nation-state as it had emerged and been universalized by the 1970s. The rise of the Ayatollahs in Iran in the wake of the Iranian Revolution of 1979 sent a powerful signal to would-be religious revolutionaries, regardless of whether Iran's shortcomings prior to 1979 could be attributed to the secular character of the Shah's rule. At the same time, within a decade or less of the Iranian revolution the end of the Cold War also brought with it increased concern about what would, by the twenty-first century, be a growing interest in 'failing' or 'failed' states.

In this context the NIEO was, for some observers, too little and too late, while for others it was too much and too early, coinciding at the same time with the growing importance of neo-liberalism. At another level, the NIEO was simply calling for changes in the 1970s that the recently universalized system of sovereign nation-states formally represented by the United Nations could not implement due to their transformative scope; the changes it envisaged ran against entrenched structures, interests, and co-opted actors and forces. Only a sufficiently profound crisis of international development could result in, and allow for, progressive and systemic alternatives of that magnitude and scope to come to the fore. From the perspective of the second decade of the twenty-first century, such crises may appear to have come and gone. It can be argued, however, that even the 'Great Recession' (dated from December 2007 to June 2009, but for many people far from over) did not have a 'sufficiently profound' impact, at least where it counted, to encourage a shift towards progressive and systemic alternatives to the established international politico-economic order of the early twenty-first century. At any rate, the call at the UN for a New International Economic Order was rebuffed. And almost forty years later the contradictions of international development are even more apparent than ever, but it is not at all clear that the United Nations was then, or is now, the forum for the serious consideration or pursuit of alternative visions of global modernity: as we have emphasized, the problem of development cannot be solved by conflating it with the developmental nation-state as it was assumed to have been universalized after 1945 under the overall auspices of the United Nations. The focus on the sovereign nation-state as the 'object of development' (Mitchell, 2002: esp. 209–43) and the vehicle for development (global modernity) is the fundamental contradiction of international development and of Third Worldism. In many ways, these contradictions are being disclosed by transnational movement politics that challenge the logic and compulsion of neo-liberal development (M. Weber 2005; 2009; McMichael 2010). This logic of neo-liberal development is organized as a global project, albeit still refracted through the mechanisms of governance and discipline enacted by states and justified in the name of national development.

**Conclusion: The Golden Age of Third Worldism**

As we have argued, the golden age of Third Worldism can be seen to have come and gone in the 1960s and 1970s. Growing disillusionment with reformist types of national development saw an increased emphasis on revolution and efforts to break with international development in its capitalist form. This shift was on the one hand provoked by growing objections to the character of US foreign policy towards the Third World in the 1960s and 1970s generally, and on the other by the failure in most cases of theories of modernization and state-guided capitalist development to deliver on their promises to the majority of people. This was parallelled by the emergence and growing appeal of dependency theory and an invigoration of Third Worldism. Dependency theory, too, for all its rich historical analysis failed to move the debates in a way that shifted the conflation of development with the state. The way in which this was played out in Africa, the Middle East and Latin America was given particular attention. The growing disappointment in the types of national development pursued from the 1940s to the 1970s also resulted in the failed attempt by a substantial number of Third World governments to use the United Nations in the mid-1970s as a forum within which they could call for and establish a New International Economic Order. However, even the relatively moderate desire to reform capitalist international development as it had been consolidated by the early 1970s came up against significant counter-pressures, and both radical and moderate brands of Third Worldism subsequently were unable to deliver on their earlier promise. At the same time, against the backdrop of the decline of Third Worldism, the late 1970s (and early 1980s) came to represent a major turning point as earlier reformist and radical ideas about national development gave way to an increasing emphasis on neo-liberalism and uneven globalization as the 'new' solution to the contradictions of international development. As also mentioned, the late 1970s saw a rising politico-religious radicalism (and/or terrorism) that challenged the secular character of the modern nation-state, a challenge manifested most obviously by the Iranian revolution. This trend was also apparent in accommodation of some politico-religious movements within secular nation-states across the Middle East, South Asia and on to Indonesia. Of course it also led to a range of violent politico-religious transnational networks that would come into their own by the early twenty-first century with sometimes devastating consequences. At the same time, others have focused attention on the rise of social movement politics in contra-distinction to a politics of neo-liberal development as pursued by states (McMichael 2010; M. Weber 2005; 2009). Meanwhile, by the 1980s, a growing number of nation-states in Northeast and Southeast Asia were increasingly seen as having successfully achieved national development. They were also seen as representing an example for the rest of the Third World. However, a highly politicized debate ensued about what kind of developmental example the East Asian economic 'miracles' represented. It is to these themes that we now turn in Chapter 4.

# 4

# Third Worldism Retreating: International Development, the End of the Cold War and the Crisis of Global Modernity

The late 1970s and the 1980s were, as already noted, characterized by a turn to neo-liberalism and 'uneven globalization', combined with the revival and then the end of the Cold War. These changes had a profound impact on international development and the Third World as they had emerged and been consolidated down to the 1970s. The shift towards neo-liberal globalization was, of course, organized in significant ways through the patterns of collaboration and resistance we have identified in our account of Third Worldism. If a distinctive form of social and political ordering emerged in this context, it took shape predominantly through the reconfiguration of the scope and reach of multilateral institutions, and the *relative* empowerment of corporate actors, and their supporting civil society organizations (CSOs; see, for example, Cutler 2003). The growing shift away from social democratically inflected models of national development towards a framework of re-regulation for neo-liberalism, which privileged markets as the prime sites of social integration, gathered political momentum; others, however, perceived this as compounding the problem of development in the Third World.

This chapter begins by examining the geo-political changes and the reorganization of international relations that set the scene for the rise of neo-liberalism and uneven globalization. This is followed by a discussion of the revival and end of the Cold War, which leads, in turn to an examination of the decline of Third Worldism. Finally we critically look at the dramatic economic emergence of a growing number of nation-states in Northeast and Southeast Asia, which were increasingly seen as successful examples of national development. There was and has been a major debate over what the developmental lessons from East Asia were in relation to national development efforts specifically and the relative failure of international development in most of the Third World more generally. We consider how such debates have both set and limited the terms of reference for the social and political problems of poverty and development in these, as well as other contexts.

## Neo-Liberalism Ascending: The Rise and Elaboration of Uneven Globalization in the Third World and Beyond

The immediate origin of uneven globalization (which has now become a multifaceted phenomenon with myriad cultural, social and political implications) is linked to the financial revolution of the late 1960s and 1970s. This was compounded by the shifts in geo-politics and the global political economy that occurred during the administration of US president Richard M. Nixon (1969–1973), which resulted in dramatic changes in international finance. The geo-political reorientation and changes to the political economy of the Cold War spearheaded by Nixon were, to a significant degree, a result of the growing political and economic problems Washington confronted that flowed from the massive escalation of its direct involvement in the Vietnam War in the 1960s. Meanwhile, by the end of the 1960s, West Germany's and Japan's economic advances had also become a source of growing concern in Washington. By the late 1960s these key Cold War allies had emerged as increasingly dynamic and globally competitive industrial nation-states. In the broader context, this had led to what came to be called in (international) political economy the 'capacity crisis', with diminishing returns on capital investments due to supply-side saturation (Amin 1997: 12–21). In addition to the pressures from the geo-political contexts, this provided additional impetus for advocates of financial liberalization and the creation of new markets and investment opportunities related directly to the removal of regulatory constraints, and the 're-regulation' for new markets and associated rights (see Amin 1997; Cerny 1990; 1993; 1997; Helleiner 1992; H. Weber 2002; 2004).

This situation, combined with the financial burden of the war in Vietnam, prompted Nixon to sanction the end of the gold standard and initiate the liberalization of the international financial regulatory order, all of which had been put in place in the wake of the Bretton Woods meeting in 1944 to ensure the stability of the global financial system. In 1944 it had been determined that one ounce of gold was equal to 35 US dollars and the US dollar in turn went on to anchor fixed monetary exchange rates worldwide. In 1971 the Nixon administration both floated the US dollar and suspended its convertibility to gold, at the same time as introducing a new 10 per cent surcharge on all imports into the United States. This eventually led to the Smithsonian Agreement that re-valued the yen by 16.88 per cent against the dollar, while the deutschmark was re-valued by 13.5 per cent against the dollar (Brenner 1998:43, 47, 116–24). The de-linking of the dollar from gold and first efforts to move away from fixed monetary exchange rates in 1971 were a decisive moment, added to by the dramatic rise in the price of oil in late 1973, which marked another important shift in the global political economy of the Cold War. It is generally assumed that the rise in oil prices at the end of 1973 was driven by the oil states of the Middle East and their opposition to Israel, and to US support of Israel in the Yom Kippur War (October 1973). However, despite Washington's public remonstrance against increases in the price of oil, there is evidence to suggest that the Nixon administration had earlier pressured the OPEC states to increase oil prices in order to undermine the economic advances of Japan and Washington's Western European allies, particularly West Germany. This was not necessarily the reason why prices were increased, but it does suggest that the Nixon administration thought that the US, with far more significant oil reserves, was better positioned than Western Europe and Japan to cope with a rise in the price of oil. The oil crisis and Nixon's termination of the global financial protocols associated with the Bretton Woods system had at least four crucial results. First, they ensured that private banks (particularly US-based banks) began to play a much greater role in global finance. Second, the national government supervision of what were increasingly becoming global financial organizations was dramatically weakened. This was a qualitative shift, the gradual spread of which over time put more and more states in a position to facilitate financial liberalization, eventually right down to the micro-level (H. Weber 2002, 2004). Third, this meant that the currency exchange rates and financial systems of other nation-states, particularly in Latin America, Africa and Asia, were increasingly influenced by trends in the financial markets in the United States. Fourth, growing competition within the banking systems of the various countries in the Organisation for Economic Cooperation and Development (OECD) was encouraged, while the government of the USA was increasingly able to more or less determine the regulatory framework for global financial markets (Gowan 1999: 4–5, 19–26).

The financial revolution was also facilitated by technological change, particularly in relation to advances in what became known as information technology. At the same time, the rise of information technology was directly linked to the research and development in the 1970s that was connected to the military imperatives of the Cold War. The combination of the computer chip with innovative new forms of communication has proven, in the view of one historian, to be the most significant 'technological innovation of the Cold War'. In fact, Odd Arne Westad goes on to argue that: 'the market revolution of the late twentieth century – or globalization if one prefers to use that term – would not have been possible without the advances in communications that the Cold War competition brought on' (Westad 2000: 559). In fact, as the Cold War came to an end it was this technological transformation, applied to the financial sector, that increasingly bound together the major centres of capitalist activity in North America, Western Europe and East Asia. This was the case even as it also reinforced long-standing exclusionary patterns of relations in those parts of the world that contained the most marginalized populations: that is in the erstwhile Third World. Thus the rise of uneven globalization has clearly been profoundly linked to the dramatic technological changes of the past 30 or 40 years facilitating the emergence of the information economy as the leading sector of the world economy, increasingly shaping and facilitating the reordering of industrial and agricultural production, political activity and social and cultural life (Castells 1996; 1997; 1998). More importantly, however, the uneven globalization centred on neo-liberalism was organized by a complex array of increasingly transnational socio-economic actors – institutions, corporations, movements and organizations. This was, in turn, linked to the growing concentration of economic control in the hands of a relatively small number of large oligopolistic transnational corporations that had emerged by the 1990s from the dramatic merger-driven and technology-facilitated changes to the global political economy (McMichael 2012: 350, 354).

Despite the widening array of transnational socio-economic forces and institutions driving uneven globalization, Washington was, and continues to be, central to the creation of an international framework for the shaping of uneven globalization in neo-liberal terms. A centre-piece of the new post-Bretton Woods order was the way in which, between 1975 and the end of the Cold War, Washington moved towards the creation of what has been termed the 'Dollar Wall Street Regime' (DWSR). No consistent use of the DWSR by Washington emerged until the administration of Bill Clinton (1993–2000). Nevertheless, by the Reagan era (1981–1988) the overall direction was, in retrospect at least, becoming increasingly clear. Concerned about inflation and industrial over- capacity in the US, the Chairman of the US Federal Reserve, Paul Volcker, who was also wary of the dollar losing too much value, embarked on his now well-known increase in interest rates in an effort to strengthen the dollar. Volcker took this path before Reagan came to office, but once Reagan became president in 1981 these measures were dramatically extended. The key elements of the Reagan administration's economic policy shift were to conduct economic policy on behalf of finance capital and to expand and utilize the new DWSR for the benefit of the US government. The former meant driving down inflation (thus strengthening the profits of financiers), deregulating the banking and financial system and dispensing major cuts in taxes to the wealthy, while attempting to drive up the value of the dollar. Meanwhile, the DWSR provided the leverage to stimulate US industrial expansion via a dramatic increase in defence spending, which was carried out against the backdrop of the Cold War revivalism of the Reagan administration. This involved pulling in large amounts of capital from overseas while running a rising budget deficit. This put the US state in the position of 'surrogate export market' for a number of major US-based manufacturers of defence-related equipment (Gowan 1999: 26–39); a trend that continues to deepen in both old and new ways down to the present day.

Meanwhile, it is still worth noting that this only became obvious in the early 1950s. Then, every year from the beginning of the Korean War to the end of the Cold War the budget of the US Defense

Department was greater than the 'combined net profits' of all US-based corporations (Miyoshi 1993:733). In fact, the US 'military-industrial complex' was also the country's single biggest employer throughout the Cold War (Walker 1995: 6). At the same time, Reagan administration officials began to extend the DWSR in an effort to address specific problems. To begin with, keeping the dollar high could have involved maintaining high interest rates in the US, unless major new sources of external funds could be attracted to invest in North American financial markets. It was under the Reagan administration that the attempt to ensure high levels of inward investment led to a major effort to wind back or eliminate capital controls in the OECD, particularly the nation-states of Western Europe and Japan (Gowan 1999: 39–41).

The debt crisis of the 1980s (triggered in part by the economic policies of Volcker and the early Reagan administration) was also central to the consolidation of uneven globalization as a more clearly defined project. The debt crisis was a key lever for the Reagan administration, with the support of the governments of Margaret Thatcher in Britain (1979–90) and Helmut Kohl (1982–98) in West Germany/Germany, in its effort to accelerate and deepen financial deregulation, trade liberalization and privatization in the Third World. At the same time, it should be emphasized that the debt crisis flowed from the rise in oil prices and the liberalization of the international financial system in the 1970s. Many of the petroleum-exporting nation-states, particularly in the Middle East, had acquired massive profits following the dramatic increase in oil prices in the 1970s. They deposited these petro-dollars in Western Europe- and North America-based banks. The banks in turn attempted to find borrowers, turning to governments in the Third World. While some countries in Asia, such as South Korea, accumulated a high level of foreign debt during the 1970s, Latin America, where economic growth had been significant in the 1960s and 1970s, was a particular focus of attention from international bankers.

By the start of the 1980s, more than 60 per cent of the total foreign debt that was owed to private banks worldwide was owed by the governments of Latin America. In 1970 the combined foreign debt for all governments in Latin America was US$2.3 billion. By 1975, the figure was US$75 billion; rising precipitously to US$229 billion by 1980 (it was US$340 billion by 1983). These figures are widely accepted across the spectrum. The global recession of the early 1980s led to a major reduction in the demand for exports from Latin America at the very moment when exports were crucial to the acquisition of the foreign exchange that was needed to make even minimal payments on the rising foreign debt. By the end of 1982, most governments in Latin America were in arrears on their debt payments. There was some concern on the part of the bankers, and some hope on the part of their critics, that governments in the region would form debtor cartels and refuse to pay their debts. However, while such a Third Worldist initiative was discussed and promoted (most notably by Fidel Castro) it did not materialize and it was abundantly clear by the 1980s that Third Worldism was in serious decline. The various indebted governments were unable and unwilling to unite in the face of strong bilateral pressure from the US and its main allies. Beginning in the early 1980s various debtor clubs were institutionalized as the IMF and the World Bank increasingly took on a central role in Latin America and beyond. The meetings of the debtor clubs, which were usually attended by IMF and/or World Bank representatives, rescheduled loans in the context of various structural adjustment agreements aimed at liberalizing, privatizing and deregulating the economies concerned. Furthermore, almost 40 per cent of the total foreign debt of the governments of the region was owed to US-based private banks. These loans were dollar-denominated and had variable interest rates. This meant that any increase in interest rates immediately affected the size of the debt (Whitehead 1984; Pastor 1987).

Mexico is a particularly good example of the connection between the debt crisis and the passing of strategies aimed at realizing national development in the form that had prevailed between the 1930s and the 1970s. In fact, the Mexican trajectory nicely reflects the overall shift from state-mediated national development to state-facilitated neo-liberal development (Babb 2001). In the Mexican case this shift was consolidated with the implementation of the North American Free Trade Agreement (NAFTA) in January 1994. NAFTA was a major turning point in the overall transformation of the political economy of Mexico and the realignment of US–Mexican relations over the previous two decades. More broadly, the incorporation of the United States, Canada and Mexico into a continent-wide free trade zone helped to anchor the post-Cold War deepening of uneven globalization and the neo-liberal ascendancy over international development. This is a trend that even the dramatic efforts to increase control over (and/or contain) the southern, and the northern, border in the name of national security, after September 2001 have impacted but certainly not reversed. Meanwhile, by the 1990s the Partido Revolucionario Institucional (Institutional Revolutionary Party – PRI), which ruled Mexico under one name or another for over 70 years down to 2000, had dismantled most of the institutional structures of state-guided national development that it had built up since the 1930s. The redistributive elements of state-mediated national development were manifested dramatically during President Lázaro Cárdenas's rule (1934–40). During his six years in office, he reallocated 47 million acres of land to over 1 million peasant families as well as establishing farming collectives, and a national bank to assist peasants. Cárdenas's successors established and pursued a concerted state-guided import-substitution industrialization programme for at least thirty years before the pressure to wind back state-guided national development started to impact significantly on Mexican political economy.

Between 1940 and the end of the 1960s the Mexican economy grew by 6 per cent a year and a significant percentage of the population experienced improved standards of living. However, as noted above, by the late 1960s cracks in the national development project were becoming increasingly apparent. The policies pursued by the government of President Luis Echeverría (1970–76), and his immediate successor, José Lopez Portillo (1976–82), reflected an incoherent populist effort to keep the national development project alive in the context of rising social tensions and pressure for political and economic reform. PRI-led national development in Mexico entered its most acute crisis in 1982. The price of oil fell by more than 50 per cent in a couple of months, dramatically exacerbating the closely entwined trends of devaluation, inflation and capital flight, along with steadily rising foreign debt repayments (the total foreign debt for Mexico by 1982 was US$85.5 billion).

During the presidency of Miguel de la Madrid Hurtado (1982–88) the Mexican government applied the structural adjustment programme that was being encouraged throughout the region and beyond. To this end, Mexico's currency, the peso, was devalued; government spending on education and health care was reduced, as was the subsidization of staple foods, while expensive imports were also cut back. Public sector companies were sold or wound up by the hundreds. Meanwhile, wage controls and dramatically rising prices reduced the purchasing power of the peso for ordinary Mexicans by at least fifty per cent (Beaucage 1998:13–16). However, it was during the administration of President Carlos Salinas de Gortari (1988–94), which culminated with the implementation of NAFTA in 1994, that state-guided national development, which had emerged in the 1930s, definitely gave way to the privatization of state enterprises and the pursuit of export-led growth. The result, in the late 1980s and 1990s, was considerable economic growth in tandem with steadily rising levels of poverty and inequality along social, ethnic and regional lines and the weakening and eventual end of one-party rule (Lustig 1998: 201–12). The PRI lost the presidency in 2000, regaining it, however, as of 2012 under the leadership of Enrique Peña Nieto. Meanwhile, in the context of the inauguration of the NAFTA, Mexico's economic liberalization project experienced a significant political challenge in the break-out of open revolt in the Chiapas region (Morten 2000; 2011). The Zapatista movement has continued its challenge to the terms of rule of the central government since.

The shift to neo-liberal economic policies and the amplification of uneven globalization was not as pronounced in Asia as it was in Latin America, or Africa. Latin American nation-states such as Mexico and Brazil had been briefly grouped with the newly industrializing countries (NICs) of East Asia (South Korea, Taiwan, Hong Kong and Singapore) in the 1970s. The debt crisis quickly undermined Mexico's and Brazil's status as economic miracles. However, the East Asian NICs, and particularly, the new second-wave NICs of Thailand, Malaysia, Indonesia and coastal China, although affected by the debt crisis, benefited far more than Latin America from the relocation of industrial production from Japan, as well as from North America and Western Europe (Wallerstein 1999: 36–7). Nevertheless, the changes of the 1980s coincided with and were connected to the uneven spread of neo-liberalism and uneven globalization in the region. In the context of the debt crisis the pressure to liberalize being exerted on governments in Asia certainly increased. For example, in Thailand, in the early 1980s, the IMF and the World Bank presided over a comprehensive structural adjustment programme. This was aimed at stabilizing the Thai economy and opening it up further to foreign investment, paving the way for the continued growth of the manufacturing sector as major Japanese corporations in particular expanded their operations southward. The structural adjustment programme in Thailand was followed in the 1980s by reform packages for other governments in the region (Dixon 1991: 33–4, 217–18).

At the same time, governments in Asia, as elsewhere, were increasingly subject to bilateral pressure from the Office of the United States Trade Representative on a wide range of issues including increased access to national markets (MacIntyre 1997:237–8). In Indonesia, as in Mexico, the decline in oil prices in the 1980s resulted in increasing debt and a decreased capacity on the part of the state to facilitate local capital accumulation. At the same time, greater use of foreign loans and foreign aid led to greater leverage on the part of the World Bank, the IMF and foreign investors. By the second half of the 1980s, important liberalizing reforms were under way in the sprawling archipelago of Indonesia. This shift in economic policy facilitated an increase in the influx of foreign capital into Indonesia in the late 1980s, much of it from Japan (as well as from South Korea and Taiwan), and the rapid rise of an export-industry sector, especially on Java (Bresnan 1993: 83). Meanwhile, in South Korea (also a major debtor by the 1980s), the rapid economic growth and the dramatic social changes of the previous twenty years had paved the way for the relative decline of the developmental state during the regime of General Chun Doo Hwan (1980–88). Although the US reinvigorated the security alliance with Seoul in the Reagan era, Washington increasingly began to question South Korea's financial and trading practices. Chun Doo Hwan responded to mounting foreign and domestic pressure by embarking on a process of economic and political liberalization. As we will see below, the liberalization of the political system was closely connected to the liberalization of the economy (Kim 2000: 2–4). In India, meanwhile, the high period of national development had passed by the 1960s, but considerable commitment to the ideas and instrumentalities associated with state-guided national development remained in place until at least the end of the 1980s (Corbridge and Harriss 2000: 143–72, 192–9).

The waning of the high modern era of national development and the ongoing consolidation of uneven globalization was also linked to a reorientation in the approach to and disbursement of US foreign aid that became increasingly apparent in the last decade and a half of the erstwhile Cold War. In the context of the US defeat in Vietnam and the wider debate about US foreign policy that resulted from the failed anti-Communist modernizing mission in one-time French Indochina, there was growing pressure to rethink US economic assistance programmes. In the 1970s this resulted in various reformist pieces of legislation under the heading of New Directions. This led briefly to an emphasis on both the basic needs of the poor and direct grassroots participation in the process of development. At the same time, the Foreign Assistance Act was amended to provide for an increased focus on human rights in the disbursement of foreign aid. However, by the late 1970s, influential free-market critics of New Directions were in the ascendant. Their views were consolidated during the Reagan administration. In the 1980s the US Agency for International Development (USAID) focused with increasing intensity on the Private Enterprise Initiative (PEI), which promoted private sector development and encouraged market-oriented reform (Adams 2000: 53–4, 68–70, 75). For example, in a 1984 policy paper, 'Private Enterprise Development', USAID asserted that: 'a society in which individuals have freedom of economic choice, freedom to own the means of production, freedom to compete in the market place, freedom to take economic risk for profit and freedom to receive and retain the rewards of economic decisions is a fundamental objective of the AID program in less developed countries'. The policy document went on to argue that: 'such a private enterprise economy is held to be the most efficient means of achieving broad-based economic development'. The main goal of USAID was said to be: 'To encourage LDCs [less developed countries] to open their economies to a greater reliance on competitive markets and private enterprise in order to meet the basic human needs of their poor majorities through broadly-based self-sustained economic growth'. Closely connected to this was an injunction about the need: 'to foster the growth of productive, self-sustaining income and job producing private enterprises in developing countries' (USAID 1984). At the same time, US foreign assistance policy in the 1980s, as in earlier periods, remained firmly grounded in geo-political calculations and strategic interests, with the percentage of foreign assistance going to development-related programmes declining and the amount spent on security-related projects rising (Adams 2000: 90–1).

This trend was readily apparent in Washington's growing involvement in Central America, following the revolutionary overthrow in July 1979 of the Somoza regime in Nicaragua. In the 1980s Central America became a crucial focus of the Reagan administration's effort to 'exorcise the ghosts of Vietnam' (LeoGrande 1998: 583–91). The nation-states of Central America were the recipients of more US economic and military aid during Reagan's first term (1981–84) than they had received in the preceding thirty years (1950–80). For example, between 1981 and 1984 the El Salvadoran government received US$ 758 million in economic aid and US$ 396 million in military aid (compared to only US$ six million in military aid in 1980). El Salvador had emerged as the recipient of more US aid than any other country in Latin America by the middle of Reagan's first term. In fact, in this period El Salvador was the third-largest US aid recipient worldwide, behind Israel and Egypt. Reflecting the ongoing strategic significance of the Middle East, Israel and Egypt received about one-third of all US foreign aid disbursed in the 1980s. Ultimately, the level of foreign aid for El Salvador in the 1980s was on a scale reminiscent of the US nation-building effort in South Vietnam in the 1960s, minus direct US military intervention (also, incidentally, minus the actual use of the term nation-building). By the end of the 1980s the US had disbursed upwards of US$ 3 billion in economic and military aid to El Salvador (the equivalent of about US$ 800,000 a day for ten years) (LaFeber 1993: 353–8).

While the economic aid to Central America in this period was driven by geo-political considerations, this did not negate Washington's focus on the liberalization of the economies of the region. In the 1980s the US combined its support for the military and proxy warfare with pressure on the governments of Central America to adopt neo-liberal economic policies. This led, among other things, to the dismantling of national institutions that had bolstered almost 50 years of Costa Rican social democracy. In El Salvador and Nicaragua, it threatened even the very limited popular economic and political gains made during the 1980s (Paige 1997: 51). This shift contributed to the rising levels of social inequality and violence in the region in the wake of the electoral defeat of the Sandinistas in 1990 and the finalization of peace agreements in El Salvador in 1992 (Dunkerley 1994). A peace agreement was also signed in Guatemala in 1996. In fact, the post-Cold War era has seen the incorporation of former guerrilla organizations (as parties) into the political process in Central America. This resulted in the FMLN – Frente Farabundo Martí para la Liberación Nacional – in El Salvador forming government over a decade after they had agreed to a peace settlement, while Daniel Ortega, longtime leader of the FSLN – Frente Sandinista de Liberación Nacional – in Nicaragua regained the presidency almost twenty years after having exited the post. In Guatemala, the URNG– Unidad Revolucionaria Nacional Guatamalteca – has remained far more marginal than the former revolutionaries in El Salvador and

Nicaragua; however, in all three polities and the region more generally the crisis of international development and the high levels of
social inequality and violence that have attended uneven globalization are all too apparent. The region has become a focus for transnational organized crime moving illegal drugs northward, as well as a
site of operations for gangs, such as Mara Salvatrucha 13 (MS-13),
which was originally formed amongst the children of El Salvadoran
refugees in Los Angeles in the 1980s. As a consequence of deporta-
tion policies and rising social inequalities, MS-13, which has built up
an unrivalled reputation for nihilism, has become what one writer
calls a 'gang without borders', at the same time as it can be viewed as
an example of the social marginalization and violence that is a major
symptom of the crisis of international development in the region and
beyond (Hagedorn 2008: 140–1).

Meanwhile, like El Salvador and Nicaragua (in broad geo-political
terms at least), Afghanistan, following the Soviet invasion in late 1979,
also became an important focus for Washington in the 1980s with
regional implications (while also serving as a staging ground for
transnational *jihadi* networks, such as Al-Qaeda). The Soviet occupation of Afghanistan (1979–89) facilitated a dramatic reorientation of
US economic and military aid to Pakistan and to a lesser extent India.
As we have seen, after 1965, President Lyndon Johnson (1963–1968)
sought to limit Washington's direct involvement in, and aid to, South
Asia in comparison to the importance that had been attached to the
region in the late 1950s and early 1960s (McMahon 1994). In 1978 US
relations with Pakistan had been weakened by the criticisms made by
President Jimmy Carter (1977–1980) of the human rights violations of
the military government of General Zia ul-Haq (1977–88) following
its ousting and execution of President Zulfikar Ali Bhutto (1971–77).
The relationship between the US and Pakistan had also been undermined by Pakistan's efforts to develop nuclear weapons. In April 1979,
in response to the Pakistani government's nuclear weapons initiative,
the Carter administration suspended US aid to Pakistan. However,
once the Soviet Union entered Afghanistan, US aid to Pakistan was
restored and then significantly increased (Jalal 1990). In the 1980s the
Pakistani military, and its main intelligence organization, the Inter-
Services Intelligence directorate (ISI), played an important role (along
with the Saudi Arabian and the Chinese governments) in supporting
the loose coalition of resistance groups (Islamic Unity of Afghan
Mujahideen) fighting the Soviet occupation (Roy 1986).

The Carter administration also attempted to improve its relations with the Indian government, under Prime Minister Morarji Desai (1977–80). The latter was trying to lessen its reliance on the USSR. Desai and Carter signed the Delhi Declaration in 1977, which restated both governments' commitment to democracy and human rights. Washington also waived restrictions on uranium sales to India. These efforts failed to put US–Indian relations on a more stable footing, once the US resumed military and economic aid to Pakistan and increasingly tilted towards China in the context of Washington and Beijing's rapprochement in the 1970s and the war in Afghanistan after 1979. In 1980, Prime Minister Indira Gandhi, who had replaced Desai, moved to improve Indian relations with the USSR. She announced a major arms deal, worth US$ 1.6 billion, with the Soviet Union in May 1980. Then in December, Leonid Brezhnev visited India and Mrs. Gandhi and the Soviet leader issued a public statement that condemned outside involvement in Southwest Asia, a clear reference to US involvement in the war in Afghanistan. The withdrawal of Soviet military forces from Afghanistan (between May 1988 and February 1989), and the subsequent end of the Cold War, led to a significant geo-political reorientation in South Asia. The end of all US aid to Pakistan by 1990 (in the context of renewed US concern about Pakistan's clandestine nuclear weapons programme) and the general deterioration of US relations with Pakistan was parallelled by improvements in US relations with India (Tahir-Kheli 1997). This trend would be reversed in the wake of the rise of Al-Qaeda and the major human cost associated with the suicide attacks on the World Trade Center in New York city (along with an attack on the Pentagon) on 11 September 2001.

## Third World Descending I: The Decline and Fall of Third Worldism

By the 1980s, political and social conditions shaped by the trends outlined above were ushering in the decline of the Third World. At the very moment when the Third World was being seen by some observers to have 'come of age', it is clear with the benefit of hindsight that the Third Worldist era was already coming to a close (Stavrianos 1981). For example, wars between the 'red brotherhood' of Vietnam, Cambodia, Laos and China in the late 1970s pointed to the decline of socialist internationalism and its close relative, Third Worldism (Evans and Rowley 1990). Meanwhile, as already mentioned, the rise of politico-religious parties and movements in the late 1970s and early 1980s (the Iranian Revolution of 1979 being exemplary of this shift) offered a return to 'religious tradition' as a way to correct the failure of the secular nation-state, whether capitalist or socialist. While this perspective viewed the secular character of the nation-state as the problem, their solution in the vast majority of cases was to reorient the nation-state so that religion could play a leading role in national politics. The challenge was and is directed at the content and character of the nation-state rather than the idea of the nation-state itself (Juergensmeyer 2008).

More broadly, as we have seen, the collective efforts under the NIEO to effect a comprehensive restructuring of the world economy in order to address the crisis of development, was countered with increasing effectiveness by neo-liberalism and proponents of market-led development policies (McMichael 2012:147–237; Prashad 2012). The debt crisis at the start of the 1980s, and the subsequent spread of neo-liberal policies and practices, meant that the UN-sponsored idea of a New International Economic Order (NIEO) that had been set out in 1974 never got off the drawing board. Instead, within a few short years, the International Monetary Fund and the World Bank were increasingly encouraging the governments of the Third World to liberalize trade, privatize their public sectors and deregulate their financial sectors (Thomas 2000; 1987). This trend also coincided with the renewal of the Cold War and the further weakening of the Non-Aligned Movement. Despite regular meetings, NAM played an increasingly limited role in international affairs during the so-called New Cold War and into the post-Cold War era (Lundestad 2005: 296–98; Morphet 1993; 1996).

Meanwhile, although there were clear shifts in the direction and geographical orientation of post-Cold War US foreign policy, there were also significant continuities in relation to uneven globalization and the nation-state system. The administration of Bill Clinton (1992-2000) emphasized at the outset that it intended to shift from containment to enlargement in an effort to amplify the overall number of democratic nation-states around the world with important implications for the erstwhile Third World (Robinson 1996; Carothers 1999). Meanwhile, the foreign aid bill that was passed by the US Congress in 1994, for example, continued, not surprisingly, to reflect a commitment to often long-standing geo-political concerns. In the year the bill was passed, Israel and Egypt received over one-third of all US foreign aid. The figure for Israel was US$ 3 billion and for Egypt it was US$ 2.1 billion, while the 1994 figure for sub-Saharan Africa as a whole was US$ 800 million (Adams 2000:110–11). This was more or less the same percentage for Israel and Egypt as they had received in the 1980s. Israel's importance to US foreign policy (and to domestic US politics) goes back many decades. Egypt, in fact, has been a major strategic outpost for Washington since 1977 when Anwar Sadat, the presidential successor to Gamal Abdel Nasser (a prominent Third Worldist), ended his government's ties to the USSR and became a central player in the US-sponsored peace process in the region. From the time of this reorientation to the end of the 1990s Cairo received at least US$ 46 billion in military and economic aid from Washington. Since the late 1970s US policy towards Egypt has viewed it as the key to making and expanding peace in the region (Owen 1999: 120–1, 133).

With the end of the Cold War, foreign aid was also directed increasingly at the former Second World. This was again for broad geo-political reasons, related particularly to a concern to improve relations with, and enhance the political stability of, a post-communist Russia that still possesses a major capacity for nuclear warfare and is the world's second largest oil exporter after Saudi Arabia (Wedel 1998:199–203). The redirection of, but limited changes to, the basis of US foreign aid policy after the Cold War makes clear the relative continuity in US strategic thinking in the 1990s. There was continued preoccupation with Russia and some of the other successor states, such as the Ukraine, that had emerged from the collapse of the Soviet Union.

In the wake of the demise of the Second World, a majority of nation-states of the erstwhile Third World were not and had not been excluded from global modernity: a majority of their citizens instead primarily continued to experience the dark side of modernity.

Throughout the 1990s, meanwhile, the Clinton administration clearly viewed Europe, East Asia/the Asia-Pacific and the Middle East/Southwest Asia as the three most important regions in the world in terms of US strategy and security. As a period of consolidation for US hegemony, the 1990s were marked by an array of US strategic geopolitical, military and economic initiatives, though the 'push-backs' in the wider world should not be discounted lightly. Our argument here, though, focuses on the challenges posed by the sustained efforts of the US (in concert with its strategic allies) to view the new post-Cold War order in global geopolitical terms. From this perspective, Latin America, Africa and South Asia were perceived as the still underdeveloped or at best developing Third World where no vital US security or economic interests were any longer at stake. Meanwhile, Europe was apparently still at the top of the list, while the Middle East/Southwest Asia was third. In this period, East Asia was regarded as number two and rising. The economic success of a number of nation-states in the region contributed to a relative decline in their explicit commitment to Third Worldism, and was elsewhere perceived to hold important lessons for the rest of the Third World. At the same time, their economic success raised security concerns for other observers. The interconnection between security and economic development was particularly obvious in the thinking of US defence planners in relation to East Asia. For example, a 1995 Department of Defense document described the US military operations in the Asia-Pacific as the 'foundation for economic growth' and the 'oxygen' of 'development' (Daniel and Ross 1999: 388–92, 402; US DoD 1995:1–2). This reflected the wider approach that perceived a close connection between China's economic development and geo-politics, as the search for threats to the US position in the world shifted increasingly to East Asia in the 1990s.

## Third World Descending II: The End of the Cold War and the Rise of East Asia

It was in East Asia, in fact, where the decline of Third Worldism had become particularly evident by the end of the Cold War. For a growing number of observers, the economic success of the NICs of Northeast and Southeast Asia by the 1980s and 1990s had called into question many of the tenets of, and the very need for, Third Worldism. For increasingly influential neo-liberals, the capitalist transformation of Asia had undermined the Third Worldist idea that the hierarchical character of the world economy was holding back economic entrepreneurship, and hence inhibited development. From this perspective and from the perspective of proponents of state-mediated development as well, the notion of a Third World – though not the political project of Third Worldism – remained relevant, as a target for even more sanguine advice on economic reform. Now, the developing countries of the Third World could become successful late developers by emulating the NICs or newly industrializing economies (NIEs) of Asia (the cogency of such comparisons, however, may not be what it is made out to be; see, for example, Grovogui 2001). At the same time, by the late 1970s successful state-mediated capitalist development in East Asia had displaced the socialist thread running through Third Worldism (Harris 1986). This process of displacement was consummated by the turn to market-oriented development on the part of the People's Republic of China and the Democratic Republic of Vietnam (both of which had pursued their versions of full-fledged state socialism previously) in the 1980s and 1990s. Third Worldism was also increasingly marginalized in Asia by efforts to promote a distinctly post-Third Worldist Pan-Asianism grounded in state-guided capitalist development (Berger 2003).

Most of the key elements of this shift are reflected in the efforts of Singaporean leader, Lee Kuan Yew (whose autobiography was entitled *From Third World to First*), to link an increasingly conservative nationalism to an equally conservative Pan-Asianism. He did this while presiding over a state-guided export-oriented industrialization project grounded in a very particular history that he, nevertheless, represented as providing development lessons for the rest of the world (Yew 2000). As with all such success stories, the human costs of development advances remain in the shadows, a feature repeating itself, if unevenly, in practically all the contexts of post-Cold War rapid development based on economic growth.

By the 1980s the then Prime Minister of Malaysia, Mahathir Mohamad, was articulating a particularly strident anti-Western Pan-Asianism that was grounded in an explicitly racial conception of national and international relations. Interestingly, however, Mahathir not only increasingly took on the mantle of the voice of Asia, but at the very moment when Third Worldism was in dramatic decline, he also attempted to position himself as a voice of the Third World (Teik 1995:332; Berger 1999). As is clear from the pronouncements of Lee Kuan Yew and Mahathir Mohamad, the increasingly dramatic rise of East Asia by the late Cold War and early post-Cold War era produced a growing effort to both explain the economic success of East Asia and extract lessons for the rest of the Third World. For the leaders of Singapore and Malaysia, along with many other observers, the key to success was a common cultural thread that was encapsulated by the notion of 'Asian values' (a list of virtues that had a striking similarity to the 'Protestant work ethic' that has been and sometimes still is deployed to explain the rise of the West, which has increasingly been codified in as dubious ways as Asia, or the East).

Meanwhile, neo-liberalism and neo-classical economics regularly pointed to the East Asian Miracle as evidence of the importance of *laissez-faire* economics. Still others talked about the developmental state and emphasized the central role of state-directed industrial policy in successful national development. Like the emergent cultural explanations for the rise of East Asia, theories of the developmental state were closely connected to the wider battle for the East Asian Miracle. The emergence of a distinctive Anglo-American tradition of developmental state theory was also linked to the broader effort in various branches of the social sciences in North America to 'bring the state back in'. While developmental state theorists challenged aspects of neo-classical economics with regard to its silence on background conditions and regulatory requirements, they also shared many of the key assumptions on which neo-classical economics rests. Like their neo-classical counterparts, theorists of the developmental state routinized the nation-state and the nation-state system and produced explanations that were ahistorical and technocratic. They originated in part in important historically grounded studies of capitalist trans-formation. However, as they rose to prominence in the 1980s and 1990s theories of the developmental state have been increasingly domesticated to the dominant neo-liberal development discourse and are characterized by a failure to understand the wider historical signif-icance of the transformation of the nation-state system. They have also failed to recognize the social and ecological consequences of 'economic' miracles, the centrality of exclusionary logics, and the limitations of their accounts of economic and social activities (see, for example, Polanyi 2001; Lacher 1999).

The origins of the idea of the developmental state are complex (Cumings 1999). At the same time, post-1945 Japan remains a crucial starting point for any effort to trace the medium- and short-term origins of the idea of the developmental state. As we have seen, up to the 1970s explanations for the economic resurgence of Japan gener-ally centred on the idea that state intervention or close interaction between business and government had been crucial to the 'Japanese Miracle' (Lockwood 1965: 503; Fairbank *et al.* 1973: 829–30). By the time neo-classical economics rose to prominence at the end of the

1970s there was far more debate about the sources of Japan's success as influential commentators questioned the state-intervention or state-guided interpretation of Japanese success in the context of efforts to pressure Tokyo to adopt more liberal economic policies (Partick and Rosovsky 1976). The resurgence of Japan and the rise of East Asia more generally also fuelled the elaboration in the 1980s of a distinctive group of theories that characterized Japan and the NICs of Asia as developmental states. These commentators usually emphasized that South Korea and Japan in particular, and Taiwan and the other NICs in a more general fashion, were economically successful because they pursued comprehensive national industrial strategies. In turn it was emphasized that these national industrial strategies were based on direct state support for large corporations using high debt–equity ratios in an effort to gain competitive advantage in overseas markets. More broadly, a developmental state was increasingly defined as a state that derived its primary legitimacy from its effectiveness at promoting and sustaining high rates of economic growth via the restructuring of national production arrangements and its strategic engagement with the changing world economy (Castells 1992: 56).

It is Chalmers Johnson's *MITI and the Japanese Miracle* that was and still is widely regarded as the central text in English involved in the promotion of the developmental state approach to East Asian industrialization (Johnson 1982). By the end of the 1980s and the early 1990s, a number of approaches to capitalist development in East Asia, emphasizing the role of a developmental state in the process of national development and inspired directly or indirectly by Johnson's work, had emerged and gained some influence. This revisionist work became increasingly policy-oriented in an effort to challenge the dominant neo-classical approach to capitalist development. This literature emerged as an important element in the wider struggle between the Japanese (state-centred) model and the US (market-oriented) model of capitalist development (Fajnzylber 1990). A growing number of theoretically sophisticated perspectives emerged out of the debate over the developmental state. However most theorists were increasingly constrained by their efforts to extract policy lessons from the East Asian experience without attempting to analyze why, in historical terms, strong institutions, or a developmental state, emerged in East Asia. They collapsed space and time in their pursuit of technical and policy lessons. Even proponents of a revised version of the developmental state, who ostensibly sought to historicize late industrialization, such as Alice Amsden in *The Rise of 'The Rest':* *Challenges to the West from Late-Industrializing Economies*, ultimately provide a highly selective analysis that continues to be ahistorical and technocratic (Amsden 2001; 1989).

Amsden's work was an important example of the academic studies of the developmental state that were influenced by Johnson's book. And whatever their shortcomings the emergence of state-centred challenges to neo-classical explanations for the rise of East Asian capitalism was an important complement to the relative recovery of development economics and the growing significance of political economy as a sub-discipline of political science by the second half of the 1980s. However, developmental state theory, like neo-classical economics, increasingly perpetuated an elite-oriented ahistorical approach to capitalist development as it moved away from an emphasis on *la longue durée* that was apparent in Johnson's excavation of the role of MITI in Japanese economic development between 1925 and 1975. A partial exception to this was the influential 1991 book on South Korea by Jung-En Woo (Meredith Woo-Cumings) (Woo 1991). Woo-Cumings's book (like her other work) provides a particularly detailed historical analysis that emphasizes the central importance of Japanese colonialism and of US Cold War imperatives in providing the overall context for the rise of an authoritarian, developmental and national security state in South Korea (Woo-Cumings 1998). In fact, Woo-Cumings's emphasis on the state and finance in South Korea draws particular attention to the way internal shifts and initiatives were conditioned and interacted with external influences such as US geo-political and economic considerations and the dynamics of the Cold War generally.

The coming of the Asian financial crisis of 1997–98 was seen by many observers as an indictment of the developmental state. However, defenders of state-guided development (and even some proponents of neo-classical economics) argued that the crisis needed to be understood primarily in terms of unregulated financial markets of which boom-bust cycles are a normal element, rather than as a result of an excess of state intervention or 'crony capitalism'. For example, in a book that was published in the midst of the Asian crisis, Linda Weiss emphasized the need to differentiate between 'state *involvement*' and 'state *transformative capacity*'. She argued that if the state was 'part of the problem' in the Asian crisis it was as a result of '*too little state capacity*, rather than too much state involvement' (italics in original: Weiss 1998: xii-xiii). Certainly the Asian crisis needs to be understood in terms of unregulated financial markets and in terms of state capacity rather than state involvement *per se*. Nevertheless, the events of 1997–98 profoundly weakened the increasingly technocratic and ahistorical image of a developmental state presiding over steady economic growth and widening prosperity, which was central to the narrative on East Asia produced by proponents of the theory of the developmental state (Kang 2002: 2–3).

In fact, the actual developmental states in East Asia were in disarray well before the crisis. For example, the state-guided national development project in South Korea (which emerged as a paradigmatic developmental state) was being undone by its own success and by the wider historical context in which it operated by the late 1980s and early 1990s, if not before. The developmental state in South Korea was able to pursue certain developmental objectives for many years because the state was particularly well insulated from the wider social order, especially from those social classes that might have challenged or undermined its developmental goals. The relative autonomy of the state in South Korea – insulated as it was from societal pressures, while benefitting from US geo-political interests in the region – and its ability to spearhead a distinctive national development effort was grounded in the very particular history of the Korean peninsula in the twentieth century. However, the success of the developmental state in South Korea led to a strengthening of various social classes whose growing political demands had dramatically weakened state autonomy by the second half of the 1980s. When this change intersected with the increasingly global, but still highly uneven, shift from national development to uneven globalization against the backdrop of the waning of the Cold War, the result was the retreat of the developmental state in South Korea. This process was repeated, with important variations, in Taiwan and elsewhere.

Furthermore, the identification of developmental states such as South Korea as a more general model by writers such as Linda Weiss and Alice Amsden also provided implicit, if not explicit, legitimation of authoritarianism and military dictatorship highlighting the connection between theories of the developmental state and early theories of military-led modernization. While the military modernization theorists were preoccupied with security and political order, advocates of the developmental state focused on the state's capacity to bring about economic development, setting out successful development under state auspices as the best guarantee for strengthening the power of the state. But both emphasized that the power and capacity of the state was the basis for social and economic development (Martinussen 1997: 239). By the 1990s most proponents of the developmental state perpetuated a technocratic, ahistorical approach to capitalist development in South Korea and beyond. Contrary to the view outlined by proponents of the developmental state (Weiss 1997; 1999), we have shown that a) the conditions of the 'model states' were highly specific, and circumscribed by factors other than state-led developmental policy; and b) the political implications of these models have been less than conducive to achieving the social and political goals to which, for instance, Third Worldism remained consistently committed (social equality, democracy, sustainability). Furthermore, the global conditions through which national development is to be achieved are institutionally circumscribed by the ideology and associated policy environments of neo-liberalism, prompting some to refer to the rise of the competition state, rather than the developmental, or welfare state (Cerny 1990; 1997).

One of the particular weaknesses of Weiss's analysis is that she defined globalization (uneven globalization) primarily, if not exclusively, in economic terms in an effort to minimize its significance (Weiss 1998: 167–87). Following an examination of trade patterns and capital flows, she concludes that there has not been nearly as much globalization as its proponents claim. In a similar vein, Robert Wade noted that: 'in the bigger national economies, more than 80 per cent of production is for domestic consumption and more than 80 per cent of investment by domestic investors' (Wade 1996: 60–1). However, it should not be assumed that trade and investment flows within national economies can simply be described as *national*, while trade and investment that moves between nation-states is *global*. As Martin Shaw has observed, what this exercise demonstrates is nothing more than that trade and capital movement are 'still measured in national and international terms'(Shaw 2000:14, 72–3, 81–2). This approach fails to address the contradictions that were apparent in state-guided national development around the world by the 1970s, and the growing pressure associated with neo-liberal politics from the 1980s onwards. Such an approach also discounts the *qualitative shifts* in globally extended systems of rule, which have been identified as incremental forms of constitutionalism for neo-liberalism based on partial and particular interests (Gill 2002; Cutler, 2003; Weber, 2006;

Higgott and Weber 2005; Robinson 1996). More broadly, since the last decade of the Cold War, the crisis of international development has been and continues to be driven by neo-liberalization conceived as the major adjustment of governance for and by markets (Jayasuriya, 2006; Peck and Tickell 2002; Peck, 2010). To return to our initial observation about the organization of the neo-liberal politics of development, its rise and amplification continues to provide the backdrop for an uneven, highly unequal and multifaceted process of economic, social, political, technological and cultural change that provides the overall context in which nation-states are increasingly oriented towards the facilitation of transnational rather than national (or international) development objectives (Mittelman 2000: 15–26; Sassen 2006). In fact, with the end of the Cold War it has become even clearer that a growing number of nation-states either never had the capacity to preside over successful national development of a capitalist or socialist derivation, or have long since lost the capacity to do so in any way proximate to the ideal typical renditions of this framework.

## Conclusion: Third Worldism Retreating

This chapter has focused on the uneven but increasingly significant organization and elaboration of the neo-liberal politics of development in the 1970s and the 1980s in the context of both the renewal and then the dramatic end of the Cold War. It was emphasized that this constituted a major shift in the theory and practice of international development and the idea of and the problems associated with the Third World. It was suggested that by the 1970s international development as it had been consolidated over the previous decades was in crisis – this was manifested by the proposal for the NIEO on the one hand, and its dramatic displacement by neo-liberalism on the other hand (a problematic ascription anyhow, given its reliance on highly unequal international divisions of labour) with neo-liberalism. This period saw a steady but uneven movement away from state-guided national development (and its implied or actual socially redistributive orientation) in the Third World and towards the ongoing effort to consolidate and universalize the 'competition state' (Cerny 1997) against the backgrop of the elaboration of uneven globalization and an ascendant neo-liberalism. Ideologically, the rise of uneven globalization and of neo-liberal politics was advocated as the necessary corrective that would facilitate development in the Third World. Significantly, the corollary of the rise of uneven globalization and the deepening of neo-liberal politics as key aspects of an increasingly global project in the 1980s was the demise of the political project of Third Worldism.

The project of Third Worldism, as argued by Prashad (2007: xv), was not 'just a place' but an emancipatory political project that sought to redress unequal relations of power in development, and also to challenge its underlying racial politics. The decline of the project of Third Worldism was in part an outcome of global social and political conjunctures (as we have outlined especially in this chapter), which, in turn, was also facilitated by some governments and/or elite groups within the Third World. By the 1990s the questions that preoccupied a growing number of students of international development had far less to do with explaining economic success and far more to do with explicating growing inequalities, the breakdown of social and political cohesion, and the resulting increased pressure on a growing number of nation-states in the Third World (most particularly in Africa, some parts of Asia and many of the smaller polities in Latin America). Thus the end of the Cold War was increasingly followed not only by the deepening of neo-liberalism and uneven globalization, but also by the emergence of new ways of classifying nation-states in the Third World. The new terms included, and were increasingly centered on, the notion of 'failing states' or 'failed states' along-side the twenty-first century resurrection and revision of ideas about 'nation-building' and modernization. This is an issue that will be addressed directly in the next chapter.

# 5

# The Resurrection of Nation-Building and Modernization: Security and International Development in the Third World after the Cold War

With the end of the Cold War, the deepening of neo-liberalism and uneven globalization and the increasingly obvious contradictions of international development, more attention was drawn to those nation-states that were characterized by high levels of either new or long-standing political and social instability, or serious economic problems, along with the degradation (or the widespread absence) of state-sponsored infrastructure. It became increasingly common, meanwhile, to talk about these nation-states as 'failing' or 'failed' states. Concerns about the potential security implications of a growing number of 'failing' and 'failed' states in the one-time Third World precipitated the emergence (even before 9/11) of a renewed emphasis on the connection between security and international development. This is the context in which the idea of 'nation-building' was resurrected, enjoying a return to prominence not seen since the early years of the Cold War. Meanwhile, in the post-Cold War era nation-building and state-building are now often used interchangeably, while 'conflict resolution', 'capacity building', 'post-conflict stabilization' and 'post-conflict reconstruction' have entered the international develop-ment lexicon, particularly in relation to the one-time Third World.

The merging of security and international development in distinc-tive post-Cold War forms is sometimes reminiscent of earlier state-guided or state-mediated capitalist and socialist nation-building efforts; however, the new approach to nation-building also reflects the ideological shift by the 1980s from state-guided national develop-ment to a focus on the strengthening of state capacity to better facili-tate neo-liberalism and uneven globalization. Also, although nation-building took on renewed salience in the early twenty-first century, the long shadow of Washington's inability in the 1960s to turn South Vietnam into a stable capitalist nation-state still hovered over US-led nation-building efforts in the Third World (Melanson 2000). Meanwhile, the more enthusiastic efforts to resurrect and/or reinvent nation-building at the start of the twenty-first century may have peaked. Even in the immediate aftermath of the suicide attacks on the World Trade Center and the Pentagon, President George W. Bush found it necessary to reassure the US public (on 25 September 2001) that the then new War on Terror (also designated as the Global War on Terrorism – GWOT – until 2009 when GWOT was dropped from US foreign policy discourse) generally and the deepening US military intervention in Afghanistan specifically would not involve, nor did they constitute, nation-building. In a somewhat coded fashion he was affirming that the US would not get involved, as it had in the 1960s, in anything resembling the war in Vietnam (a long struggle that became central to Cold War rivalries and Third Worldism in the 1960s and 1970s). By early 2002, however, Washington was not only engaged in what was increasingly perceived as nation-building in Afghanistan, but the Pentagon had begun planning the military inva-sion of Iraq.

A decade later, it appears that the Global War on Terrorism was never as 'global' as originally anticipated. In the case of Latin America, for example, it has proven difficult if not impossible to view trends in the region as having any connection to violent politico-reli-gious actors and movements in the Middle East and South and Southeast Asia (even the latter region has proved less than fertile ground for Al-Qaeda and other like-minded organizations). Meanwhile, the US has pulled back from (and/or out of) Iraq (which never had an Al-Qaeda problem until after the US got there) and Afghanistan, and the struggle against transnational terrorist networks looks set to continue as primarily an intelligence, police and covert operations effort (Overseas Contingency Operations – OCO). This was the general, but not always seen as sufficient, approach prior to 9/11, and there appears to have been a return to this position. Of course, there are major institutional byproducts, the benefits of which will continue to be debated. For example, the US Department of Homeland Security (DHS), which was set up in late 2001, defines 'national security' in broad terms and possesses sweeping powers in relation to the rights of both citizens and foreign nationals. Meanwhile, although two major US military operations (Afghanistan and Iraq) were conducted under the umbrella of the Global War on Terrorism, the relationship between these two wars and Al-Qaeda, or other transnational *jihadi* terrorist networks was never straightforward. In fact, as previously noted, in the case of Iraq, Al-Qaeda did not emerge there until after the US had invaded and occupied the erstwhile secular dictatorship of Saddam Hussein (1979–2003). Transnational networks have cells in strong nation-states and in weak nation-states: in the 'First World' and the 'Third World'. Their transnational character underlines the problems associated with the widespread practice of identifying transnational terror networks with 'Third World' politics or grievances. In the case of strong nation-states they generally try to operate beyond the reach of the 'state', while in the case of weak nation-states they may take refuge or set up a base (and recruit from the local population) to take advantage of the relative absence of effective central government; in either case, they are maintaining their presence *aside* from the respective state's capacity to police them effectively (unless they are actively supported by the state).

There continues, then, to be a concern that 'failing' or 'failed' states in the Third World, especially those with geo-political or international economic significance, provide a setting in which transnational politico-religious terrorist networks or transnational criminal organizations can prosper. Unfortunately the most common response remains the dubious effort to resurrect nation-building (while changing the name to 'post-conflict stabilization and reconstruction').

This chapter begins with an overview of the debate about post-Cold War nation-building and efforts to characterize and understand the problems that plague 'failing' or 'failed' nation-states in what for many is still associated with the Third World. We also examine the related effort to generate solutions aimed at stabilizing and reconstructing the nation-states concerned; for the practitioners of nation-building, this often raises the question as to whether or not they were ever unified and stable polities in the first place. For our critical analysis, however, it also raises the question of whether the criteria for stability or unity deployed in such contexts are sufficiently clear, rather than merely posited on the basis of political prejudice. The second section examines the limits of, and problematic assumptions underlying, both historical and contemporary approaches to nation-building in the Third Word by focusing on US nation-building efforts in Iraq in the wake of Operation Iraqi Freedom in March 2003. This is done in the context of an explicit discussion of and with reference to the dramatic failure of the US nation-building effort in South Vietnam in the 1960s and early 1970s, a topic that was discussed from a slightly different angle in Chapter 3. In this instance the historical significance of the wars in Vietnam to Third Worldism and its centrality to the nation-building debate justifies such a high degree of focus here. The third and final section looks at nation-building in Afghanistan since the US-led Operation Enduring Freedom (OEF) overthrew the Taliban government in late 2001; the Taliban remain as a complex 'insurgency', while, OEF has ostensibly been brought to a close as of 2014. The cases in this chapter span the Cold War and post-Cold War era, while also reflecting a broad spectrum of 'state success' and 'state failure' in the Third World.

## 'State Failure' in the Third World: The Theory and Practice of Nation-Building in the Post-Cold War Era

'State-building' (as the antidote to 'state failure') in the Third World is being defined here as an externally driven, or at least externally facilitated, attempt by one or more nation-states to either establish, consolidate or recuperate a state's sovereignty over an internationally recognized national territory. Post-Cold War nation-building (state-building) efforts have been or are also a concern of a large and loose network of non-government organizations (NGOs) generally focused on humanitarian assistance and foreign aid with a social orientation alongside private companies and contractors whose work ranges from the provision of security to the building or repairing of basic infrastructure. These transnational organizations and corporations operate under the auspices of the relevant branch (if it exists) of the specific national government, national military institution, as well as local constabulary and police organizations in polities where there is a high degree of 'state failure' and a perceived need for post-conflict stabilization and reconstruction. State-building in theory and practice has also been used to describe efforts by national elites to create and consolidate a sovereign territorial state and mobilize the population around a shared sense of national identity.

In fact, while our preoccupation is with the externally driven rather than the internally driven notion of nation-building: there is an obvious overlap between the two and both are linked to diverse pursuits of modernization strategies and international development centred on the sovereign nation-state. Following our definition, state-building can encompass formal foreign military occupation; advice and assistance in relation to counterinsurgency; foreign involvement in, or leadership of, post-conflict stabilization and reconstruction; the disbursement of significant quantities of foreign military and economic aid; and the use of peacekeepers or stabilization forces provided by the US, British, French, and other nation-states under the auspices of the United Nations. Meanwhile, the North Atlantic Treaty Organization (NATO) and the European Union have taken on state-building responsibilities in recent years.

It should be emphasized that the increase in state-building efforts sanctioned, and/or spearheaded by the United Nations and the use of troops and advisers from numerous UN member nation-states is a departure from the Cold War era. During much of the Cold War, externally facilitated nation-building efforts were primarily US- or Soviet-sponsored operations with limited actual UN involvement (Berger and Reese 2010: 451–71). For example, UN intervention in the Congo (July 1960 to June 1964) was the organization's largest nation-building effort during the entire history of the Cold War. The Opération des Nations Unies au Congo (ONUC) was far more extensive than UN involvement in the Korean War (1950–53). And despite the official support of the UN, both going to war against North Korea and then engaging in the stabilization and protection of South Korea in the aftermath were overwhelmingly US operations, while North Korea navigated a complex relationship with Moscow and Beijing. It was not until the post-Cold War era that the UN would again intervene anywhere in the world on the scale of either the Korean War in the early 1950s or its operations in the Congo in the early 1960s. In fact, the Korean case only received UN sanction because the USSR was boycotting the UN Security Council at the time, a mistake they made sure not to repeat (von Hippel 2000). Throughout the Cold War the Security Council was hamstrung by the ability of either Washington or Moscow to veto any initiative the other might sponsor. The 1990s, then, saw a dramatic expansion of UN-sanctioned state-building, peace keeping and humanitarian intervention, but some major conflicts and the efforts that followed, such as the ousting of Saddam Hussein (1979–2003) and the full-scale occupation of Iraq, were initially notable for the complete absence of the United Nations. The initial US intervention in Iraq was organized around a 'coalition of the willing' and had no formal UN involvement although the UN did become involved in the aftermath of Operation Iraqi Freedom (OIF).

While the renewed enthusiasm for state-building in the Third World may have peaked at some point in the first decade of the twenty-first century, it is clear that there is currently a growing number of observers and policymakers at the United Nations, or in the relevant branches of the governments of the US and other major powers, or located at various international organizations, not to mention NGOs, private contractors and think tanks, who are increasingly preoccupied with development and security in the Third World. It is also safe to say that (given the relative centrality of the United Nations and elected or appointed officials from sovereign nation-states in all of this), the theory and practice of state-building which they have used to frame the problem of 'state failure' is articulated in relatively narrow technocratic and instrumental terms. As we have already suggested, however, 'state failure' is best seen as a symptom of the wider global crisis of development. The problem of 'state failure' in the post-Cold War era is grounded in a combination of the profound limitations that flowed from the universalization of the nation-state system over much of the preceding century (the world-historical shift from colonial empires to nation-states) and the boom-bust cycles of global capitalism. By contrast, the key concerns with regard to the breakdown and collapse of (nation-)states in the post-Cold War era is still focused on preventing or containing 'state failure' and operates on the assumption that it is possible to devise interventions in order to 'rescue' 'failing' states, and ensure they became stable and prosperous units in both the nation-state system and the globalizing world economy. The perspective taken here is that contrary to the main approaches to 'failing' or 'failed' states, the crisis of international development and 'state failure' are, of course, *not* external, but internal to neo-liberalism and uneven globalization.

One central concern of this debate as it emerged in the 1990s was whether state collapse stemmed from a scarcity of natural resources, or from their abundance under simultaneous conditions of weak capacity. For example, Thomas Fraser Homer-Dixon argued that resource scarcity drives elites to 'capture' natural resources, alienating powerless groups who respond by taking up arms (Homer-Dixon 1999). Other observers argue that it is the abundance, not the shortage, of natural resources that is the key to violent conflict and state collapse (Soysa 2000; Hauge and Ellingsen 2000; Lomborg 2000; Gleditsch 2000). Furthermore, according to this latter view, civil conflict for some participants may be of more economic benefit than peace. For example, David Keen argued that: 'there may be more to war than winning' (Keen 2000:26). In his detailed study of Colombia, Nazih Richani noted that under certain identifiable conditions, 'war systems', or 'systems of violence', emerge that are self- perpetuating, making it much harder to end or at least mitigate conflict within nation-states (Richani 2002: 3–4).

The view that civil wars and endemic political violence (along with a complete lack of public order in 'failing' or 'failed' nation-states) are still primarily caused by the pursuit of economic gain on the part of key combatants was given its most well-known and most reductive rendition in a series of World Bank studies carried out under the leadership of Paul Collier and Anke Hoeffler. Using a broad statistical analysis of virtually all civil wars worldwide since the mid-1960s, they concluded that variables such as regime type, economic mismanagement, political rights, and levels of ethnic homogeneity or heterogeneity were statistically irrelevant to explaining the causes of civil wars. Their study concluded that economic factors were the crucial explanatory variable (Collier 2000; Collier and Hoeffler 2000).

In their analysis, low economic growth rates and low incomes predispose nation-states to civil war. In one of their many controversial conclusions, however, they argue that they found no strong connection between high levels of socio-economic inequality and civil conflict that could escalate to full-scale civil war and 'state failure'. They also emphasized that polities that were highly dependent on the export of primary commodities and were populated by large numbers of young men, with limited or no education, were also highly susceptible to civil conflict and political instability, and were characterized by profound limits on the state's capacity to exercise sovereignty over its national territory. Their overall conclusions were that political grievances were not directly connected to the outbreak of civil wars. In their view, nation-states that contained significant cohorts of poorly educated youths and readily accessible natural resources were particularly susceptible to civil conflict and the emergence of rebels driven primarily by powerful economic incentives ('greed') rather than political motives ('grievance') to use violence to acquire wealth (Collier 2000; Collier and Hoeffler 2000; Collier 2003).

While the 'greed and grievance' argument satisfied some observers, its reliance on quantitative analysis and its economic determinism was challenged in many quarters. If the first decade of the twenty-first century found us looking out on a world in which the nation-state system was becoming increasingly dysfunctional, its second decade saw the number of 'failing' or 'failed' states increasing. This encouraged a growing number of commentators (some of whom got an early start) to situate their analysis of civil conflict, national instability and 'state failure', as well as their expectations (or lack thereof) for post-conflict transitions and their prescriptions on how to manage them, within an historical and politico-economic context (Reno 1998).

A particularly self-conscious effort to go 'beyond greed and grievance' was mapped out early on by Karen Ballentine and Jake Sherman (Ballentine and Sherman 2003b). At the outset they emphasize that while there has been and continues to be considerable agreement that the dynamics of civil conflict can only be understood with reference to economic factors, what remains to be clarified is why, when and how (much) economics matters. Furthermore, the highly normative character of the 'greed and grievance' model is intertwined with an easily challenged terminological imprecision that contributes to considerable disagreement about its usage and relevance. Ballentine and Sherman conclude that the 'greed theory of civil war' is undermined from the outset by the fact that it is grounded in statistics. It also clearly implies that the inhabitants of weak or 'failing' nation-states of the Third World appear to be more susceptible to 'greed' than individuals, institutions and corporations based outside the Third World. In the final analysis, it also conspicuously fails to ask pertinent questions about *whose* greed may bear the greatest responsibility for the lamented insecurities. Consider in this context, for instance, the arms trade in the Kivu region in sub-Saharan Africa, the effects of water privatization in Bolivia or Ghana, or recent trends in 'land grabbing' that affect subsistence and small-scale farmers across the world, resulting in food deprivation and destitution.

Generally, this literature's virtually complete reliance on quantitative (statistical) analysis (and the often dubious veracity of the statistics collected) serves to generate propositions about the role of economic factors that at best can really only be viewed as 'probabilistic' assessments rather than as a definitive argument or predictive theory about the cause of, or future risk of, civil conflict. Most importantly, Collier's approach fails to provide any actual description or analysis of the always complex dynamics of civil conflict in 'specific real-world instances'. For Ballentine and Sherman, it was 'essential' to move 'beyond greed and grievance' when seeking to understand the causes of and how to devise policies for the prevention of civil conflicts; to reverse impending 'state failure'; to facilitate nation-building; and to enhance security at the sub-national or transnational level as well as promote international development generally (Ballentine and Sherman 2003a: 4–5).

Regardless of the improvements advocated by Ballentine and Sherman, the most influential descriptions of and prescriptions for nation-building and international security in the post-Cold War era continue to avoid or at least downplay issues of history, culture and identity, in favour of a quantitative and technocratic approach. This, in turn, is linked to an even more fundamental problem: as the dominant theories on development and security emerged and were revised and reconfigured, they continued to treat the nation-state as the natural unit of analysis. The vast majority of the growing array of theories and policy proposals seeking to explain and facilitate conflict resolution through state-building continue to be based on the assumption that nation-states are the pre-ordained units of a wider international order (committed to national and international development). This is underpinned by the assumption that capitalism, or the dominant and still romanticized conception of liberal capitalism, reflects a normal or even natural step in the evolution of the post-Cold War order, a step a growing number of nation-states in the once and future Third World will eventually take.

By contrast (and this point is central to rethinking the Third World) it should be emphasized that the nation-state system and the particularities of liberal (or neo-liberal) capitalism that facilitate the deepening of uneven globalization are not the consequences of some natural or evolutionary process. They are the results of a process of ongoing change driven by historical contingency and conjuncture, as well as socio-economic and political conflict and compromise in and through continuous and contiguous relations of inequalities. To reiterate, the fact that 'we are where we are' in the contemporary global political economic order (centred on the universalization of the nation-state system – and international development – overlaid by neo-liberalism and uneven globalization) does not mean there was anything inevitable about how we got here. Nor does it mean there is anything natural or pre-ordained about the overall contours of international development and world politics as they manifest themselves in the early twenty-first century. It is safe to say (and it needs to be said repeatedly) that although in theory nation-states have been and continue to be seen as the main vehicles for the achievement of global modernity, in practice this continued preoccupation with the (nation)-state is riddled with contradictions.

This widespread view is reinforced by the fact that at the global or even the regional level (although there is, as we will see in Chapter 6, a renewed emphasis on regional frameworks for development and/or security) there are no systemic alternatives to international development or to uneven globalization in its liberal capitalist form. This inability or unwillingness to think beyond the crisis-ridden terms of reference provided by national and international development is readily apparent in virtually all of the analytical and policy-oriented literature on nation-building down to the present. A particularly good example, (not new, but still representative down to the present) is Francis Fukuyama's edited book, *Nation-Building: Beyond Afghanistan and Iraq* (Fukuyama 2006c). Fukuyama relied on broad technocratic prescriptions, but at least one key point of his introduction ('Nation-Building and the Failure of Institutional Memory'), which is reiterated in his conclusion ('Guidelines for Future Nation-Builders'), identifies a useful problem that resonates down to the present and beyond. At both the outset and the end he emphasized 'the relatively weak degree of institutional learning on the part of the U.S. government concerning approaches to nation-building'. Furthermore, although in his view the United Nations 'may have done a bit better in preserving institutional knowledge, it has also suffered from short memory and disorganization at the start of each new effort' (Fukuyama 2006a:231–2).

This is one of the two most important points of the book. The second point, which was central to both Fukuyama's approach and that of a number of contributors, such as Larry Goodson (on Afghanistan), is the idea that a sufficiently robust long-term commitment to nation-building in the face of 'state failure' will serve to modernize and develop the polity in question and make it a stable and prosperous part of the nation-state system and the globalizing world economy (Fukuyama 2006b). For example, Goodson emphasizes that the 'final' and 'most important' lesson that can be derived from the experience of nation-building in Afghanistan is that successful 'nation-building requires sustained, determined engagement by the international community and often leadership by the United States'. In his view 'a foundation for the rebuilding of Afghanistan has been laid' and 'now it is time to finish the job' (Goodson 2006:167). By contrast, it should be clear by now that we (that is the authors of this book) view widespread 'state failure' (and the civil conflict and violence that go with it), as well as the massive numbers of people living in abject poverty worldwide (despite over half a century of pursuing global modernity) as the unfortunate if not disastrous results of the unequal power relations through which the promises of global modernity have thus far (for better and often for worse) been realized (Saurin 1995; McMichael 2010). This is a global and systemic crisis that has been compounded by neo-liberalization and is at the centre of the vagaries of the 'contemporary global order' generally and the erstwhile Third World more specifically. To make the point somewhat differently we are saying in no uncertain terms that the continued fixation on the nation-state and the unwillingness to confront 'state failure' as a consequence of decades of dubious international development and security policies represents perhaps the most important challenge we face when trying to seriously address contemporary development and security problems.

### From South Vietnam to Iraq: The Limits of Nation-Building and International Development in the Third World

The profound contradictions that are central to both historic and contemporary nation-building in the Third World can be illustrated by the discussion of two of the most prominent examples of nation-building from 1945 to the present: Vietnam and Iraq. Vietnam emerged out of eight years of war (1946–54) with its French colonizers and another twenty years of US military escalation, culminating in defeat for the

latter in 1975. In the wake of the Second World War the most important areas of French Indochina fragmented into the nation-states of the
Republic of Vietnam and the Democratic Republic of Vietnam from
the mid-1950s to the mid-1970s. North and South Vietnam were eventually united in 1975, but only after they had been scoured by decades
of war against the global backdrop of the Cold War. The erstwhile
French protectorates of Laos and Cambodia, meanwhile, were drawn
into the Vietnam War in numerous direct and indirect ways, while
they also ended up mired in particularly violent wars of national liberation. The widespread warfare that afflicted late-colonial French
Indochina into the Cold War era reflected the increasingly stark
contrast between an obstinate French colonial government on the one
hand and a committed revolutionary Vietnamese nationalist movement on the other. When the French embarked on a major military
effort to hold onto French Indochina they came up against, and were
eventually defeated by, a determined national liberation movement
led by Ho Chi Minh and the Vietnamese Communist Party. The struggle from 1946 to 1954 moved up and down the combined registers of
national liberation, decolonization and the increasingly Manichean
geopolitics of the Cold War (Berger 2004b).

   Washington supported the French effort to restore themselves as
the colonial overlords of Indochina out of concern about the dominant
role that Vietnamese Communists played in the war of national liberation and also because it wanted France's support for its post-1945
approach to the Cold War in Western Europe. With French defeat in
Vietnam in 1954 the US moved to backstop the contrived government
of South Vietnam. As noted in Chapter 3, economic and military aid
worth at least 2 billion dollars was transferred between 1954 and 1961
to the Ngo Dinh Diem regime (1955–63) in South Vietnam. Within a
decade or so, however, South Vietnam would increasingly become the
touchstone of failure and defeat in relation to both counterinsurgency
and nation-building in the Third World, while revolutionary
Vietnamese nationalism (centred on North Vietnam) would become a
major current of Third Worldism down to the 1980s. Despite, or
because of the profound shortcomings of the Diem regime, there was
a steady and dramatic escalation in the number of US ground troops in
the south between 1964 and 1968. By the late 1960s there were
around 500,000 Americans in the south, with as many as one and a
half million more playing supporting roles across Southeast Asia. In
the wake of the 1968 Tet Offensive launched by the Vietnamese

Communists, President Lyndon B. Johnson put a stop to deploying any more US troops, while also making it clear that he was not going to run for re-election. This paved the way for a new President-elect, Richard M. Nixon, to come to office by the end of 1968. Nixon promised to end the war with honour, bring U.S. troops home and also to 'Vietnamize' the war (Berger 2004a).

Between 1969 and 1973, the Nixon administration slowly but steadily wound down the presence of US ground troops. With the US withdrawal more or less complete by 1973, it was only a matter of time until the fall of Saigon in April 1975 and the complete victory of the North over the South, which led quickly to reunification under the Democratic Republic of Vietnam. In South Vietnam, the steady escalation of troops had not contributed to effective nation-building. In fact, the growing US military presence and the military and economic aid that went with it helped ensure that the regime in Saigon and the large but ineffective Army of the Republic of Vietnam (ARVN) the US helped to consolidate in the South became increasingly corrupt and utterly dependent on Washington, while the political legitimacy of successive governments in South Vietnam spiralled downward. The US inability in the 1950s and 1960s to create a nation-state called South Vietnam out of the wreckage of part of former French Indochina, an enterprise that was grounded in the increasingly enthusiastic Cold-War-driven redrawing of already dubious colonial or national boundaries, remains a much debated cautionary tale. It is safe to say that by the late 1970s South Vietnam, which had lost independence in 1975, came to symbolize the profound limits of US nation-building in the Third World generally and the constraints on Washington's ability to project power in Southeast Asia more specifically. US failure in South Vietnam encouraged Washington to pursue less direct forms of nation-building and 'regime change' at the same time as the scale and scope of Washington's involvement in Southeast Asia was (and remains) geopolitically and economically crucial: that is, the US is still the most important geopolitical and economic actor in the region and beyond regardless of the vicissitudes of the Cold War. The fear at the time (late 1960s and early 1970s) that South Vietnam was one of those places where Washington was losing a global struggle for the Third World against the now defunct Soviet Union and its allies appears with the benefit of hindsight more misplaced than ever.

Nevertheless, in part as a result of the Vietnam War, it was not, in fact, until Operation Iraqi Freedom, which was launched in March 2003, that the US became involved in anything even close to its commitment in South Vietnam in the 1960s and early 1970s. Within a year of the invasion and occupation of Iraq, the US was viewed by many commentators as bogged down in an incipient civil war and suffering from a classic case of 'mission creep' (Ricks 2007). As in the case of South Vietnam a generation earlier, Iraq rapidly became representative of the limits of nation-building in the Third World. A dismal political effort by the US at the outset exacerbated the military conditions on the ground, while the inability of the military to establish security hindered political efforts to establish effective governance beyond Baghdad (Ricks 2007; Bremer and McConnell 2006). This sense of failure was widespread until late 2007 and 2008 when the new head of Central Command, General David Petraeus, presided over the launch of the so-called 'surge' in Iraq. Commentators inside and outside the Pentagon and the White House were convinced that civil war (or communal violence) was a foregone conclusion and Iraq was on the way to becoming as lost a cause as South Vietnam had been for an earlier generation of would-be nation-builders. However, with newly acquired political and military commitment, the US military dusted itself off from years of combating a violent insurgency and demonstrated a newfound resolve to go into contested areas under the auspices of an operational mandate based upon a 'clear, hold', and 'build' strategy (Ricks 2009).

A year later, for reasons that have been and will continue to be much debated the surge (which involved the insertion of at least 20,000 more US troops into strategic locations such as parts of Baghdad) appeared to have brought the situation under control. In the wake of the surge US forces were withdrawn from major urban centres and focused on 'advise and assist' missions designed to allow the withdrawal of the vast majority of US personnel and pass leadership to an elected government of Iraq, which had the final say in relation to the operational activities of the Iraqi military forces. The ability of Iraq's central government to maintain the gains from the surge remains to be seen, but no one doubts the amount of effort expended to provide the political space necessary for reconciling differences between political, ethnic and religious factions that remain fixtures of the Iraqi political landscape. Ultimately Iraq continues to rest on a fragile balance of coercion and consensus against the backdrop of ongoing reconciliation and accommodation efforts between the Sunni, Shia, and Kurdish populations. Economic diversification and the redistribution of wealth are major sticking points unlikely to go away any time in the near future. Meanwhile, there is evidence that in the case of Iraq, violence decreased before the surge even started because of the passing of sovereignty to the Baghdad government and/or letting the local military and police, ineffective though they might have been in many places, actually do the work.

The centre is sort of holding in Iraq, but it is still far too soon to tell (just a decade or so after the initial enthusiasm of Operation Iraqi Freedom in early 2003) if a stable nation-state of Iraq will emerge out of Washington's nation-building effort that formally started in March 2003 and carried on for almost ten years. Even setting aside the pernicious impact of the civil war in Syria on Iraq and the fact that Iraq remains in a region of volatile peace since at least the establishment of the United Nations at the end of World War Two, it is not at all clear that the current constitutional arrangements have the capacity required for the necessary reconciliation efforts. The history of the Iraqi trajectory suggests that it still faces some very serious obstacles, not the least of which is the emergence of a sufficient sense of national identity amongst the majority of the population capable of sustaining some form of unity in the face of differences which will (and probably ought to) persist. For example, Toby Dodge argues that since its establishment as a nation-state in the wake of the First World War Iraq has been profoundly shaped by 'four interlinked structural problems'. First, the Iraqi trajectory has been characterized for its entire history by the state's use of 'extreme levels of organized violence'; second, there is a sustained pattern of using 'state resources' and state patronage to acquire the 'loyalty' of key social groups; third, the state has been able to use the considerable revenue acquired from the oil industry to strengthen state autonomy; and fourth, there has been an ongoing and pronounced pattern whereby the Iraqi state has recreated and exacerbated ethnic and communal demarcations as a 'strategy of rule'. For Dodge, these dynamics have reinforced the 'domestic illegitimacy' of the Iraqi state, as well as its 'military adventurism beyond its own borders' (Dodge 2003:169–70). To be sure, the factors Dodge identifies are the hallmarks of a significant number of former British colonies; in this regard they testify to the particular challenges of state formation faced. However, as we have seen above, these challenges are now also refracted through the shifting constellations of an altered development across the one-time colonial world context centred on neo-liberalism and uneven globalization.

This history of violence in Iraq in particular is grounded in its emergence, under British tutelage, out of the wreckage of the Ottoman Empire after the First World War. The boundaries and institutional arrangements that were set in place were primarily designed to serve British geo-political and imperial interests (E. Karsh and I. Karsh 1999; McCarthy 2001). Before Britain, through the League of Nations, secured the mandate to govern Iraq (formed out of the three former Ottoman provinces of Basra, Baghdad and Mosul). Prior to this, the territory concerned did not constitute a single political community. There were no systems of centralized government, education, military command or any of the institutions by which a *nation-state* is commonly defined and administered in the region, which the British named formally as Mesopotamia and then Iraq. In addition, the three erstwhile Ottoman provinces (mentioned above) that became Iraq were among the most ethnically and religiously diverse parts of a sprawling empire that had been centuries in the making and unmaking and then disappeared in any formal sense quite quickly when the guns fell silent at the end of World War One. Arabic speakers constituted 75–80 per cent of the population, while Kurdish speakers made up 15–20 per cent of Mesopotamia as it became Iraq in 1920. Within the Arab population a further division continues to exist between two of the more distinct branches of Islam: that is the divide between the Sunni and the Shi'a. The population of the region of the late Ottoman empire that became Iraq was therefore segmented from the outset into at least three distinct politico-religious or politico-ideo-logical communities: the Arab Shi'a, the Arab Sunni and the Kurds (Tripp 2000).

Britain's first step in creating the new Iraqi state was the installation in August 1921 of Amir Faisal (a Hashemite) as Iraq's king, a constitutional feat without local precedent. The British also laid out a constitution that gave a freshly minted Iraqi parliament sufficient power to bring down a cabinet, but this was counterbalanced by granting the king the right to confirm all laws, to call for general elections and to prorogue parliament. Formal independence came in 1930, which led to membership in the League of Nations in 1932 and increasingly drew attention to the new nation-state's fragility, while ushering in a period of widespread disillusionment with the consti-

tutional system and growing demands for social reform. In 1933
King Faisal died and his politically indifferent son Ghazi assumed
the throne. In 1936 the Bakr Sidqi coup, the first military intervention in Iraqi politics, ushered in a reformist government interested in
more rapid economic and social development. Initially the reform-
ers appeared strong but within ten months the rising opposition, led
by landlord-sheikhs and Arab nationalists, forced the regime to
resign: this was followed by a series of less overt military interventions in Iraqi politics. King Ghazi was killed in a car accident in
1939 and his three-year-old son Faisal II took the throne under the
regency of 'Adb al-Ilah. However, the role of the monarchy (a
British invention) in Iraqi politics had, by this time, already declined
significantly.

Nevertheless, British influence over Baghdad remained significant
until the revolution of July 1958 when a group of young army officers
led by 'Abd al-Karim Qasim seized power. Faisal II and 'Abd al-Ilah
were executed, the monarchy was terminated and a Revolutionary
Council was formed, which withdrew Iraq from the US-backed
Baghdad Pact and established close ties with the Soviet Union and the
Eastern bloc. Britain's oil concessions were also revoked. Qasim was
overthrown by a Ba'th Party (Arab Renaissance Party) coup in 1963,
but the latter regime lasted only nine months. A palace coup then
brought 'Abd al-Salam 'Arif to power (after his death in a plane crash
in 1966 he was succeeded by his brother 'Abd al-Rahman 'Arif). In
1968 a second Ba'th Party coup brought Ahmad Hasan al-Bakr and
Saddam Hussein (who were relatives and both from the town of
Tikrit) to power. Their dominance was secured by force – through a
series of trials, executions and arrests. A new constitution declared
Iraq part of the wider Arab 'nation', as well as an Islamic state and a
socialist society. In the new regime Hassan al-Bakr held the offices of
president and prime minister and was also the chairman of the newly
formed Revolutionary Command Council (RCC), with Saddam
Hussein as vice-chairman. Associates and kinsmen from Tikrit were
appointed to key positions in all the organizations that propped up the
government.

By the early 1970s Saddam Hussein had emerged as the real force
behind the regime. His power derived from his authority within the
civilian ranks of the Ba'th Party, his control of a Ba'th militia, and his
position as head of a complex network of security agencies. In 1972
the Ba'th regime nationalized all oil production in the country. At the

same time, the 'increasingly significant Iraqi national oil industry could only be maintained and expanded with initial external, primarily Soviet and French, help. This was an event of major political and economic importance and was both popular and well-timed as the government gained control of Iraq's oil resources on the eve of the momentous price revolution that accompanied the 1973 Arab–Israeli war. Enriched by the tremendous influx of oil revenue, the regime carried out major economic and social reforms. Even though the Ba'thist state had consolidated power through the use of extreme violence and terror, this level of prosperity and redistribution enabled the regime to create a base of public acceptance. In 1976 Hussein, who had no military background, appointed himself a general in the army. Hussein's insertion into the military hierarchy reduced the importance of al-Bakr, and in 1979 the latter resigned. Hussein immediately succeeded him as president, secretary general of the Ba'th Party, chairman of the RCC, and commander-in-chief of the armed forces.

However, as Dodge argues, Saddam Hussein's lengthy period in power from 1979 to 2003 'must be understood less as the cause of Iraq's violent political culture – or even of Iraq's role as a source of regional instability – and more as the symptom, albeit an extremely consequential one, of deeper long-term dynamics within Iraq's political sociology' (Dodge 2003:170). Thus Britain's profoundly flawed effort early in the twentieth century to construct an ostensibly post-colonial, but absolutist-monarchical 'nation-state' out of three former Ottoman provinces continues to be central to any understanding of post-Saddam Iraq in the twenty-first century (Dodge 2003: x–xii). As this book goes to press and for the foreseeable future it is still far too soon to tell whether Iraq, given its numerous historical fractures, will stabilize as a functioning, even prosperous, nation-state in the wider post-Cold War and post-9/11 nation-state system. Regardless of what proponents of peace and prosperity might hope for (and it is assumed that genuine peace and prosperity are broadly desired even if viewed as unattainable) there are few signs that the conflict-ridden Middle East if not beyond is the place where strong regional and/or multilateral institutions can deliver security and development any time soon. If such a perspective requires confirmation: we need look no further than Afghanistan over the same period.

## The Example of Afghanistan: International Development and the Limits of Nation-Building in the Third World

In fact, it can be argued that the notion of 'failing' or 'failed' states, while useful at one level, does not really capture the complexity of 'state failure' in relation to the crisis of international development and the limits of nation-building in the Third World. For example, some commentators have argued that Taliban-ruled Afghanistan (before the arrival of the US in late 2001) 'was not' a 'failed state'. What it was (and is still) 'is a partially failed and partially connected state' that operates at the 'interstices' of uneven globalization via drug trafficking, counterfeiting and the training and planning of acts of terrorism (Weber *et al.* 2007:50), while a significant part of the population has seen primarily the dark side of modernity. At the same time, as we entered the second decade of the twenty-first century there was a growing awareness that the Taliban and Al-Qaeda are now (or again) gaining a greater or lesser degree of support from opium cultivation and its processing and shipping. Afghanistan is regularly reported as the source of 90 per cent of the world's heroin consumption. After years of apparently limited public concern, Washington generally, and the Drug Enforcement Administration (DEA) more specifically, began to draw attention to the fact that Al-Qaeda and the Taliban are financed in part at least by the opium/heroin trade and that the US needs to make a greater effort to curtail or eliminate opium growing and heroin production (Peters 2009).

Going after the drugs, however, is an endless quest in terms of both stopping their flow and/or cutting the cord, thick or thin, that connects the heroin trade to Al-Qaeda and the Taliban. For example, US-backed nation-building and counterinsurgency operations against the *Fuerzas Armadas Revolucionarias Colombianas* (FARC) in Colombia (the hub of the regional and global cocaine trade and another nation-state that has been prominent on the failed state index in years past) were funded and justified on the grounds that defeating the FARC would help win the 'war on drugs'. Furthermore, after 9/11 the FARC was also formally listed as a terrorist organization to incorporate a Cold War-style Marxist guerrilla organization into the Global War on Terrorism (GWOT). This was always a dubious connection and Latin America or the Americas more broadly (apart from the US itself), never fitted well with the idea of a Global War on Terrorism, a term that from 2009 began to be wound back by the administration of US president Barack Obama.

In fact, the wider backdrop to and limits of rolling up Al-Qaeda and winning the war against the Taliban is the need to realize that Afghanistan has never existed as a unified nation-state with a strong and legitimate central government and that situation is not going to change soon, if ever. Afghanistan has never been close to being ruled in a fashion where the central government actually exercised control across the polity as a whole. In fact, when you go back to the nineteenth century and earlier, there was no Afghanistan in terms of a sovereign nation-state. Even today it is more of a sovereign nation-state on paper than it is on the ground. The contemporary nation-state of Afghanistan has never really controlled its territory; and its claims to being a sovereign nation-state are derived from external recognition.

Afghanistan as it is currently constituted emerged out of the vagaries of the Duranni Empire, established in 1747 by Ahmad Shah Durrani and centred on Kandahar. The capital was later moved to Kabul, by which time the Duranni Empire was in decline. In the second half of the nineteenth century it was at the centre of the so-called 'Great Game' as the Russian Empire to the north and the British Indian Empire to the southeast encroached on the region and vied for control. Until the early twentieth century, Afghanistan served primarily as a buffer state between the two rival imperial powers, with the British exercising a degree of indirect control over the government in Kabul. The kingdom achieved full independence, on 19 August 1919, when it successfully terminated any vestige of British control in the aftermath of a third war between British India and Afghanistan.

The literal translation of Afghanistan is Land of Afghans and prior to the nineteenth century it referred primarily to the southern region inhabited by the Pashtuns, while the kingdom as a whole was known as the Kingdom of Kabul. During the process of centralization and expansion the name Afghanistan was adopted as the name for the entire kingdom and was referred to as such in treaties with Persia and the British Indian Empire. When it was formally recognized as an independent state in 1919, Afghanistan was the name it continued to use, which was later enshrined in the country's constitution in 1923. Thirty years earlier, in 1893, the British had demarcated what became known as the Durand Line as the boundary between Afghanistan and British India. The line ran through the middle of Pashtunistan. Then, when Pakistan and India emerged as independent nation-states out of the break-up of British India in 1947, the Afghan government, as mentioned above, refused to recognize the Durand Line and continues to refuse to do so (Rubin 2002: 45–58).

From the 1930s to the early 1970s, Afghanistan experienced a period of relative political stability under King Zahir Shah. In 1973, Mohammed Daoud Khan led a bloodless coup against his brother-in-law the king and established Afghanistan as a republic with himself as the first president. This, as it transpires was the beginning of a downward political spiral. Mir Akbar Khyber, a prominent figure in the People's Democratic Party of Afghanistan (PDPA) was killed by government troops while most of the leadership was arrested. Fearing that the Daoud government was planning to eliminate the PDPA, those members of the leadership (which included a military wing) who remained at large launched an uprising. Daoud was killed, and the key figure to emerge in the wake of this revolt was Nur Mohammad Taraki, who became both prime minister and president of the newly minted Democratic Republic of Afghanistan, while also serving as general secretary of the PDPA. From 1978 onwards the PDPA government launched major land reform, loosened restrictions on 'freedom of religion' and brought women into political life. In Kabul and other cities, most people either welcomed the PDPA or adopted a position of ambivalence. However, the government's secular initiatives and its preoccupation with women's rights did not go down well in the countryside, where Afghan peasants held to conservative Islamic practices such as restricting the rights of women (Rubin 2002: 58–78).

The PDPA's popularity in the country was in the balance from the outset, at the same time as internal party politics were fractious. In March 1979 Field Marshall Hafizullah Amin took over as prime minister and vice-president of the Supreme Defence Council. Taraki was initially allowed to remain president, but on 14 September, Taraki was ousted by Amin, with the former being killed in the process. This led the Soviet Union, a key ally of the PDPA government, to intervene to try and end the internal PDPA infighting and stabilize the regime. On 24 December 1979 some 100,000 Soviet troops rolled into Afghanistan, with as many as 200,000 troops in the country at the height of what became a decade-long occupation. The Kremlin also supported the killing of Amin, who was replaced by Babrak Karmal. When the Soviets withdrew in 1989, estimates of the number of Afghan civilians who had died ranged from 600,000 to two million, while more than five million had gone into exile in Pakistan and elsewhere. In 1979, US president Jimmy Carter initiated the covert funding of the Mujahideen, the broad-based opposition group that was fighting the Soviet-backed government. The Mujahideen was comprised of an array of factions that generally articulated some form of conservative 'Islamic' ideology. Once the Soviet troops left Afghanistan, Washington and its allies cut off their support and made no effort to aid the rebuilding of the war-ravaged polity. Meanwhile, Moscow continued to support President Najibullah, who had served as the head of the Afghan Secret Service during the occupation, until the early months of 1992, at which point the Kremlin ended its sales of oil to the Najibullah regime, and Najibullah himself was killed as Kabul fell to the Mujahideen. Subsequent infighting between the various factions of the Mujahideen escalated, ushering in a revitalized era of warlordism (Rubin 2002: 111–280).

By the mid-1990s the Taliban had emerged as a unified military and politico-religious force. With considerable support from the government of Pakistan they captured Kabul in 1996 and declared the Islamic Emirate of Afghanistan. By late 2000 the Taliban controlled most of the country. The Taliban introduced a range of restrictions: they drove women out of the work force, universities and schools, while former supporters of the PDPA were hunted down and eliminated. The Taliban continued to consolidate their position until late 2001, when a US-led military force (Operation Enduring Freedom – OEF) overthrew the Taliban government because it had been providing safe harbour for those deemed responsible for the 9/11 attacks on the US (Crews and Tarzi 2008). A large number of Taliban were either killed, captured or scattered across their support base, or took sanctuary along the rugged parts of the Afghanistan–Pakistan border or within Pakistan itself. In the past ten years the Taliban have regained momentum inside Afghanistan and Pakistan, while Al-Qaeda and other *jihadi* networks have turned the Afghanistan–Pakistan border into a focus of the ongoing struggle within Islam pitting moderates against violent politico-religious organizations. The latter also challenge the US and its allies well beyond the region in various ways even as the US moves to withdraw militarily from Afghanistan by 2014. While the central Afghan government continues to function, it was and is profoundly corrupt and continues to not only have to deal with a Taliban insurgency but also with established warlords.

Afghanistan has entered the second decade of the twenty-first century further scoured by war and no less united or stable than before. Nor does it possess much in the way of the robust infrastructure and institutional capacity that are required if it is to function as a sovereign nation-state. Its strongest linkage with the rest of the world is its central role in the heroin trade. The writ of the government in Kabul does not extend outwards in a fashion that comes close to controlling the bulk of the territory over which it is supposed to rule. Meanwhile, some of the most expensive real estate in the world can be found in downtown Kabul. Afghanistan remains characterized by ethnic fractures and unrepentant warlordism, while refusing to recognize the legitimacy of its current border with Pakistan: much of it runs through a region that neither the Afghan government nor the Pakistani government is able to control effectively. If there was ever an ostensibly sovereign territorial nation-state that exemplifies the limits of nation-building, while making clear the contradictions and even crisis of the nation-state system in the erstwhile Third World, observers need look no further than Afghanistan. It also needs to be noticed that Afghanistan *never really operated as* an effective nation-state, and that aspirations to live in such an arrangement have been (and in many cases still are) scarce. It reflects in an extreme fashion the profound shortcomings of the still powerful idea that it is the sovereign nation-state individually and collectively that signify global modernity and is the primary means by which development in the Third World and elsewhere can be successfully pursued.

## Conclusion: The Resurrection of Nation-Building and Modernization

Post-Cold War theories and practices of nation-building in the Third World have a complicated history. For example, as has been suggested, nation-building in the early Cold War era established certain precedents which were characterized not least by contiguities with the politics of the colonial era, although these were to some extent overlaid by the connection between development and security as characterized by the emergence of the bipolar geopolitical framework of the Cold War. Once the Cold War was over, nation-building underwent reconceptualizations and renewals in the light of the contradictions of international development, neo-liberalism and uneven globalization, which in turn began to be seen within the parameters of an increasingly problematic modernization project (cue, for instance, the global environmental crisis). In the wake of the 'peaceful revolutions' in Eastern Europe, the 1990s inculcated a shift away from theories of modernization that looked at development and security with a focus on state capacity-building and centralized legitimate force. Instead, the focus turned towards civil society actors as drivers of both development 'from below' and security through pluralistic 'civility' (Kaldor 2003; Keane 2001). However, the state-centred security framework returned with a vengeance after 9/11, as the link between international development and security was resurrected in the form of nation-building at the same time as it continued to be debated and rethought. Despite a range of alternative ideas about development and/or security, and despite the fact that empirically the 'international system' had always comprised numerous examples of juridical statehood far removed from the ideal-type of the nation-state, the dominant international approach to development and security rests once more on assumptions that may well prove to be the main obstacles to realizing the goals of stability and development. As our analysis has shown, 'incomplete' statehood cannot be understood as a symptom of a particular stage of growth (see, for instance, Jackson 1990; Collier 2007); rather these instances are expressions of the organization of the historically contingent project of global modernization and its contradictions of the nation-state system (Saurin 1995, 1996).

As this chapter has made clear, development and security are once again framed by pre-eminent geopolitical actors in national and international terms. More specifically national development and national security have been reified in relation to the unevenly universalized system of sovereign nation-states. At the same time, the existence of major, if still marginalized challenges to the dominant conceptions of development and security (Shah 2009), testify to the increasing difficulties faced by attempts to reconcile social, political and ecological integration with the institutional architecture of the international system. These newer approaches, which include a focus on social and environmental issues, and questions of gender inequality, to name just a few examples, are reflected in the day-to-day actions of countless peoples and organizations around the world, cross-cutting borders and boundaries, and reshaping both inclusion and exclusion in novel ways (see, for example, Thomas and Weber 1999; Sparke 2006; Barndt 1997; Perez and Berger 2009). They do hold out some hope in the face of the consequences and implications of decolonization, the universalization of the nation-state system, the coming and eventual passing of the Cold War, the rise and fall of Third Worldism, and the crisis of international development. It is beyond the scope of this book to examine and discuss the full range of alternatives to the dominant narratives on global modernity and international development. It is, however, worth noting that while there are many dissident approaches to security and development they have not yet produced a comprehensive alternative political imaginary that could successfully displace the institutionally entrenched nation-state system as the dominant mode of integration worldwide (even though many of these dissenters challenge the latter's policies, such as the privatization of water, or healthcare; see, for example, Thomas and Weber 2004; Morgan 2011).

One possible option by which to gradually move beyond the privileged focus on the nation-state as the key to development is taken up in Chapter 6 in which we outline a new agenda for processing the challenges of the contradictions of global modernization that emphasizes possible regional development-security frameworks for progress. It does this particularly by addressing the need for the dispersal of sovereignty – that is, political authority needs to be far more multi-tiered and responsive than it currently is. This is not a catch-all solution, but at its best it is an incipient (even potentially systemic) challenge to and dramatic revision of the current institutions for international development and security. It may seem too tepid for some and too radical for others, as well as being seen as unrealistic by many. As we will make clear, it is not a complete and impregnable alternative, but the basis for a new and open-ended agenda that will continue to require rethinking and experimentation.

# 6

# A New Agenda for Negotiating Global Modernity: A Regional Development-Security Framework after Third Worldism

We have seen that Third Worldism has lost its political significance, at least as a comprehensive political project. Today's crisis of the Third World is not only tied to the exhaustion of a political project that sought to redress the effects of colonial rule and ongoing post-colonial exploitation and material deprivation; the concept also no longer has much utility as a descriptive category that gives meaning and substance to relevant prescriptions for negotiating the depth and breadth of the implications of global modernity and development. This problem is (as we have argued throughout the book) rooted in the widespread and continued commitment to the modern nation-state and the nation-state system as the embodiment of the institutional means by which to achieve development. In more than one sense, our review of the project of Third Worldism has shown that its political constitution was always oriented in terms that pointed beyond the advancement of the conditions of individual nation-states, and towards collective political struggles reaching through 'statist' understandings of socio-political organization. In that sense, at least, Third Worldism was a *regionalist* project aimed at global transformation. That this faltered in its more radical outlook has to be contextualized; the global transformation of political economic relations signalled by the rise of neo-liberalism, and its associated development policies, circumscribes one important trend here, with continuing salience. The end of the Cold War, as we have seen, is another central feature of changing conditions, which affected the reconfiguration of Third Worldism, and the notion of advocating and implementing alternative pathways to modernization.

Instead of stressing 'the end of the nation- state', however, we have argued that the nation-state system is in the midst of a transformative crisis (Castells 1997, 1998; Cerny 1990, 1997; Hameiri 2009, 2013). Reconfigurations of statehood mean that the emergence of the 'competition state', while not necessarily already a comprehensive outcome, is certainly in the process of 'globalizing'. Related to this is the deepening of market-disciplinary rule and the reconfiguration of social bonds (Cerny 1997: 274), which in turn meets with counter-pressures (see, for instance, the recent emergence of the Occupy movement), and/or socio-political crisis tendencies (see Eastern Europe, or parts of Southeast Asia; on the latter, see Carroll 2010). The increases in interdependency initially hailed as the rise of a post-Cold War new liberal world order, have, through the associated global organizations such as the WTO, inaugurated new political conflicts over distribution, economic opportunity, social well-being and ecological implications.

The effects of these changes have been understood in terms of the dispersal of governance authority into multi-tiered constellations, in and through which rule and rules are conceived and applied to contexts and populations in increasingly 'post-sovereign' modes. Such dispersals, though, have borne both the ideological and actual disciplinary imprints of an underlying proto-neoliberal consensus, thus contributing to the creation and reproduction of further inequalities and exclusions. This type of regionalist-oriented multi-level governance is not hegemonic socially and has been subject to various counter-political pressures globally (Gill 2002; Bieler 2011).

Simultaneously, the ensuing socio-political conflicts in the post-Cold War order are increasingly policed by military means, marking out one site in which the nation-state re-asserts institutional capabilities, though not any comprehensive *political* vision aimed at providing redress, reform and positive change. As we have seen in our discussions of the recent wars in Iraq and Afghanistan, the *absence* of a plausible political project has marred the renewed appetite for interventionism.

In this context a new approach is required to capture and understand these dynamics and consider their significance for development. Our objective in this chapter is not to offer a comprehensive elaboration or an exposition of a systemic alternative. This would be counter to the democratic impulse that underscored the vision of Third Worldism itself, and such an approach would most likely fall short of tackling the complex problems of development as we have reconstructed them in this volume.

This chapter nevertheless does make a tentative effort to sketch a plausible alternative for a reconfigured approach to negotiating global modernity, which we suggest could take the form of regional development-security frameworks with progressive orientations. We attempt to outline political possibilities based on our analyses above, which we consider to have potential in a context in which more radical political solutions perhaps lack feasibility, despite the fact that some such projects are also underway, often carried forward by social movements or non-state actors (see, for instance, the politics of the 'global food sovereignty' movement; McMichael 2008). Our objective here is to elaborate the features of regional frameworks for development and security that may have the potential to stand as an open-ended (and ultimately, someday even a systemic) alternative that could meet the challenge of the current crisis of global modernity and international development. The existence of this crisis is reflected in the acceptance in many quarters of the view that we live in a world characterized by a growing number of 'nation-states in crisis' and the prospect of societal collapse that goes with it. These tendencies are already in some cases (such as sub-Saharan Africa and large parts of South and Southeast Asia) attributed to regions (Berger and Reese, 2010), thus adding to the *prima facie* plausibility of the reconfigured regionalist approach we sketch here.

This chapter looks at rethinking the Third World and meeting the challenge of development in a way that includes recasting the contemporary conception of national sovereignty in favour of more formal multi-tiered forms of political authority, a number of contemporary examples of which exist and could, to a lesser or greater degree, be built on. For instance, in the case of the European Union (EU) the dispersal of national sovereignties at least to some extent holds out the potential of reanimated forms of democratization and more inclusive and comprehensive politics (Hameiri 2013: 321). The EU has the potential for this, though its embrace of deepening democratization has been slow and very uneven (it does, however, comprise some elements of redistributive measures and strategic planning at a genuinely regional level). The focus of multi-tiered political authority should not be solely the pursuit of economic development (as it is conventionally measured) and the delivery of security to corporations and the protection of private property, which, as we have argued above, is presently the dominant approach. A shift to a multi-tiered approach to political authority ought to be premised on the recognition that local lived experiences are already connected to regional and global structures and relations. However, there is increasingly a legitimacy gap in the terms of governance (cf. Cerny 1997) and especially so in the context of the rise of neo-liberal development. A formal shift in political authority could expand conceptions of who belongs to a political community (thus enhancing the political conditions for social obligations to be extended to previously excluded classes and communities) and it would also create the possibility of more substantive democratic participation. The latter could entail affording the opportunities for social groups to 'have the right to define their own rights' and rules and regulations, which has been an emerging point of reference of those deprived of basic rights, from the right to water (Morgan 2011:110) and even to the city (Patel 2009:111–56), to diverse polities (including, for instance, indigenous ones). It is enhancing this democratic provision as well as the substantive conditions for redistribution and recognition of difference that we consider as a possible option entailed by a multi-tiered approach to political authority oriented within regional contexts. In substantive terms, this means that development has to be about the protection of civil and human rights (Grovogui 2011), along with the calibration and re-calibration of the obligations of 'citizens' both collectively and individually (in relation to taxation and legal systems) and the delivery of basic needs (for example, schools and universities, roads, law enforcement, emergency services and health care, as well as access to water and electricity), and more than a modicum of the provision of collective goods. In short this can entail citizenship understood even more explicitly as a 'compact' that involves rights, responsibilities and recognition (cultural, social and political). The regional development-security frameworks we are considering would have to move beyond key elements of conventional international relations as embodied for instance by the United Nations (UN). A new agenda for negotiating global modernity would involve the institutionalization of a dialectical relationship between global governance (such as that embodied by the UN) and regional facilitation of development-security frameworks centred on open-ended and multi-tiered approaches to political authority. Also, although keeping in view (global) modernity, we are highlighting the importance of identity, customs, culture and tradition; thus, it is clear that addressing the continuous substantive fallout of the legacies of colonialism and post-colonial subjection would need to be central to the development-security frameworks we anticipate, both at the levels of their regional institution, and at the level of global governance. These issues need to be regarded through a more refined lens, as they may provide the vectors through which development and security can be more effectively achieved. This is not to suggest that in other cases, attachments to specific versions of 'revisionist' conceptions of culture and identity (for instance) have not been obstacles to progressive change as conceived for our purposes. Tradition and custom are constantly reinvented, while the crisis of development exemplified in many parts of the world reflects the dark side of global modernity rather than its absence (cf. McMichael 2010).

The case for regional development-security frameworks is a plausible one, given that the post-Cold War era has seen the creation, renaming and/or strengthening of a wide range of regional development and security organizations. Some of these organizational-regional reorientations hold out more promise than others; one could go into this issue by comparing, for instance, the development and human insecurity implications of the North American Free Trade Agreement (NAFTA) on the one hand, and the political possibilities reflected in the strengthening of the EU on the other hand. Another case, the Organization of African Unity, which was established in 1963, displayed only a minor degree of effectiveness into the 1990s. Then in 2002 it was renamed and re-launched as the African Union (AU), modelled, on paper at least, on the EU, with regional development and security foci. Some observers go so far as to argue that, as with the EU, the African Union 'is certain to experience many difficult challenges and a long period of adjustment before it succeeds in fulfilling' its objectives of a regional common market and a unified set of governing institutions that result in a United States of Africa (Keylor 2008: 448). These aspirations and the naïve assessment provided by William Keylor are brought low by the profound difficulties that the reinvigoration of AU-focused regionalism faces at this point in time. However, it would be equally inappropriate to overlook the real gains the AU has made in addressing, albeit in a serious but limited fashion, both conflicts and developments in recent years (see, for example, Grovogui 2011).

For a regional development-security approach to work, the question of national sovereignty requires critical attention, and a diverse range of actors would have to be brought together in effective institutional settings. This, of course, implies a reconfiguration of sovereignty that moves away from its focus on what are 'neo-absolutist' conceptions in tune with the premises of classical International Relations towards more comprehensive models based on popular sovereignty (M. Weber 2007). The latter can more likely be realized at this particular point in time in regional contexts. Once a broad spectrum of stakeholders are brought together, they would have to address themselves to regional problems based on the assumption that the region is the most appropriate level for dealing with many pressing issues, while also formally delegating development-security efforts upwards and downwards based on a far more multitiered notion of political authority. The strengthening of regional frameworks would have to be advanced alongside an emphasis on strengthening local participation too. There is a need at all levels to recognize our common humanity, but also to recognize the diversity within that commonality and the need to protect people as much as possible not only from the threats of violent conflict, but also from the cruelties entailed in historic and ongoing inequality and the contemporary 'successes' of neoliberal economics.

To this end this chapter starts with a return to, and amplification of, our earlier discussion of the idea of the sovereign modern territorial nation-state, which remains far too central to development policy generally and various regional organizations more specifically. In particular we look at the debate about the nation-state and its profound limitations as a naturalized and often rigid collection of political institutions and arrangements. In this context, we then turn to a discussion of the crisis of the system of sovereign nation-states as a whole. In the third and final section of this chapter we focus on the proposed alternative embodied in the idea of open-ended regional development-security frameworks for progress. Ultimately we argue that at this juncture rethinking the Third World would mean a sustained commitment to new or revised forms of development- and/or security-oriented regionalism, whether they are relatively entrenched, as in the case of the EU, somewhat looser regional organizations such as the Asia Pacific Economic Cooperation forum (APEC), or more deliberately alternative but not unproblematic forms of regionalism such as the Alianza Bolivariana para los Pueblos de Nuestra América-Tratado de Comercio de los Pueblos (ALBA-TCP) (cf. Morgan 2011: 114–17) and the African Union (AU). Whatever the myriad shortcomings of contemporary regional development and/or security organizations, they provide an often already existing framework (both minimalist and maximalist) via which we can rethink the Third World and begin to pursue a far more inclusive form of global modernity with a far broader range of benefits and opportunities (and obligations) than is offered by the sovereign nation-state in most parts of the world. Ultimately, the agenda we are outlining here would require an in-depth and ongoing consideration of regional integration, which already has and continues to be a subject of intense critical debate (Jayasuria 2009; Hameiri 2013, 2009). That debate, which is far from over, is beyond the scope of this book insofar as it would be impossible to give regionalism and its relationship to development the thorough consideration it deserves without producing another book in the process. For this reason this chapter has the modest goal of ending our rethinking of the Third World, by clarifying how regional development-security frameworks can be part of a new agenda for negotiating global modernity that moves beyond the continued focus on the sovereign nation-state as it was universalized after the Second World War.

## The Sovereign Nation-State in Crisis: Ethnicity, Nationalism and Global Modernity

The apparent failure of the sovereign nation-state to deliver on its post-1945 promise saw renewed interest in clarifying and defining state formation and its relationship to nationalism and the 'nation'.

A famous definition of the modern nation that remains an important starting place for understanding the rise to prominence of the sovereign nation-state in the twentieth century actually comes from Joseph Stalin, who presided over the brutal consolidation of the Union of Soviet Socialist Republics from the 1930s until his death in 1953. Writing in the early decades of the twentieth century, Stalin argued that 'a nation is a historically constituted, stable community of people, formed on the basis of a common language, territory, economic life, and psychological make-up' that is reflected 'in a common culture' (quoted in Hutchinson and Smith 1994: 18–21). While Stalin's definition is relatively unproblematic, his implementation of his ideas about nationalism and state-formation involved extremely high levels of violence and left a complex and bloody legacy in the former Soviet Union, which became known as the Second World from 1945 down to its demise in 1989–91. The Soviet dictator remains a potent, primarily negative icon of the Cold War worldwide, whose only 'intellectual' contribution to Marxism may well have been his basic efforts at addressing the 'national question'. As we have seen, this was a question that remained relatively marginalized in the discourses in and around the superpowers and their allies during the Cold War, even though it was highly important aspect of the ongoing struggles around decolonization and national liberation in the 'Third World' during the same period.

As has also been noted earlier in this book, the end of the Cold War and the resurgence of nationalism stimulated renewed interest in the subject in 'Western' academia. Nationalism was divided by some observers into three broad analytical categories: primordial, ethnic and modern. Primordial conceptions of nationalism guided nationalist movements and reinforced popular ideas about nationalism as natural and rooted in a shared past during the rise and fall of Third Worldism. By the 1960s the primordial interpretation of nationalism was increasingly challenged by the view that the 'nation' is a modern phenomenon and any effort to see it as having existed in timeless fashion down through history is ahistorical. While this occurred at a time when Third Worldism was in the ascendant, in retrospect at least it was also starting to show serious problems as a result of having been built on the idea of a collectivity of sovereign territorial nation-states in tension with a constituted reality that was characterized by high levels of inequality between and within the growing number of sovereign nation-states in this period.

In contrast to both the primordial and the modern conception of nationalism, there is a third approach, which focuses on ethnicity. The ethnic perspective rejects primordialism and emphasizes that nations are strictly speaking modern creations, but while they are not culturally deterministic, ethnic approaches perceive far more continuity than the modernists. They seek to 'contextualize the emergence of nations within the larger phenomenon of ethnicity which shaped them', although what is meant by 'ethnicity' varies from author to author (Hutchinson 1994: 7–9). Anthony Smith's work is still probably the best known and the most relevant to any discussion of ethnicity and modern nationalism. Writing in the late 1980s he argued that 'the central difficulties of both state-making and nation building stem from the nature and intensity of ethnic ties and sentiments'. Furthermore, the 'lack of ethnic foundations and resilience can unmake states and dismantle nations as much as any inept elite activities or geopolitical calculations'. Smith emphasized that the 'central difficulty of "nation building"' in the Third World, particularly in the Middle East, Asia and Africa was the 'lack of any shared historical mythology and memory on which state elites can set about "building" the nation'. In his view the 'nation' (as a key element of the sovereign nation-state) can only successfully emerge 'from the central fund of culture and symbolism and mythology provided by shared historical experiences' (Smith 1989: 258–9). And even that is a necessary but far from sufficient condition as we move through the second decade of the twenty-first century.

Contemporary nation-states that reinforce Smith's emphasis on the centrality of ostensibly shared cultural roots to 'nations' and the creation of nation-states include, for example, Thailand. Formerly Siam, the rise of the sovereign nation-state of Thailand is said to have flowed from a relatively homogeneous ethnic 'base' centred on a dynastic heritage that provided the historic material for the construction of a modern nation-state. Thailand is somewhat unusual insofar as the dominant historical trend in what would become the Third World was the establishment of colonial rule during which the foreign rulers classified the local people along ethnic lines, establishing a social order which brought different ethnic groups into a divided and hierarchical system of power. As colonialism passed its zenith, many different ethnic groups were for a time, at least, able to set their various conflicts aside; however, even as the nationalist movements in question were about to wrench the state from the grasp of the colonizers, ethnic rivalries re-emerged and often led in short order to military dictatorships and communal violence. Smith draws a major distinction between those 'new states' without an 'ethnic core' and those with one. While most nation-states in Southeast Asia, for example, may have a core *ethnie*, most African states and a number of states in the Middle East do not. In the mid-1980s he argued that 'the state system and state boundaries since 1945 have held remarkably firm, despite continued pressures from ethnic movements'. Nevertheless Smith concluded that where an 'ethnic core' is absent, the formation of a modern nation-state is unlikely if not impossible. In fact, even '*with* an ethnic core, there remain severe problems' as it becomes part of the foundation of a modern sovereign territorial nation-state (Smith 1989: 252–4, 260–2; 1993: 7–8).

Smith's emphasis on an ethnic base (in the sense of providing the historical material for nationalism) is important. However, there are also strong grounds for rejecting the idea that modern nation-states, or similar forms of sovereign institutions that may come in their wake, need ethnic cores, or that ethnic differences are an inevitable basis for conflict within nation-states. David Laitin argues that the evidence to support the assumption that there is a close 'relationship between ethnic difference and violence' is actually lacking despite the popular tendency to assume the contrary. He argues that the dynamics underlying ethnic-communal conflict and civil war, while mobilized and affirmed by appeals to ethnicity, are caused by a 'weak' state that cannot deliver a range of basic services to its citizens, at the same time as it is unable to provide effective law enforcement, especially on the margins. Based on detailed quantitative research supported by thorough qualitative analysis, Laitin argues that the common assumption that national and ethnic differences are intrinsically 'dangerous' is incorrect. The widespread concern to eliminate or at least mitigate 'civil violence' is generally (although not always) a causal factor driving state-building. Meanwhile, there is, Laitin notes, a tendency to focus 'far more on the few cases of communal violence than on the normal situation of ethnic peace' (Fearon and Laitin 2003: 75–90; Laitin 2007: 21–3).

There is not necessarily as much difference between the ethnicists and the modernists as the tripartite typology sketched out above implies. To be sure, Smith's approach does still conceptualize ethnicity in a far more fixed fashion than modernists such as

Benedict Anderson (discussed in Chapter 1). Anderson's approach, which is reinforced by Laitin's analysis in many ways, rests on the assumption that modern nationalisms have been created in the context of complicated dynamics of historical change: that is the process that carried us from a world of empires to a world of sovereign nation-states. Also, as we noted at the outset, the delineation between the nation and the state is extremely important. The state is mainly a 'political-legal concept', while the nation is what some observers have characterized as 'primarily psycho-cultural'. Therefore, states may exist when there is no nation (Afghanistan or the Congo). Conversely, a nation may exist when no legally recognized state does (such as Palestine or Somalia). It is only when both the state and the nation not only exist but are bound by a range of mutually reinforcing obligations and benefits that the ideal-typical modern nation-state exists in a meaningful fashion. Returning to the beginning then, a working definition of the modern nation-state needs to bear in mind the complexity and contested character of the 'nation' and the difference between 'nation' and 'state'. However, as a point of departure the modern nation-state can be defined as a historically grounded community of people, generally, but not always, sharing a common language, located within a clearly defined territory, and sharing at the broadest level at least a common political and cultural framework capable of accommodating ethnic differences. Furthermore, they are recognized by other modern nation-states as sovereign and discrete entities within a wider system of nation-states worldwide. After 1945 this was, as already noted, the backdrop for the rise and fall of the Third World down to the end of the Cold War.

## The System of Sovereign Nation-States in Crisis

The crisis of the nation-state system emerges out of the historical context of the rise of nationalism and the universalization of the system of sovereign nation-states in the twentieth century. Furthermore, as has been argued, the connection between development and security was embedded in the international system as it emerged from a world of empires to a world of sovereign nation-states, a majority of which were in the erstwhile Third World and garnered a position of collective influence in international relations

through organizations such as the UN. For example, the development-security connection is central to Paul Kennedy's (2006)
historical overview of the UN, entitled *The Parliament of Man: The
Past, Present, and Future of the United Nations*. His book, which
was a product of his earlier participation in the writing of a perform-
ance-oriented report for the United Nations, stakes out a middle path
between shelving the UN and radically transforming it in favour of
'a United Nations organization, duly modified from the world of
1945, but still recognizable to its founding fathers, and still dedicated to their lofty purposes' (Kennedy 2006: xvii). While emphasizing the dramatic changes in geopolitics and the pressing array of
global development and security problems, he argues that 'perhaps'
the 'most important' of all contemporary 'challenge[s]' facing the
UN (and its more important members) is 'how to deal with failed
states'.

Kennedy's call for reforms thus not only prescribes changes to
the make-up and character of the Security Council but also links
security to development. He emphasizes that there has been much
consternation in the General Assembly of the UN and beyond that it
'focuses too much on security and not enough on development'.
This is a problem that is clearly reflected in the low priority the UN's
Economic and Social Council has compared to the Security Council.
Kennedy offers a wide range of piecemeal reforms as a means of
adjusting the UN to deal with the new world order. Despite his
recognition of the importance of the problem of state failure, his
prescriptions remain narrowly technocratic. Furthermore, he ends
with what can only be described as a platitude, arguing that 'the
boulder is only halfway up the mountain, and much effort is needed
if it is to be moved further' (Kennedy 2006: 246, 265, 269–79, 290).

In many ways Kennedy's optimistic defence of the United
Nations provides us with the perfect opportunity to suggest forward-
movement in an alternative direction that acknowledges the existence of the UN, but promotes regional development security frameworks for progress and views a reconfigured UN provision of global
governance in dialectical relation with that. The UN, particularly the
General Assembly, provided a stage for Third Worldism in the
context of the latter's emergence as a political force from the
Bandung Conference in 1955. The subsequent decline of the
General Assembly as a forum for progressive global governance,
inaugurating also the ebb of Third Worldism itself, testifies to the

inadequacies of UN governance, which, as we argue, makes a reorientation to regionalism necessary. Given the UN's record, a new regional approach ought to look for legitimacy elsewhere than the New York-based bureaucratic edifice that has grown and spread over the past sixty years. Even though the UN retains certain critical functions (such as its role in providing platforms for food security or global health care), it remains too often in a stalemate over crucial issues associated with the development and security needs of the majority of the world's population. A new orientation to a political regionalism thus offers a greater potential for addressing the 'dark side' of global integration, while remaining compatible with retaining the capacity to coordinate through UN global governance where and when appropriate.

It is important to note that very powerful interests and political and socio-economic forces continue to remain strongly invested in the international status quo. This is the context in which the governments of sovereign nation-states and observers of international relations, international development and international security, and/or proponents of deepening global modernity, continue to regard the UN as a key actor, or a forum for a crucial collection of national actors, in this overall process. However, despite the vision and hope that attended the establishment of the UN it is now increasingly constrained in addressing the problems thrown up by global social integration and its contradictions and exclusions (not least with regard to the implications of global environmental change).

Following the creation and amplification of the UN there was also a rising tendency to focus on national development in an international context, while neglecting the actual complexity of the new nation-states and the consequences of the universalization of the nation-state system. Some commentators certainly draw attention to the history of state-formation and the vagaries of nationalism, not to mention the connection between nation-building, or state-building, and economic development. However, they virtually all end up accepting the technocratic parameters of contemporary nation-building and state-building discourses and the juridical (*de jure*) or constitutional legality of nation-states. This has ensured that the sovereignty of extant or new nation-states is enshrined by the UN. This is a discourse that continues to naturalize the nation-state and the nation-state system, often overlooking or ignoring the *de facto* reality of a world of sovereign nation-states in favour of the *de jure*, or juridical sovereignty of nation-states worldwide regardless of the divergences in actual functionality that are readily apparent from nation-state to nation-state. Where 'national development' is still understood in such terms which allow analysts to attribute the causes of 'underdevelopment' to formally recognized, discrete national units, the *actual* constitutive dynamics of the 'problem of development' are missed. Contemporary prescriptions for nation-building or state-building in the Third World, as it is still routinely described (in the post-Cold War and post-9/11 era), have limited or no prospects for success if they fail to locate what they are doing in a far more critical and historical context.

Most importantly, the 'rules of the game' changed dramatically after 1945. The establishment of the UN and the onset of the Cold War represented a fundamental shift in the spread and significance of 'national sovereignty'. As we have seen, for the next thirty years, regardless of what side of the Cold War one was on, decolonization, national liberation and the establishment of sovereign nation-states with membership in the UN swept aside those colonial empires that had survived the vagaries of the Second World War. By the 1970s, a process begun during the First World War (if not earlier) saw a world of *de facto* and/or *de jure* empires give way to a world of *de facto* and/or *de jure* nation-states. In the Cold War era these nation-states became, among other things, the potential building-blocks of the Third World and/or Third Worldism. It is important to recognize that it is in this context that the formation of a political project of Third Worldism which transcended national outlooks took on its significance and potency.

With regard to the period prior to the Second World War, Charles Tilly has argued that 'war made the state and the state made war'. In particular the financial imperatives of war making in Europe over an extended period of time led to heightened levels of economic extraction, mobilization and repression, and where successful resulted in the formation of strong states and latterly 'nation-states' (Tilly 1975; Tilly 1992: 12; Porter 1994: 192–3, 240–1). The end of the Second World War, the establishment of the UN and the growing momentum of decolonization had profound and unforeseen implications in relation to the push for and the whole idea of a Third World in the context of the Cold War, and the universalization of the nation-state system. In relation to the period prior to 1945, following Tilly, Brian Taylor and Roxana Botea have also argued that strong national states emerged over an extended historical period and were consolidated as a result of the imperatives of interstate warfare. This has meant that for warfare to lay the groundwork for strong national states in the post-1945 era they needed to possess a necessary (but not always sufficient) amount of national-political 'coherence', such as occurred in Europe over a period of centuries. Importantly in the post-1945 era 'war now takes place in a state system that has already been created'. Warfare between states no longer works to 'create' the nation-state system. At the same time, the juridical (or *de jure*) sovereignty provided by the UN does not actually create modern nation-states in the Third World (Taylor and Botea 2008: 28–9). Whatever the merits of such historiography, its limitations are thrown into stark relief once the contexts of state-formation in the post-colonial world are considered in more depth and detail (Pasha, 2013: esp. 145–65).

The late twentieth century has in fact been characterized by the deepening of the crisis of the nation-state system alongside the inbuilt cyclical economic crises of liberal and neoliberal capitalism and uneven globalization. Instead of the international economy expanding in spatial terms, since the 1970s the various financial, trading and production networks that connect economic regions have been getting deeper and stronger, even though such increases in interconnectedness need to be carefully analysed. This process of *relative* regional exclusion, however, does not simply involve the economic neglect of a particular region or economies. Instead, it comprises their *integration* through new forms of extractive relations, rendering the margins thus created in the first instance even more precarious. In turn, it also entails the increasing elaboration of humanitarian networks and activities by the UN and a range of aid organizations in those regions, and with often less than unambiguously positive implications. There are also important peace-keeping and nation-building initiatives by outside governments in these marginalized regions, sometimes under UN auspices and at other times operating under the authority of a particular national government or group of national governments, or a regional organization (Bellamy *et al.* 2004; 188–268). These parts of the world (often unified by the continued use of the Third World as a descriptive and prescriptive category) have not, as we have already emphasized, been left out of global modernity; rather they have experienced its negative (or dark) side.

In the post-9/11 world the UN and its peace-keeping efforts in the Third World are profoundly constrained component of a wider post-Cold War order still centred on the United States (a United States that has its own wide range of financial and institutional problems that may not reflect 'state failure' but certainly require more attention than they appear to be receiving (see Katzenstein 2005). This is a post-Cold War order in which political instability, terrorism and criminality and 'failing' nation-states in various parts of the erroneously labelled Third World have precipitated the emergence (even before 9/11) of a renewed emphasis on the connection between development and security, while also to a greater or lesser degree viewing poverty and underdevelopment as a threat to global order. This shift is embodied in the growing links between strategies of conflict resolution, social reconstruction and foreign aid policies. While the United States and other OECD governments have been engaged in the post-Cold War nation-building effort that this reorientation represents, this task is also being shifted to new or reconfigured networks that combine national governments, military establishments, myriad private companies and contractors and NGOs (Duffield 2001).

## Beyond the System of Sovereign Nation-States: Regionalism, Internationalism and Negotiating Global Modernity

Since at least the end of the Cold War, regional economic and political initiatives have emerged as part of either an effort to advance a liberal politico-economic order, or to mitigate the impact of uneven globalization on the sovereign nation-state. Regional organizations have, to varying degrees, allowed sovereign nation-states to strengthen their position in a globalizing world, while providing a transitional framework for the processing of uneven globalization at a sub-global, but transnational level (cf. Hameiri 2013). Many regional efforts also strengthen (owing to their 'reconfigurations of sovereignty') smaller sovereign nation-states in relation to more powerful nation-states, while allowing for the dispersal of sovereign prerogatives and political competencies to the sub-national level. Regional integration up and down the regional-national-local register has the potential to facilitate everything from commerce to culture in an institutionalized, but ideally open-ended, equitable,

and increasingly participatory fashion. However, regional organizations and regional integration have to date been very uneven, and
those parts of the world where states are weak or failing are often
considered to have weak regional organizations also. The idea we
pursue here sees a more ambitious role for regional development-
security frameworks than what is currently on offer in existing
regional organizations.

The proposal we investigate has the potential to mark an altered
point of departure for policy design and implementation.
Simultaneously, it offers pathways for emphasizing the importance
of popular sovereignty rather than the state-centred conceptions that
have been integral to the reproduction of the international order.
This section first outlines reasons for the utility of the regional
development-security framework, then makes clear that there are
some contemporary prospects for seriously considering a new
approach to progressive forms of regionalism oriented towards
negotiating modernity worldwide in more inclusive terms.

Even the more hard-case examples of states in crisis, such as the
Democratic Republic of the Congo, Somalia and Afghanistan, are
clearly best understood and addressed as regional problems. In each
case, a reactive crisis-response approach is often utilized to deal
with insecurity, and to promote institution-building with little or no
input, not only from the people who live within the borders of the
state concerned, but also from the nation-states in the immediate
region and/or their citizens. As each new crisis demonstrates, a
policy focus on the individual state can lead to a certain degree of
increased development security, but this progress soon becomes
constrained by an inability to address the global and transnational
dimensions by which such crises are reproduced. This focus obliter-
ates the unequally co-constituted transnational dynamics of crises
tendencies as such (Shah 2009). Most commentators and policymakers are aware of the first phenomenon, 'spill-over', even if their
analyses of this continues to be constrained by state-centrism
(Byman and Pollack 2007). Few, however, have picked up on the
'co-production of crises' idea (though this has some precursors in
Marxist, dependency, world systems and post-colonial thinking, see
Grovogui 2002). As one author has observed, '(t)he domain of the
state is seen to be one of accommodation and contest by innumer-
able and contending sites of power embedded in society at the
regional and sub-regional levels' (Jalal, in Callahan 2003: 12). State

crises have the potential to quickly move to regional levels due to the degree of connectivity between the state and other regional actors. As a result, a change in economic policy, the level of political stability, and social change taking place within one state all have a profound impact upon the region as a whole. In this context we can take Benjamin Miller's definition of a region as our point of departure for what follows. For Miller, a region is a construct based on two conditions: '(1) a certain degree of geographical proximity' (to which we might add crucial developmental consequences and opportunities); and '(2) strategic interaction or security interdependence' (Miller 2007: 41). This definition of a region suggests a level of social and political connectivity already available as a resource for development and security.

State-centrism in political analysis continues to detract from exploring the political possibilities that regional organisations can engender. An example of this is the contemporary discourse about 'weak' or 'failing' states, which focuses attention once more on a single specific institutional understanding of socio-political integration. Terms such as 'failing' or 'failed' states, used to describe the weaker state-actor, add to the perception that there was once a viable, even strong state in place. While some states in crisis may have possessed more capacity in the past, there are, as we have made clear, just as many that have been weak and under pressure since they gained independence, owing mainly to their structural positioning within the world economic relations against which the project of Third Worldism first emerged, articulated its most coherent challenges (see the discussion of the New International Economic Order in Chapter 3), and upon which it ultimately foundered. National independence sometimes coincided with failure as weak post-colonial institutions provided the main vectors for civil and ethnic conflict (for example in Sudan and Burma). Meanwhile, there are many states that were never unified even in the colonial era ('buffer states' such as Afghanistan and Ethiopia). The broad-based solidarity espoused by the project of Third Worldism, which also in a sense affirmed the Third World as a political region, was on the one hand built on a recognition of these problems, as it was directed at overcoming them through a vision which precisely transcended state-centred analysis and practice. As we have argued below, this legacy continues, and as we are suggesting here, it may influence the formation of regional development-security frameworks significantly.

The starting point, then, is to recognize that many states labelled as failed or failing were never stable self-sustaining entities of governance in the image of the 'nation-state' to begin with, and their insecurities were significantly constituted through global and transnational flows and forces (cf. Saurin 1995; Grovogui 2002; Shilliam 2008; Shah 2009). A legacy of the colonial period was that there existed, in some cases, no functioning compact between the 'government state' and its 'citizens nation' (see also Mamdani 1996). A shift in emphasis towards the regional hence reflects the acknowledgement of where the centre of gravity of development and security frameworks could more plausibly be.

The strength of institutions and infrastructure represents the pooled resource capacity of the region, consisting mainly of the fiscal, institutional and economic capability which member states may possess to contribute to the advancement of the regional development-security framework. Consensus represents cooperative action at the regional level of governance, as well as the degree of popular support among the domestic constituency of each member state. Additionally, contributions from global actors, international organizations or nation-states are rolled up as regional attributes of either political support (consensus) or investment/aid to include security force assistance (capacity). Capacity and consensus respectively drive the formulation of policy. The success of regional assistance could further serve to reinforce capacity through creating conditions for its expansion across the region. Successful regional policy could also serve to further shape regional consensus as the people in both the key crisis zones and the region as a whole begin to benefit from development and security. While the national state may sometimes be the level at which this policy is implemented, regionally oriented policy must be flexible due to the dynamic processes allowing for a shifting of political authority upwards from the nation-state to the regional framework, and downward to the level of popular participation. Such a framework would have to be organized in a fashion that ensures policy input from the national and local level through channels that are open and understood by all concerned.

The regional development-security framework could take advantage of both the geographical proximity and international connectivity critical in ensuring the formation and maintenance of the necessary political will for negotiating regional development-security framework(s), while losing sight neither of the specific needs of any given locality, nor of the dialectical relation with the global flows into which it articulates. It also provides a template for the management of resources at the regional level. Such frameworks may also have the capacity to address many of the current challenges to state-building through clear delineations of authority, the pooled capacity of a region, and the fundamental importance of working towards consensus for regional stability. Focused policy design and implementation are necessary corollaries of successful regionalization in this vein, in order to balance the interaction among regional member states with their competing domestic requirements. Multilateralism is an inherent component of negotiating and maintaining the regional development-security framework, while its orientation would have to be towards the promotion of a clearly defined though open-ended direction. Through multilateralism at the regional level (and reaching towards transnationalism), the regional framework has the capacity to set and monitor time-lines, and effectively regulate the acquisition and distribution of resources for development and security.

Security provisions such as non-aggression pacts or security assistance grounded in a regional framework may provide the critical time and space necessary for the political and institutional development both of the nation-states concerned and more importantly of the open-ended regional framework that will make things easier in the medium term. Additionally, the pursuit of common platforms for defensive capabilities produces benefits for all member states, facilitates inter-operability in the conduct of security measures, and minimizes the potential for intra-regional conflict. Cooperation at this level is not utopian. It may require a certain degree of vision and a serious level of commitment, but it also potentially offers an effective strategy for assisting specific nation-states and enhancing stability in the region as a whole.

A renewed contemporary shift towards more regional political organisations in the sense we are suggesting here can draw on some significant changes in the resources available for achieving both more effective governance and greater enhanced participation, including advances in information technology, and the opportunities these provide for intensified networking and information sharing. While it is incumbent on political analysts to heed the potential adverse implications of the spread of these technologies (from surveillance to the creation of more and more salient 'digital divides'), there is also reason to think that their deployment, if purposefully handled, can contribute to the goals of the progressive regionalism we have outlined. The crucial question, then, is how well technology is managed and utilized, and to what ends. Technologies have potentials to enhance productivity in a positive manner, if their introduction and mainstreaming proceeds in line with broader social goals around employment, welfare and equitable participation.

Linked to these technological advances is the reconfigured understanding of education as a key resource for handling the main challenges of the present and the future. There has been a recent shift towards more comprehensive frameworks for life-long learning and educational transformation, and these, too, could and should be accommodated centrally in the new regionalist framework.

Finally, increasingly there are the intellectual resources available for conceptualizing practical alternatives to the dominant framing of development in terms of neo-classical economic premises. Heterodox economists have raised a paradigmatic re-appraisal of cooperative arrangements and approaches in terms of their capacity to deliver superior outcomes in distribution, participation, effectiveness and sustainability (see, for example, Ostrom 1990). The regionalist framework we envisage could more easily accommodate corresponding projects and trials than is the case in either state-centred or multilateral (global) growth-based approaches to poverty reduction and development. With such resources included, some of the institutional experimentation of earlier Third Worldism can live on productively and with promise.

It stands to reason that regional frameworks are not new. There are numerous historical precedents, not least from the context of indigenous governance (Crawford 1994). Examples such as these are pertinent reminders that alternative political constellations comprising regional aspects have been part of the framework of addressing problems of security and development among peoples not constrained by our notions of sovereignty, or methodological territorialist assumptions. A focus on indigenous politics is instructive here, particularly for our purpose of highlighting the transformative potential of a post-sovereign regionalist framework. In many cases, the Third Worldist project, inflected as it was towards emancipatory nationalism, enabled the centrist conception of state governance against which many indigenous populations have continued to struggle. These struggles have engendered limited success in recent years at the level of multilateral institutions (UN 2007), though such success remains constrained significantly by the sovereign prerogatives of 'host-states' (Shaw 2002; Strakosch 2014). With a regionalist 'post-sovereign' constellation, new pathways would be opened for accommodating and engaging different polities within regions.

Building on the lens opened by the example of indigenous struggles, we can include other groups, classes or identities for which the 'state' has turned more and more into the source of problems, discriminations and/or persecution. Among those vulnerable in these ways are, for instance, migrant populations, for whom the architecture of territorial sovereignty constitutes severe risks, disempowerment and disciplining force (see, for instance, in relation to NAFTA, Perez and Berger 2009; Suliman 2014). The potential of regional political arrangements not only reflects a greater array of political identities and possibilities, but also provides for enhanced capacities for the identification and pursuit of common goals (such as sustainability); hence objectives can provide responsiveness well beyond the constraints of the nation-state model (for example, see Katzenstein 2005: 195).

## Conclusion: A New Agenda for Negotiating Global Modernity

Any serious analysis of the problems of contemporary state-formation suggests that recasting it within a regional framework yields better potential than current practices, taking into account the local particularities of development and security, as well as global power relations. Many of the current failures and future challenges associated with nation-state-centred development already need to be understood in relation to their regional and global contexts. The creation or amplification of regional frameworks, with a strong component of innovative institution-building and diplomatic reframing regarding how groups' or individuals' participatory power can be harnessed, offers realistic prospects for achieving the objectives associated with overcoming contemporary contradictions of development and insecurity in the future. Regional cooperation can generate enhanced capacities, broader consensus for political action and ideally more focused policies for consolidating and strengthening political associations and social objectives in the region. We have suggested that the 'Third World' no longer has the required political or developmental significance it once did. Along with national liberation and the Cold War, it belongs to a historically specific conjuncture during which its project, Third Worldism, resonated profoundly, and provided the prospect (that often went unrealized) of addressing longstanding grievances, inequalities, and conflicts comprehensively, and with lasting effect. The passing of this historical conjuncture has signalled not the end of political pressure regarding the goals and objectives of Third Worldism, but its reorientation to new, different institutional and geo-political realities.

# Conclusion: Rethinking the Third World

As we have argued in this book, the rise and fall of the idea of the Third World and pursuit of the political project of Third Worldism from the 1950s down to the present entailed significant political transformations. The latter included the gradual universalization of the nation-state system in the context of the uneven and challenging working-through of the legacies of colonialism. The widespread hopes that the post-Second World War era would eventually be characterized by increasingly broad and ongoing improvements in development and security did not materialize and have not yet done so. A large number of nation-states in Asia and Africa (as well as the Americas) often based their optimistic visions for their future on the project of Third Worldism, aiming to collectively carry forward over decades sometimes complementary and sometimes specific versions of an inclusive, but yet to be fleshed out, shift in global social, political and economic relations. However, this gave way to the consolidation of inequalities, further exclusions and renewed conflicts. As we have seen, Third Worldism was at the centre of the wider geopolitics of the Cold War and the highly politicized debate about how to engage with the post-colonial ordering of global modernity. Over twenty years out since the end of the Cold War, the Second World (the USSR and its clients-allies) have exited the world stage with no serious prospects of returning as a serious systemic alternative to neo-liberalism and uneven globalization. In the absence of the Second World the notion of the Third World as both a location and a project has lost whatever relevance it may have had in an earlier era.

That said, for the relatively few remaining proponents of state socialism, as for their counterparts who emphasize the benefits of a romanticized version of liberal capitalism, the dominant development discourse remains grounded in a narrow conception of the Third

World as a still large collection of nation-states that continue to be in need of development. It also continues to be characterized by a complete failure to adjudicate the contradiction between national development efforts on the part of sovereign nation-states on the one hand and the ascendancy of neo-liberalism and uneven globalization since the 1980s on the other hand. The idea that there is a need to move beyond a focus on the nation-state (or a collective of nation-states such as those that aligned themselves with what became known as Third Worldism) as the means by which development can be achieved is not new. There are, as we have seen, a range of alternatives on offer that at least imply that there is a fundamental problem at the centre of international development. As noted above, however, since the end of the Cold War there have been no systemic alternatives with sufficient traction in comparison to an expanding set of often highly focused ground-level alternative approaches (mentioned or discussed in the Introduction and elsewhere), the majority of which do not even begin to address the question of political ordering or look beyond the sovereign nation-state as the primary focus of development efforts.

This Conclusion briefly restates the main elements that facilitate a rethinking of the Third World, reiterating the main aspects of the idea of the Third World from its inception down to the present including the rise and fall of Third Worldism. Significantly we also draw attention to some of the more important, albeit ultimately implausible, contemporary efforts to recycle Third Worldism in the twenty-first century. The second part of the Conclusion restates the main elements that characterized the decline of Third Worldism at the end of the Cold War, and revisits briefly the contradictions of international development and world politics against the backdrop of the crisis of global modernity. This will also include a reminder of the more recent and highly problematic resurrection of nation-building that was examined in detail in Chapter 5.

We also discuss concerns about and enthusiasm for the regional organizations that have emerged as a counterpart (explicitly or implicitly) to either a fixation with the national or in relation to uneven globalization in the post-Cold War era. Some of these regional efforts even articulate a tepid variation of Third Worldism; one of the most well-known is the Beijing Consensus, a project that offers ostensible leadership by the People's Republic of China to a host of other nation-states by following the authoritarian and hybrid socialist-capitalist model pursued by mainland China since the late 1970s

(Halper 2010). In the third and final section below we return to the discussion (outlined in some detail in Chapter 6) of the possibility of moving beyond the limits of conventional understandings of international and national development (and the Third World) by considering the possibility of regional development-security frameworks for progress. As noted, such approaches would involve the recalibration of conceptions of national sovereignty with an emphasis on open-ended and multi-tiered notions of where political power and authority ought to best be lodged in order to facilitate more inclusive forms of development and human prospects. With such an approach, it becomes at least possible to jettison monolithic and 'partially universalist' conceptions and practices of modernity and modernization. It could be seen as an opportunity to facilitate more progressive politics, not least by drawing on the practices and experiences of social movements, indigenous peoples, peasant activists and other politically engaged transformative agents. It is these political actors who have often been central to pointing out the contradictions we have outlined above, but have at the same time also been central in devising and practising alternatives to the dominant conception of development. In addition, all of these groups have gained their political experience in decidedly transnational settings, and forged linkages on the explicit basis of challenging nation-state-centered forms of governance. As a brief glance at different regionalist projects will readily confirm, much of this 'transnational movement expertise' has informed and substantively shaped political engagement with, for instance, regional trade agreements at all levels. Consider, for example, the NAFTA case, which, as a result of transnationalized contestation, especially by labour and environmental groups, had to be reconceived to include side-agreements and special institutional provisions (though these have not ended the politics of contestation!). The implications of such political social movement dimensions at the level of institutional development have long been noted under the header of a shift from multilateralism to 'complex multilateralism' (O'Brien *et al.* 2000; Thomas and Weber 1999). In the context of a strengthening of regional development-security frameworks, these 'post-sovereign' political formations are important potential contributors.

In the light of such insights, it is clear that the numerous contemporary regional approaches (new and old) of the post-Cold War era (and this includes the European Union, which is setting the agenda for the deepening of regional organizations) do not go nearly as far as we are suggesting. It is, of course, worth noting that the focus on regionalism is not new; at the same time there is no compulsive logic, which could or will ensure that regional efforts avoid the re-occurrence of potentially key problematic elements or flaws typical of earlier attempts to turn Third Worldism's political project into a regional and/or global institutional reality. In contrast to Third Worldism, the regional alternative we are proposing is about comprehensively revising and redistributing political authority; something centralizing (and often not particularly democratic) post-colonial nation-states have often had little or no interest in doing. However, the new multi-tiered regionalism still underscores something that proponents of various versions of Third Worldism were aware of from the outset: independent sovereign nation-states could not and cannot achieve progress without recourse to larger political associations.

On the potential of important shifts towards regional development-security frameworks, it is worth recalling that the relatively small number of nation-states that did make significant progress after 1945, such as in parts of Northeast and Southeast Asia, not to ignore large parts of Europe, did so in relationship to implicit or explicit forms of security- and development-oriented regionalism, or at least profound levels of bilateral or multilateral linkages to other sovereign nation-states and to the key geopolitical actors of the Cold War, the US and the USSR. The proponents of Third Worldism did realize that national success depended on some sort of regional framework (expressed in Third Worldism). We also make the point that the Third World has long since lost its value as a useful descriptive and/or prescriptive term for achieving a more inclusive global modernity and those who remain committed to it are putting far too much faith in the notion of the Third World and in the role of the sovereign nation-state as both a symbol of and means by which to achieve development and security for the vast majority of its citizens. This problem is simply compounded by the usage of the term Third World as interchangeable with poverty and underdevelopment.

## Global Modernity I: The Third World and the Rise and Fall of Third Worldism

As we have seen the actual term 'the Third World' was first used in 1952 by Alfred Sauvy, a French demographer. However, it was the

Bandung Conference of 1955 that appears to have really kick-started the idea of the Third World in relation to the First World centred on the US and the Second World centred on the USSR in the Cold War. Importantly, as M. K. Pasha has noted (Pasha 2013: 148): 'In Bandung's shadow, the "Third World" was no longer' regarded as a 'pejorative term, but as a positive marker and virtue, a political alternative to colonialism and the hegemonic grasp of the two superpowers'. Following Bandung, the term was often used to generate unity among a growing number of non-aligned nation-states that wanted to avoid taking sides in the Cold War. As we have seen, the idea of a Third World and Third Worldism was promoted by influential anticolonial nationalists, such as Jawaharlal Nehru and Sukarno, who called for a political non-alignment and a distinct path, or paths, to global modernity that followed neither the liberal capitalism of the First World or the state socialism of the Second World.

Meanwhile, in academia as well as among policymakers in both of the Cold War blocs, the idea of a Third World was severed from the political project of the Non-Aligned Movement (NAM) and Third Worldism, and became central to a growing body of academic and policy-oriented work on economic development and underdevelopment. Since the 1960s cohort after cohort of development specialists and policymakers have explicitly or implicitly taken a romanticized version of a modern and developed North America (and/or Western Europe and laterally Japan and parts of East Asia), where the problems of development are seen to have been more or less solved, as a conceptual yardstick for development policy. The Third World was increasingly and comprehensively represented as underdeveloped, while the conditions of 'underdevelopment' became separated from the historical processes which had constituted them.

The idea of a Third World was refracted through the establishment of organizations such as the NAM in 1961. Following the Sino-Soviet split in 1960, Third Worldism also had its Soviet and Maoist varieties. The former was seen as incorporating those governments in the Third World, which were allied with the USSR. This Moscow-oriented Third Worldism sought to establish a broad front between the Second World and the Third World against the First World. The Maoist variant articulated a Beijing-oriented Third World, in which China was part of the Third World, against the First World, of which the USSR (the Second World) was also perceived to be a part. Meanwhile, rapidly and dramatically between the 1940s and the 1970s, a range of new nations based on former colonies in Asia, Africa, the Middle East and Oceania, emerged, a trend, which saw the membership of the United Nations (UN) rise from 51 to 156 nation-states by 1980. As a result Third World governments in general gained greater influence at the UN and this led (as we have seen) to a formal call by the United Nations in April 1974 for a New International Economic Order (NIEO) led by the socialist-oriented government of Algeria (Thomas 1985: 129). The advance of this more radical, but justice-oriented, re-imagining of political economic relations coincided with the rise, on the other end of the political spectrum, of neo-liberalism under the tutelage of the Reagan and Thatcher administrations (Prashad 2012: 16:17).

By the beginning of the 1980s initiatives associated with the NIEO were in retreat as the British government, particularly during Margaret Thatcher's premiership (1979–90) and the US government, especially during the presidency of Ronald Reagan (1981–88), sought to reinvigorate the Cold War and downplay the North–South conflict. In the case of the latter they argued that economic growth rendered obsolete any demands or requirements for policies aimed at the redistribution of wealth or the restructuring of the international economic order (except to realize economic growth). This outlook was backed up by North American and West European power over the International Monetary Fund (IMF) and the World Bank in the context of the newfound leverage provided by the debt crisis and the international recession of the early 1980s. In these circumstances the United Nations generally and the United Nations Conference on Trade and Development (UNCTAD) and the United Nations Development Program (UNDP) more specifically, increasingly became conduits for uneven globalization and neo-liberal development, rather than the earlier idea of state-led (and redistribution-oriented) national development as the cornerstone of international development and of successful Third Worldism (for a good discussion of these dynamics see Prashad 2012: 166–85).

## Global Modernity II: International Development, World Politics and the Contemporary Recycling of Third Worldism

Meanwhile, the contemporary recycling of Third Worldism, while providing inspiration to some, is at best a disappointing and superficial revision, if not a travesty of the earlier project. One of many important efforts is the growing interest in and support for the Beijing Consensus. As its name implies, it emerged as one obvious counterpart (or challenge) to the Washington Consensus, which in its early post-Cold War phase embodied the key elements of neo-liberalism and uneven globalization (the usage of the term Washington Consensus has now passed although neo-liberalism and uneven globalization continue to hold the high ground in international development and world politics). Nevertheless the challenge is out there and clearly encapsulated in books such as Halper's (2010) *The Beijing Consensus: How China's Authoritarian Model Will Dominate the 21st Century*. It is worth noting, however, that the author makes very clear some of the profound challenges faced by the People's Republic of China in managing its 'domestic' affairs and the profound limits that do and will continue to prevent it from emerging as a genuine global power leading a large entourage of client-allied nation-states in the wider geo-political landscape.

Another major challenge to the Washington Consensus and, perhaps, an attempt to reshape Third Worldism through a revised development discourse (from above) has been the so-called post-Washington Consensus (PWC). The basic premise of the PWC is that lessons have been learnt about the adverse effects of technocratic neo-liberalism, with its emphasis on macro-economic structural adjustment, and rapid labour market restructuring as preconditions for growth. The rhetoric of the PWC emphasizes state ownership of development processes, and understates the continuing role of various conditional restraints, and of investor-driven private-sector liberalization. However, as has been shown in quite some detail, as well as in comprehensive studies of the PWC's policy instruments, such as the Poverty Reduction Strategy Papers (PRSPs), the substance of PWC-driven development policies are still aligned tightly with the parameters of the Washington Consensus, despite the refashioned political rhetoric implying otherwise (Gill 2002; McMichael 2012: esp. 215–49; Jayasuriya 2006; Soederberg 2014; Weber 2006, 2010)

If such contemporary (implicit or explicit) versions of Third Worldism are in trouble their problems began well before the end of the Cold War, even if they did not become so manifestly obvious until the last decade of the twentieth century. Certainly, the end of the Cold War at the start of the 1990s saw an effort (if not a very convincing effort in our view) in some quarters to revitalize the idea of a Third

World), while others felt that the idea of a Third World had lost its analytical and political utility. The former argue that the new circumstances of the post-Cold War era could still be clarified and progress made via the elaboration and reconfiguration of the idea of the Third World. Critics of this idea emphasize that the spatial divisions of the Cold War era between the First, Second and Third Worlds had become practically useless by the 1990s compared to their relative usefulness in an earlier era.

## Global Modernity III: A Way Forward and the Regional Development-Security Framework?

Meeting the challenge of development and security, or a more inclusive global modernity if you will, in the context of the contradictions of state-centred development and associated relations of instability and inequality, is likely to require a move beyond theories and practices that remain grounded in the framework of the universal sovereign nation-state system. As noted before and discussed in Chapter 6, a comprehensive elaboration of a fully detailed, planned and negotiated development-security framework for progress, is beyond the scope of this particular book; however, by elaborating some elements of a new framework it was hoped that we could signal the outlines of a new challenge, and provoke new directions for debate. What was laid out was an open-ended proposal based on some immanent possibilities reflected in the rise of development and security oriented regionalism. What was emphasized was the potential value and the positive possibilities entailed in multi-tiered forms of political authority organized through regional frameworks. This could build in more flexibility in relation to political authority and facilitate a move away from the fetishizing of the sovereign territorial nation-state, which as a signifier and a means to carry us towards an inclusive and humane global modernity increasingly lacks resonance.

As noted in Chapter 6, at least since the end of the Cold War regional economic political and/or security initiatives have taken on new importance echoing in some cases older, post-colonial regionalisms (such as Pan-Africanism) as part of an effort to process the implications of neo-liberalism and uneven globalization, and the lack of nation-state-centred capacity to deliver positive and progressive forms of modernity. Regional organizations themselves, of course, contain the same contradictory neo-liberal development model, hence regional solutions, too, have the potential to become as inequitable and conflict prone as many contemporary nation-states. For instance, forms of regional integration oriented predominantly in terms of facilitating economic growth through trade liberalization and investor guarantees have been conducive to further increasing wealth gaps, zones of conflict and political contestation. In this context, there is more than ever a need for politically astute regional solutions that view the way forward as the pursuit of development and security within a regional framework, without losing sight of the substantive challenges involved in avoiding the reproduction of the contradictions of nationalist and neoliberal conceptions of development. Such a regional approach would offer a well-grounded understanding of the dynamics of the problems of specific nation-states, by setting them in a regional context, which is in turn (at least at this juncture) a more appropriate level to both understand and deal with the crisis of global modernity and the repeated failure of development and security efforts.

At this point it is hoped that as part of a rethinking of the Third World there would be great benefit in a shift in international development and world politics in the direction of a far more inclusive form of global modernity than predominates at this time in history. Paramount in all this, following on from the discussion above, is the procedural requirement for the creation or amplification of new regional development-security frameworks. To work as initiatives that mediate global modernity in the interests of the majority, these regional frameworks would have to block out the re-admittance of authoritarian or technocratic approaches to development and security that characterized the Cold War and/or post-Cold War era. The perspective taken here is that creating the contours of novel, much more inclusive and comprehensive regional development-security frameworks could be indispensable to rethinking the Third World and the future achievement of more inclusive and progressive forms of global modernity.

## Conclusion: Rethinking the Third World

This book has sought to both review and rethink the idea of the Third World between the 1950s (in the context of the histories of imperialism and colonialism, and the politics of decolonization) and the present, including a discussion of the decline of Third Worldism, against the backdrop of the end of the Cold War, the revitalization of the link between development and security after 9/11, and the crisis of global modernity.

Our rethinking of the Third World through an analysis of the political project of Third Worldism has been animated by the significance of the project's profound and lasting transformative influence in world political affairs. In substantive terms, Third Worldism successfully raised resistance to colonial rule and exploitation that had been justified in terms of racial hierarchies and reflected in practices comprising the most brutal politics of subjugation; as we have shown, these successes must also be seen in the context of tendencies towards reproducing pernicious forms of 'developmentalism', affecting not least, for instance, indigenous peoples, peasants, and /or minorities and dissidents. That said, the politics of race and racism would be undeniably more pronounced than they still are had it not been for Third Worldism. It is in this sense that we can appreciate that its beginnings were not linked to origin myths about nation-states, but struggles for emancipation from racialized colonial rule and imperialism, which had entailed enslavement and subjugation through forced labour systems and relations of expropriation. (Shilliam 2008, 2012: Grovogui 1996). The eventual project of Third Worldism carried forward both the passion and the hope associated with earlier forms of struggle for emancipation against racism and colonialism. Yet, it was to be a paradoxical project: the formal equality held out by the promises of nation-statehood was ultimately not able to wholly undermine the substantively unequal political and economic relations which persisted regardless. They were compounded by the broader political-economic framework conceived in terms of 'catch-up' that had already naturalized inequality in terms of a temporalizing logic, drawing on concepts such as the 'development ladder'. The fact that development, or the problem of development, came to be associated first and foremost with the Third World only served to further entrench the idea of 'development stages' as natural in comparison to other, ostensibly developed states. The contradictions of framing development in this fashion has come to increasing prominence in the twenty-first century.

It is against this background that we have briefly outlined a new agenda for an open-ended global modernity. We have sketched out a regional development-security framework for progress that could, in our view, help carry the pursuit of progress beyond preoccupations with the sovereign nation-state as the 'object of development' (Mitchell 2002: esp. 209–43).

This agenda still has one obvious link to an earlier Third Worldism: they both share the assumption that sovereign nation-states are rarely if ever able to pursue progress on their own and successfully pursue a more inclusive global modernity: the history of nation-states has always been in relation to bilateral and multilateral relationships between other sovereign nation-states (relationships that are sometimes implicit and at other times explicit). The obvious lessons learnt from this process were already prevalent at the moment of the formal independence of Third World states (hence their collective call for the NIEO). What we add to these approaches (among other aspects) is the close scrutiny of the nation-state and the idea of national development itself. However, our objective in so doing is not to assume that a different scale of political organization necessarily holds the solution, nor do we wish to romanticize regions. The critical potential of this approach lies in shifting the development discourse from the current foci on measuring and homogenizing the nation states based on comparative assessments of standardized performances towards more pluralistic political arrangements comprising more equitable and humane possibilities. It is in this sense that rethinking the "Third World' is, and must also be about critically reflecting on the politics of global development (cf. Saurin 1996; McMichael 2010). What we add in our study (among other aspects) is a critical reappraisal of the nation-state and the idea of national development itself. For all its contradictions, the political project of Third Worldism was in its heyday a radical political project that sought to significantly reframe global political relations. That radical vision and the politics that went with it still resonate down to the present day.

# Bibliography

Abernethy, D.B. (2002) *The Dynamics of Global Dominance: European Overseas Empires, 1415–1980* (New Haven: Yale University Press).

Adams, F. (2000) *Dollar Diplomacy: United States Foreign Assistance to Latin America* (Aldershot: Ashgate).

Adas, M. (1989) *Machines as the Measure of Men: Science, Technology, and Ideologies of Western Dominance* (Ithaca: Cornell University Press).

Alfred, T. (1999) *Peace, Power, Righteousness. An Indigenous Manifesto* (Oxford: Oxford University Press).

Amin, S. (1997) *Capitalism in the Age of Globalization* (London: Zed Books).

Amin, S. (2006) 'The Millennium Development Goals: A Critique from the South, *Monthly Review*, 57:10, 1–15.

Amsden, A.H. (1989) *Asia's Next Giant: South Korea and Late Industrialization* (New York: Oxford University Press).

Amsden, A.H. (2001) *The Rise of "The Rest": Challenges to the West from Late-Industrializing Economies* (New York: Oxford University Press).

Anderson, B. (1992) *Imagined Communities: Reflections on the Origin and Spread of Nationalism*, 2nd edn (London: Verso).

Anderson, B. (1998) *The Spectre of Comparisons* (London: Verso).

Anderson, P. (1984) 'Modernity and Revolution', *New Left Review*, I.

Anderson, P. (1998) *The Origins of Postmodernity* (London: Verso).

Ash, T.G. (2004) *Free World: America, Europe, and the Surprising Future of the West* (New York: Vintage).

Babb, S. (2001) *Managing Mexico: Economists from Nationalism to Neoliberalism* (Princeton: Princeton University Press).

Ballentine, K. and Sherman, J. (2003a) 'Introduction', in Ballentine, K. and Sherman, J. (eds), *The Political Economy of Armed Conflict: Beyond Greed and Grievance* (Boulder: Lynne Rienner).

Ballentine, K. and Sherman, J. (eds) (2003b) *The Political Economy of Armed Conflict: Beyond Greed and Grievance* (Boulder: Lynne Rienner).

Baran, P. (1957) *The Political Economy of Growth* (New York: Monthly Review Press).

Barndt, D. (1997) 'Bio/cultural Diversity and Equity in Post-NAFTA Mexico (or Tomasita Comes North While Big Mac Goes South)', in Drydyk J.and Penz, J. (eds), *Global Justice, Global Democracy* (Winnipeg: Fernwood Publishing).

Beaucage, P. (1998) 'The Third Wave of Modernization: Liberalism, Salinismo, and Indigenous Peasants in Mexico', in Phillips, L. (ed.), *The Third Wave of Modernization in Latin America: Cultural Perspective on Neo-Liberalism* (Wilmington, DE: Scholarly Resources Books).

Bedford, K. (2007) 'The Imperative of Male Inclusion: How Institutional Context Influences World Bank Gender Policy', *International Feminist Journal of Politics* 9:3, 289–311.

Bellamy, A.J., Williams, P. and Griffin, S. (2004) *Understanding Peacekeeping* (Cambridge: Polity Press).

Benjamin, J.R. (1987) 'The Framework of U.S. Relations with Latin America in the Twentieth Century: An Interpretive Essay', *Diplomatic History,* 11, 91–112.

Berger, M.T. (1995) *Under Northern Eyes: Latin American Studies and US Hegemony in the Americas 1898–1990* (Bloomington: Indiana University Press).

Berger, M.T. (1996) 'Southeast Asian Trajectories: Eurocentrism and the History of the Modern Nation-State', *Bulletin of Concerned Asian Scholars,* 28.

Berger, M.T. (1999) 'APEC and Its Enemies: The Failure of the New Regionalism in the Asia-Pacific', *Third World Quarterly,* 20, 1013–30.

Berger, M.T. (2000) '(De)Constructing the New Order: The Path to Democratic Capitalist Modernity and the Social and Cultural Contours of the Patrimonial State in Indonesia', in Souchou, Y. (ed.), *House of Glass: Culture, Modernity, and the State in Southeast Asia* (Singapore: Institute of Southeast Asian Studies).

Berger, M.T. (2003) 'The New Asian Renaissance and Its Discontents: National Narratives, Pan-Asian Visions and the Changing Post-Cold War Order', *International Politics,* 40, 195–221.

Berger, M.T. (2004a) *The Battle for Asia: From Decolonization to Globalization* (London: Routledge).

Berger, M.T. (2004b) 'Decolonizing Southeast Asia: Nationalism, Revolution and the Cold War', in Beeson, M. (ed.), *Contemporary Southeast Asia: Regional Dynamics, National Differences* (Basingstoke: Palgrave Macmillan).

Berger, M.T. and Reese, J.Y. (2010) 'From Nation-States in Conflict to Conflict in Nation States: The United States of America and Nation Building from South Vietnam to Afghanistan', *International Politics,* 47, 451–71.

Bieler, A. (2011) 'Labour, new social movements and the resistance to neo-liberal restructuring in Europe', *New Political Economy,* 16(2), 163–83.

Bose, S. (1997) 'Instruments and Idioms of Colonial and National Development: India's Historial Experience in Comparative Perspective', in Cooper, F. and Packard, R. (eds), *International Development and the*

*Social Sciences: Essays on the History and Politics of Knowledge* (Berkeley: University of California Press).

Bremer, P.L. and McConnell, M. (2006) *My Year in Iraq: The Struggle to Build a Future of Hope* (New York: Simon & Schuster).

Brenner, R. (1998) 'Uneven Development and the Long Downturn: The Advanced Capitalist Economies from Boom to Stagnation, 1950-1998', *New Left Review*, I.

Bresnan, J. (1993) *Managing Indonesia: The Modern Political Economy* (New York: Columbia University Press).

Breuilly, J. (1985) *Nationalism and the State* (Manchester: Manchester University Press).

Bury, J.B. (1955) *The Idea of Progress: An Inquiry Into Its Origins and Growth* (New York: Dover Publications). (First published 1920.)

Byman, D.L. and Pollack, K.M. (2007) *Things Fall Apart: Containing the Spillover from an Iraqi Civil War* (Washington, DC: Brookings Institution Press).

Callahan, M.P. (2003) *Making Enemies: War and State Building in Burma* (Ithaca: Cornell University Press).

Calvert, P. and Calvert, S. (1996) *Politics and Society in the Third World: An Introduction* (London: Harvester Wheatsheaf).

Cammack, P. (2002) 'The Mother of All Governments: The World Bank's Matrix for Global Governance', in R. Wilkinson and S. Hughes (eds), *Global Governance: Critical Perspectives* (London: Routledge).

Carothers, T. (1999) *Aiding Democracy Abroad: The Learning Curve* (Washington, DC: Brookings Institution Press).

Carroll, T. (2010) *Delusions of Development: The World Bank and the Post-Washington Consensus in South East Asia* (Basingstoke: Palgrave Macmillan).

Castells, M. (1992) 'Four Asian Tigers With A Dragon Head: A Comparative Analysis of the State, Economy and Society in the Asian Pacific Rim', in Appelbaum, R.P. and Henderson, J. (eds), *States and Development in the Asian Pacific Rim* (Newbury Park: Sage).

Castells, M. (1996) *The Rise of the Network Society (The Information Age: Economy, Society and Culture, Volume 1)* (Oxford: Blackwell).

Castells, M. (1997) *The Power of Identity (The Information Age: Economy, Society and Culture, Volume II)* 2nd edn (Oxford: Blackwell).

Castells, M. (1998) *End of Millennium (The Information Age: Economy, Society and Culture, Volume III)* (Oxford: Blackwell).

Cell, J.W. (1992) *Hailey: A Study in British Imperialism, 1872–1969* (Cambridge: Cambridge University Press).

Cerny, P.G. (1990) *The Changing Architecture of Politics – Structure, Agency and the Future of the State* (London: Sage).

Cerny, P.G. (1993) 'The Political Economy of International Finance', in

Cerny, P.G (ed.), *Finance and World Politics: Markets, Regimes and States in the post-hegemonic era* (Aldershot: Edward Elgar).

Cerny, P. G. (1997) 'Paradoxes of the Competition State: The Dynamics of Political Globalization', *Government and Opposition*, 32, 251–74.

Chakrabarty, D. (2000) *Provincializing Europe – Postcolonial Thought and Historical Difference* (Princeton: Princeton University Press).

Chang, H.-J. (2002) *Kicking Away the Ladder: Development Strategy in Historical Perspective* (London: Anthem Press).

Chatterjee, P. (1986) *Nationalist Thought and the Colonial World: A Derivative Discourse* (London: Zed Books).

Chatterjee, P. (1993) *The Nation and Its Fragments: Colonial and Postcolonial Histories* (Princeton: Princeton University Press).

Clapham, C. (1998) 'Degrees of Statehood', *Review of International Studies*, 24, 143–57.

Collier, P. (2000) 'Doing Well out of War: An Economic Perspective', in Berdal, M.R. and Malone, D.M. (eds), *Greed and Grievance: Economic Agendas in Civil Wars* (Boulder: Lynne Rienner).

Collier, P. (2003) B*reaking the Conflict Trap: Civil War and Development Policy* (Washington, DC: World Bank and Oxford University Press).

Collier, P. (2007) *The Bottom Billion* (Oxford: Oxford University Press).

Collier, P. and Hoeffler, A. (2000) *Greed and Grievance in Civil War* (New York: Oxford University Press and the World Bank). (First published 1999.)

Conklin, A. (2000) *A Mission to Civilize: The Republican Idea of Empire in France and West Africa, 1895–1930* (Stanford: Stanford University Press).

Cooper, F. (1996) *Decolonization and African Society: The Labor Question in French and British Africa* (Cambridge: Cambridge University Press).

Cooper, F. (1997) 'Modernizing Bureaucrats, Backward Africans, and the Development Concept', in Cooper, F. and Packard, R. (eds), *International Development and the Social Sciences: Essays on the History and Politics of Knowledge* (Berkeley: University of California Press).

Cooper, F. (2005) *Colonialism in Question – Theory, Knowledge, History* (Berkeley: University of California Press).

Cooper, F. and Packard, R. (1997) 'Introduction', in Cooper, F. and Packard, R. (eds), *International Development and the Social Sciences: Essays on the History and Politics of Knowledge* (Berkeley: University of California Press).

Corbridge, S. and Harriss, J. (2000) *Reinventing India: Liberalization, Hindu Nationalism and Popular Democracy* (Cambridge: Polity).

Cowen, M.P. and Shenton, R.W. (1996) *Doctrines of Development* (New York: Routledge).

Crawford, N. (1994) 'A security regime among democracies: Cooperation among Iroquois Nations', *International Organization,* 48(3): 345–385.

Crews, R.D. and Tarzi, A. (eds) (2008) *The Taliban and the Crisis of Afghanistan* (Cambridge, MA: Harvard University Press).

Cribb, R. (1999) 'Nation: Making Indonesia', in Emmerson, D.K. (ed.), *Indonesia Beyond Suharto: Polity, Economy, Society, Transition* (London: M.E. Sharpe).

Cumings, B. (1999) 'Webs With No Spiders, Spiders With No Webs: The Genealogy of the Developmental State', in Woo-Cumings, M. (ed.), *The Developmental State* (Ithaca: Cornell University Press).

Cutler, C. (2003) *Private Power and Global Authority – Transnational Merchant Law in the Global Political Economy* (Cambridge: Cambridge University Press).

Daniel, D.C.F. and Ross, A.L. (1999) 'US Strategic Planning and the Pivotal States', in Chase, R.S., Hill, E.B. and Kennedy, P.M. (eds), *The Pivotal States: A New Framework for US Policy in the Developing World* (New York: Norton).

Darby, P. (1987) *Three Faces of Imperialism: British and American Approaches to Asia and Africa 18701970* (New Haven: Yale University Press).

Davis, M. (2006) *Planet of Slums* (London: Verso).

Deutsch, K.W. (1953) *Nationalism and Social Communication: An Inquiry into the Foundations of Nationality* (Cambridge, MA: Harvard University Press).

Dirlik, A. (1994) *After the Revolution: Waking to Global Capitalism* (Hanover: Wesleyan University Press).

Dixon, C. (1991) *South East Asia in the World Economy* (Cambridge: Cambridge University Press).

Dodge, T. (2003) *Inventing Iraq: The Failure of Nation-Building and a History Denied* (New York: Columbia University Press).

Doty, R.L. (1996) *Imperial Encounters: the Politics of Representation in North-South Relations* (Minneapolis: University of Minnesota Press).

Duara, P. (1995) *Rescuing History from the Nation – Questioning Narratives of Modern China* (Chicago: University of Chicago Press).

Duffield, M. (2001) *Global Governance and the New Wars: The Merging of Development and Security* (London: Zed Books).

Dunkerley, J. (1994) *The Pacification of Central America: Political Change in the Isthmus, 1987–1993* (London: Verso Books).

Elias, J. (2008) 'Struggles over the Rights of Foreign Domestic Workers in Malaysia: The Possibilities and Limitations of "Rights Talk"', *Economy and Society*, 37(2): 282–303.

Elias, J. (2014) 'Davos Woman to the Rescue of Global Capitalism: Post-Feminist Politics and Competitiveness Promotion at the World Economic Forum', *International Political Sociology*, 7:2, 152–69.

Eller, J.D. and Coughlan, R.M. (1993) 'The Poverty of Primordialism: The Demystification of Ethnic Attachments', *Ethnic and Racial Studies,* 16.

Enloe, C. (2000) *Bananas, Beaches and Bases: Making Feminist Sense of International Politics* (Berkeley: University of California Press).

Ertman, T. (1997) *Birth of the Leviathan: Building States and Regimes in Medieval and Early Modern Europe* (Cambridge: Cambridge University Press).

Escobar, A. (1995) *Encountering Development – The Making and Unmaking of the Third World* (Princeton: Princeton University Press).

Esteva, Gustavo (1992) 'Development', in Wolfgang Sachs (ed.), *The Development Dictionary* (London: Zed Books).

Evans, G. and Rowley, K. (1990) *Red Brotherhood at War: Vietnam, Cambodia and Laos Since 1975* (Thousand Oaks: Verso Books).

Fairbank, J., Reischauer, E. and Craig, A. (1973) *East Asia: Tradition and Transformation, Revised Edition* (Boston: Houghton Mifflin).

Fajnzylber, F. (1990) 'The United States and Japan as Models of Industrialisation', in Gereffi, G. and Wyman, D.L. (eds), *Manufacturing Miracles: Paths of Industrialization in Latin America and East Asia* (Princeton: Princeton University Press).

Fearon, J.D. and Laitin, D.D. (2003) 'Ethnicity, Insurgency and Civil War', *American Political Science Review,* 97(1), 75–90.

Ferguson, N. (2006) *The War of the World* (New York: Penguin Books).

Fieldhouse, D.K., (1982) 'Decolonization, Development, and Dependence: A Survey of Changing Attitudes', in Gifford, P., Louis, W.R. (eds), *The Transfer of Power in Africa: Decolonization, 1940–1960* (New Haven:Yale University Press).

Fukuyama, F. (2006a) 'Guidelines for Future Nation-Builders', in Fukuyama, F. (ed.), *Nation-Building: Beyond Afghanistan and Iraq* (Baltimore: The Johns Hopkins University Press).

Frank A. G., (1966) *The Development of Underdevelopment* (New York: Monthly Review Press).

Frank A. G., (1967) *Capitalism and Underdevelopment in Latin America* (New York: Monthly Review Press).

Fukuyama, F. (2006b) 'Lessons of Nation-Builders', in Fukuyama, F. (ed.), *Nation-Building: Beyond Afghanistan and Iraq* (Baltimore: The Johns Hopkins University Press).

Fukuyama, F. (ed.) (2006c) *Nation-Building: Beyond Afghanistan and Iraq* (Baltimore: The Johns Hopkins University Press).

Furnivall, J.S. (1939) *Netherlands India: A Study of Plural Economy* (Cambridge: Cambridge University Press).

Furnivall, J.S. (1948) *Colonial Policy and Practice: A Comparative Study of Burma and Netherlands India* (Cambridge: Cambridge University Press).

Furnivall, J.S. (1991) *The Fashioning of Leviathan: The Beginnings of British Rule in Burma* (Canberra: Australian National University).

Gay, P. (1967) *The Rise of Modern Paganism, Volume 1 of The Enlightenment: An Interpretation* (London: Weidenfeld & Nicolson).

Gay, P. (1970) *The Science of Freedom* (London: Weidenfeld & Nicolson).

Gellner, E, (1983) *Nations and Nationalism* (Oxford: Basil Blackwell).

Gershoni, I. and Jankowski, J. (1997) 'Introduction', in Gershoni, I., Jankowski, J. (eds), *Rethinking Nationalism in the Arab Middle East* (New York: Columbia University Press).

Ghani, A. and Lockhart, C. (2008) *Fixing Failed States: A Framework for Rebuilding a Fractured World* (New York: Oxford University Press).

Gill, S. (2002) 'Constitutionalizing Inequality and the Clash of Globalizations', *International Studies Review,* 4, 47–65.

Gleditsch, N.P. (2000) 'Armed Conflict and Environment', in Diehl, P. and Gleditsch, N.P. (eds), *Environmental Conflict: An Anthology* (Boulder: Westview).

Goodson, L.P. (2006) 'Lessons of Nation-Building in Afghanistan', in Fukuyama, F. (ed.), *Nation-Building: Beyond Afghanistan and Iraq* (Baltimore: The Johns Hopkins University Press).

Gowan, P. (1999) *The Global Gamble: Washington's Faustian Bid for World Dominance* (London: Verso).

Grovogui, S.N. (1996) *Sovereigns, Quasi Sovereigns, and Africans. Race and Self-Determination in International Law* (Minneapolis: University of Minnesota Press).

Grovogui, S.N. (2001) 'Come to Africa: A Hermeneutics of Race in International Theory', *Alternatives,* 26, 425–48.

Grovogui, S.N. (2002) 'Regimes of Sovereignty: Rethinking International Morality and the African Condition', *European Journal of International Relations,* 8 (3), 315–38.

Grovogui, S.N. (2011) 'To the Orphaned, Dispossessed, and Illegitimate Children: Human Rights Beyond Republican and Liberal Traditions', *Indiana Journal of Global Legal Studies*, 81:1, 41–63.

Guha, R. (1997) *Dominance without Hegemony- History and Power in Colonial India* (Cambridge, MA: Harvard University Press).

Habermas, J. (1985) 'Modernity: An Incomplete Project', in Foster, H. (ed.), *Postmodern Culture* (London: Pluto Press).

Hagedorn, J.M., (2008). *A World of Gangs: Armed Young Men and Gangsta Culture.* (Minneapolis: University of Minnesota Press).

Hall, R.B. (1999) *National Collective Identity: Social Constructs and International Systems* (New York: Columbia University Press).

Halper, S. (2010) *Beijing Consensus: How China's Authoritarian Model Will Dominate the Twenty-First Century* (New York: Basic Books).

Hameiri, S. (2009) 'Beyond Methodological Nationalism, but where to for the Study of Regional Governance?', *Australian Journal of International Affairs,* 63(3), 430–41.

Hameiri, S. (2013) 'Theorizing Regions through Changes in Statehood –

Rethinking the Theory and Method of Comparative Regionalism', *Review of International Studies* 39(2), 313–35.

Hardt, M. and Negri, A. (2001) *Empire* (Cambridge, MA: Harvard University Press).

Harris, N. (1986) *The End of the Third World: Newly Industrializing Countries and the Decline of an Ideology* (London: I. B. Tauris).

Harvey, D. (1989) *The Condition of Postmodernity* (Oxford: Basil Blackwell).

Hauge, W. and Ellingsen, T. (2000) 'Causal Pathways to Conflict', in Diehl, P. and Gleditsch, N.P. (eds), *Environmental Conflict: An Anthology* (Boulder: Westview).

Havinden, M.A. and Meredith, D. (eds) (1996) *Colonialism and Development: Britain and its Tropical Colonies, 1850–1960* (London: Routledge).

Headrick, D.R. (1981) *The Tools of Empire: Technology and European Imperialism in the Nineteenth Century* (New York: Oxford University Press).

Headrick, D.R. (1988) *The Tentacles of Progress: Technology Transfer in the Age of Imperialism, 1850–1940* (New York: Oxford University Press).

Helleiner, E. (1992) *States and the Re-emergence of Global Finance* (Ithaca: Cornell University Press).

Higgott, R. and Weber, H. (2005) 'GATS in Context: development, an evolving lex mercatoria and the Doha Agenda', *Review of International Political Economy,* 12, 434–55.

Hindess, B. (2007) 'The Past is Another Culture', *International Political Sociology,* 1, 325–38.

Hobsbawm, E. (1994) *The Age of Empire: 1875–1914* (London: Abacus).

Hollister, W., McGee, S. and Stokes, G. (2000) *The West Transformed: A History of Western Civilization, Volume I, to 1715* (Fort Worth: Harcourt Brace).

Homer-Dixon, T.F. (1999) *Environment, Scarcity, and Violence* (Princeton: Princeton University Press).

Hoselitz, B. F. (1952) 'Non-Economic Barriers to Economic Development', *Economic Development and Cultural Change,* 1, 8–21.

Huntington, S.P., (1968) *Political Order in Changing Societies* (New Haven: Yale University Press).

Hutchinson, J. (1994) *Modern Nationalism* (London: Fontana Press).

Hutchinson, J. and A.D. Smith (eds) (1994) *Nationalism* (Oxford: Oxford University Press).

Ichiro, T. (1997) 'Colonialism and the Sciences of Tropical Zones: The Academic Analysis of Difference in "the Island Peoples"', in Barlow, T.E. (ed.), *Formations of Colonial Modernity in East Asia* (Durham: Duke University Press).

Inikori, J.E. (2002) *Africans and the Industrial Revolution in England: a*

*Study in International Trade and Economic Development* (Cambridge: Cambridge University Press).

Jackson, R.H. (1990) *Quasi-States: Sovereignty, International Relations and the Third World* (Cambridge: Cambridge University Press).

Jalal, A. (1990) *The State of Martial Rule: The Origins of Pakistan's Political Economy of Defence* (Cambridge: Cambridge University Press).

Jayasuria, K. (2006) *Statecraft, Welfare, and the Politics of Inclusion* (Basingstoke: Palgrave Macmillan).

Jayasuria, K. (2009) 'Regulatory Regionalism in the Asia-Pacific', *Australian Journal of International Affairs*, 63(3), 335–47.

Johnson, C.A. (1982) *MITI and the Japanese Miracle: The Growth of Industrial Policy, 1925–1975* (Stanford: Stanford University Press).

Jowitt, K. (1993) *New World Disorder: The Leninist Extinction* (Berkeley: University of California Press).

Juergensmeyer, M., (2008), *Global Rebellion: Religious Challenges to the Secular State, from Christian Militias to Al Qaeda* (Berkeley: University of California Press).

Jung, W.B. (1988) *Nation Building: The Geopolitical History of Korea* (Lanham: University Press of America).

Kaldor, M. (2003) 'The Idea of Global Civil Society', *International Affairs*, 79, 583–93.

Kang, D.C. (2002) *Crony Capitalism: Corruption and Development in South Korea and the Philippines* (Cambridge: Cambridge University Press).

Karsh, E. and Karsh, I. (1999) *Empires of the Sand: The Struggle for Mastery in the Middle East, 1789–1923* (Cambridge, MA: Harvard University Press).

Katzenstein, P.J. (2005) *A World of Regions: Asia and Europe in the American Imperium* (Ithaca, NY: Cornell University Press).

Keane, J. (2001) *Global Civil Society* (Oxford: Oxford University Press).

Kedzie, C.R. and Aragon, J. (2002) 'Coincident Revolutions and the Dictator's Dilemma', in Allison, J.E. (ed.), *Technology, Development, and Democracy: International Conflict and Cooperation in the Information Age* (Albany: State University of New York Press).

Keen, D. (2000) 'Incentives and Disincentives for Violence', in Berdal, M.R. and Malone, D.M. (eds), *Greed and Grievance: Economic Agendas in Civil Wars* (Boulder: Lynne Rienner).

Kennedy, P. (1989) *The Rise and Fall of the Great Powers: Economic Change and Military Conflict 1500 to 2000* (London: Fontana).

Kennedy, P. (2006) *The Parliament of Man: The Past, Present, and Future of the United Nations* (New York: Random House).

Kertzer, D.I. (1988) *Ritual, Politics, and Power* (New Haven: Yale University Press).

Keylor, William R. (2008) *A World of Nations: The International Order*, second edn (New York: Oxford University Press).

Kilcullen, D. (2009) *The Accidental Guerrilla: Fighting Small Wars in the Midst of a Big One* (New York: Oxford University Press).

Kim, S.S. (2000) 'Korea and Globalization (Segyehwa): A Framework for Analysis', in Kim, S.S. (ed.), *Korea's Globalization* (Cambridge: Cambridge University Press).

Kingston, P.W.T. (1996) *Britain and the Politics of Modernization in the Middle East, 1945–1958* (Cambridge: Cambridge University Press).

Knock, T.J. (1992) *To End All Wars: Woodrow Wilson and the Quest for a New World Order* (New York: Oxford University Press).

Krasner, S.D. (1985) *Structural Conflict: The Third World Against Global Liberalism* (Berkeley: University of California Press).

Lacher, H. (1999) 'The Politics of the Market: Re-reading Karl Polanyi', *Global Society,* 13, 313–26.

LaFeber, W. (1993) *Inevitable Revolutions: The United States in Central America* (New York: Norton).

Laitin, D.D. (2007) *Nations, States, and Violence* (New York: Oxford University Press).

Lake, A. (1993) *From Containment to Enlargement* US Department of State Dispatch 4.

Larson, B. (2004) *Trials of Nation Making: Liberalism, Race, and Ethnicity in the Andes, 1810–1910* (Cambridge: Cambridge University Press).

Latham, R. (1997) *The Liberal Moment: Modernity, Security and the Making of Postwar International Order* (New York: Columbia University Press).

Lee, J.M. (1967) *Colonial Development and Good Government: A Study of the Ideas Expressed by the British Official Classes in Planning Decolonization 1939–1964* (Oxford: Clarendon).

LeoGrande, W.M. (1998) *Our Own Backyard: The United States In Central America, 1977–1992* (Chapel Hill: University of North Carolina Press).

Lockwood, W.W. (1965) 'Japan's New Capitalism', in Lockwood, W.W. (ed.), *State and Economic Enterprise in Japan* (Princeton: Princeton University Press).

Lomborg, B. (2000) 'Resource Constraints or Abundance', in Diehl, P. and Gleditsch, N.P. (eds), *Environmental Conflict: An Anthology* (Boulder: Westview).

Louis, W.R. (1984) *The British Empire in the Middle East, 1945–1951: Arab Nationalism, the United States, and Postwar Imperialism* (Oxford: Clarendon).

Lugard, F.D. (1922) *The Dual Mandate in British Tropical Africa* (London: Blackwood).

Lundestad, G. (2005) *East, West, North, South: Major Developments in International Relations Since 1945* (London: Sage).

Lustig, N. (1998) *Mexico: The Remaking of an Economy* (Washington, DC: Brookings Institution Press).

MacIntyre, A. (1997) 'South-East Asia and the Political Economy of APEC', in Rodan, G., Hewison, K. and Robison, R. (eds), *The Political Economy of Southeast-Asia: An Introduction* (Melbourne: Oxford University Press).

Malley, R. G. (1996) *The Call from Algeria: Third Worldism, Revolution, and the Turn to Islam* (Berkeley: University of California Press).

Mamdani, M. (1996) *Citizen and Subject: Contemporary Africa and the Legacy of Colonialism* (Princeton: Princeton University Press).

Martin, T. (2001) T*he Affirmative Action Empire: Nations and Nationalism in the Soviet Union, 1923–1939* (Ithaca: Cornell University Press).

Martinussen, J. (1997) *Society, State and Market: A Guide to Competing Theories of Development* (London: Zed Books).

Mazower, M. (1998) *Dark Continent: Europe's Twentieth Century* (London: Allen Lane).

McCarthy, J. (2001) *The Ottoman Peoples and the End of Empire* (New York: Oxford University Press).

McMahon, R.J. (1994) *The Cold War on the Periphery: The United States, India, and Pakistan* (New York: Columbia University Press).

McMichael, P. (2008) 'Peasants make Their Own History, But Not Just as They Please …', *Journal of Agrarian Change*, 8:2&3, 205–28.

McMichael, P. (2010) 'Changing the subject of development', In McMichael, P. (ed.), *Contesting Development: critical struggles for social change* (New York: Routledge).

McMichael, P. (2012) *Development and Social Change: A Global Perspective* (London, New York: Sage).

Melanson, R.A. (2000) *American Foreign Policy Since the Vietnam War: The Search for Consensus from Nixon to Clinton,* 3rd edn (New York: M. E. Sharpe).

Mill, J. (1820) *The History of British India* (London: Baldwin, Cradock & Joy).

Miller, B. (2007) *States, Nations, and the Great Powers: The Sources of Regional War and Peace* (New York: Cambridge University Press).

Mintz, S. W. (1986) *Sweetness and Power: The Place of Sugar in Modern History* (Harmondsworth: Penguin).

Mitchell, T. (2002) *Rule of Experts – Egypt, Techno-Politics, Modernity* (Berkeley: University of California Press).

Mittelman, J.H. (2000) *The Globalization Syndrome* (Princeton: Princeton University Press).

Miyoshi, M. (1993) 'A Borderless World? From Colonialism to Transnationalism and the Decline of the Nation-State', *Critical Inquiry,* 19.

Morgan, B. (2011) *Water on Tap – Rights and Regulation in the Transnational Governance of Urban Water Services* (Cambridge: Cambridge University Press).

Morphet, S. (1993) 'The Non-Aligned in "The New World Order": The Jakarta Summit, September 1992', *International Relations,* 11.

Morphet, S. (1996) 'Three Non-Aligned Summits – Harare 1986; Belgrade 1989 and Jakarta 1992', in Dunn, D.H. (ed.), *Diplomacy at the Highest Level: The Evolution of International Summitry* (London: Palgrave Macmillan).

Morris-Suzuki, T. (1994) *The Technological Transformation of Japan: From the Seventeenth to the Twenty-First Century* (Cambridge: Cambridge University Press).

Morten, A. D. (2000) 'Mexico, Neoliberal Restructuring and the ELZN – a Neo-Gramscian Analysis', in Gills, B. K. (ed.) *Globalization and the Politics of Resistance* (Basingstoke: Palgrave Macmillan).

Morten, A. D. (2011) *Revolution and the State in Modern Mexico* (London: Rowman & Littlefield).

Moteff, J. (1998) *Critical Infrastructures: A Primer, CRS Report for Congress* (Washington, DC: Congressional Research Service).

Murphy, C.N. (1983) 'What the Third World Wants: An Interpretation of the Development and Meaning of the New International Economic Order Ideology', *International Studies Quarterly,* 27.

Nandy, A. (2002) 'The Beautiful, Expanding Future of Poverty: Popular Economics as a Psychological Defense', *International Studies Review,* 4, 107–22.

Nasser, G.A., (1955) *Egypt's Liberation: The Philosophy of the Revolution* (Washington, DC: Public Affairs Press).

Nkrumah, K., (1966) *Neo-Colonialism: The Last Stage of Imperialism* (New York: International Publishers).

Nisbet, R. (1980) *History of the Idea of Progress* (London: Heinemann).

O'Brien, R., Goetz, A.M., Scholte, J.A. and Williams, M. (2000) 'Complex Multilateralism: MEIs and GSMs', in O'Brien, R. *et al.* (eds), *Contesting Global Governance: Multilateral Institutions and Global Social Movements* (Cambridge: Cambridge University Press).

O'Brien, R. and Williams, M. (2007) 'European Expansion', in O'Brien, R. and Williams, M. (eds), *Global Political Economy – Evolution and Dynamics* (Basingstoke: Palgrave Macmillan).

Office of the President of the United States (1996) *A National Security Strategy of Engagement and Enlargement* (Washington, DC: US Government Printing Office).

Ostrom, E. (1990) *Governing the Commons* (Cambridge: Cambridge University Press).

Owen, R. (1999) 'Egypt', in *The Pivotal States: A New Framework for US Policy in the Developing World* (New York: Norton).

Paige, J.M. (1997) *Coffee and Power: Revolution and the Rise of Democracy in Central America* (Cambridge, MA: Harvard University Press).

Partick, H. and Rosovsky, H. (1976) 'Japan's Economic Performance: An Overview' and 'Prospects for the Future and Some Other Implications', in

*Asia's New Giant: How the Japanese Economy Works* (Washington, DC: Brookings Institution Press).

Pasha, M.K. (2013) 'The "Bandung Impulse" and International Relations', in Seth, S. (ed.) *Postcolonial Theory and International Relations – a critical introduction* (London: Routledge).

Pastor, R.A. (ed.) (1987) *Latin America's Debt Crisis: Adjusting to the Past or Planning for the Future?* (Boulder: Lynne Rienner).

Patel, R. (2007) *Stuffed and Starved – the battle for the world food system* (Brooklyn: Melvin House Publishing).

Patel, R. (2009) *The Value of Nothing: How to Reshape Market Society and Redefine Democracy* (New York: Picador).

Peattie, M.R. (1984) 'Japanese Attitudes Toward Colonialism, 1895–1945', in Myers, R.H. and Peattie, M.R. (eds), *The Japanese Colonial Empire, 1895–1945* (Princeton: Princeton University Press).

Peck, J. (2010) *Construction of Neoliberal Reason* (Oxford: Oxford University Press).

Peck, J. and Tickell, A. (2002) 'Neoliberalizing Space', *Antipode,* 34, 380–404.

Perez, M.A. and Berger, M. (2009) 'Bordering on the Ridiculous: MexAmerica and the New Regionalism', *Alternatives–Global, Local, Political,* 34, 1–16.

Peters, G. (2009) *Seeds of Terror: How Heroin is Bankrolling the Taliban and al Qaeda* (New York: St Martin's Press).

Polanyi, K. (2001) *The Great Transformation – the political and economic origins of our time* (Boston: Beacon Press). (First published 1944.)

Porter, B.D. (1994) *War and the Rise of the State: The Military Foundations of Modern Politics* (New York: The Free Press).

Prakash, G. (1995) 'Introduction: After Colonialism', in Prakash, G. (ed.), *After Colonialism: Imperial Histories and Postcolonial Displacements* (Princeton: Princeton University Press).

Prashad, V. (2007) *The Darker Nations: A People's History of the Third World* (London: The New Press).

Prashad, V. (2012) *The Poorer Nations: A Possible History of the Global South* (London: Verso).

Prebisch, R. (1950) *The Economic Development of Latin America and its Principle Problems* (New York: United Nations Department of Economic Affairs).

Rajagopal, B. (2003) *International Law from Below: Development, Social Movements and Third World Resistance* (Cambridge: Cambridge University Press).

Rashid, A. (2008) *Descent into Chaos: The United States and the Failure of Nation Building in Pakistan, Afghanistan, and Central Asia* (New York: Viking).

Reno, W. (1998) *Warlord Politics and African States* (Boulder: Lynne Rienner).

Richani, N. (2002) *Systems of Violence: The Political Economy of War and Peace in Colombia* (Albany: State University of New York Press).

Ricks, T.E. (2007) *Fiasco: The American Military Adventure in Iraq* (New York: The Penguin Press).

Ricks, T.E. (2009) *The Gamble: General David Petraeus and the American Military Adventure in Iraq, 2006–2008* (New York: The Penguin Press).

Rist, G. (1996) *The History of Development: From Western Origins to Global Faith* (London: Zed Books).

Robertson, A.F. (1984) *People and the State* (Cambridge: Cambridge University Press).

Robinson, W.I. (1996) *Promoting Polyarchy: Globalization, US Intervention, and Hegemony* (Cambridge: Cambridge University Press).

Rodney, W., (1972) *How Europe Underdeveloped Africa* (London: Bogle-L'Ouverture Publications).

Roeder, P.G. (2007) *Where Nation-States Come From* (Princeton: Princeton University Press).

Rojas, C. (2002) *Civilization and Violence – Regimes of Representation in 19th Century Colombia* (Minneapolis: University of Minnesota Press).

Rostow, W.W. (1960) *The Stages of Economic Growth: A Non-Communist Manifesto* (Cambridge: Cambridge University Press).

Roy, O. (1986) *Islam and Resistance in Afghanistan* (Cambridge: Cambridge University Press).

Rubin, B.R. (2002) *The Fragmentation of Afghanistan: State Formation and Collapse in the International System*, 2nd edn (New Haven: Yale University Press).

Rubin, B.R. and Rashid, A. (2008) 'From Great Game to Grand Bargain', *Foreign Affairs,* 87.

Said, E. (1995) *Orientalism* (New York: Penguin). (First published 1978.)

Sachs, J. (2005) *The End of Poverty: Economic Possibilities for Our Time* (New York: The Penguin Press).

Sassen, S. (2006) *Territory, Authority, Rights: From Medieval to Global Assemblages* (Princeton: Princeton University Press).

Saurin, J. (1995) 'The End of International Relations? The State and International Theory in the Age of Globalization', in MacMillan, J. and Linklater, A. (eds), *Boundaries in Question: New Directions in International Relations* (London: Pinter).

Saurin, J. (1996) 'Globalisation, Poverty and the Promises of Modernity', *Millennium Journal of International Studies,* 25, 657–80.

Seth, S. (2013) 'Postcolonial Theory and the Critique of International Relations', in Seth, S. (ed), *Postcolonial Theory and International Relations – A Critical Introduction* (London: Routledge).

Seton-Watson, H. (1977) *Nations and States: An Enquiry into the Origins of Nations and the Politics of Nationalism* (London: Methuen).

Shah, K. (2009) 'The Failure of State-Building and the Promise of State Failure: Reinterpreting the Security-Development Nexus in Haiti', *Third World Quarterly,* 30, 17–34.

Shaw, K. (2002) 'Indigeneity and the International', *Millennium Journal of International Studies,* 31(1), 55–81.

Shaw, M. (2000) *Theory of the Global State: Globality as an Unfinished Revolution* (Cambridge: Cambridge University Press).

Shilliam, R. (2008) 'What the Haitian Revolution Tells Us about Development, Security, and the Politics of Race', *Comparative Studies in Society and History,* 50:3, 778–808.

Shilliam, R. (2012) 'Forget English Freedom, Remember Atlantic Slavery: Commercial Law and the significance of Slavery for Classical Political Economy', *New Political Economy,* 17, 591–609.

Shiva, V. (2009) *Soil Not Oil* (London: Zed Books).

Smith, A.D. (1989) 'State-Making and Nation Building', in *States in History* (Oxford: Blackwell).

Smith, A.D. (1993) *The Ethnic Origins of Nations* (Oxford: Wiley-Blackwell).

Soederberg, S. (2014) *Debt-fare States and the Poverty Industry: Money, Discipline and the Surplus Population* (London: Routledge).

Soysa, I. de (2000) 'The Resource Curse: Are Civil Wars Driven by Rapacity or Paucity?', in Berdal, M.R. and Malone, D.M. (eds), *Greed and Grievance: Economic Agendas in Civil Wars* (Boulder: Lynne Rienner).

Sparke, M. (2006) 'A Neoliberal Nexus: Economy, Security and the Bio-politics of Citizenship on the Border', *Political Geography,* 25, 151–80.

Stalin, J. (1994) 'Marxism and the National Question', in Hutchinson, J. and Smith, A.D. (eds), *Nationalism* (Oxford: Oxford University Press).

Standing, G. (2011) *The New Dangerous Class* (London: Bloomsbury Academic).

Stavrianos, L.S. (1981) *Global Rift: The Third World Comes of Age* (New York: William Morrow).

Steinberg, J.B. (2003) *Information Technology and Development: Beyond Either/Or* (Washington, DC: Brookings Institution Press).

Stokes, E. (1959) *The English Utilitarians and India* (Oxford: Clarendon).

Strakosch, E. (2014) 'Politics of Indigenous Development', in Weber, H. (ed.), *Politics of Development* (London: Routledge).

Suliman, S. (2014) 'The Politics of Migration and the North American Free Trade Agreement', in Weber, H. (ed.), *Politics of Development* (London: Routledge).

Tahir-Kheli, S. and Council on Foreign Relations (1997) *India, Pakistan, and the United States: Breaking With the Past* (New York: Council on Foreign Relations).

Taylor, B.D. and Botea, R. (2008) 'Tilly Tally: War-Making and State-Making in the Contemporary Third World' *International Studies Review,* 10.

Teik, K.B. (1995) *Paradoxes of Mahathirism: An Intellectual Biography of Mahathir Mohamad* (Kuala Lumpur: Oxford University Press).

Therborn, G. (1995) *European Modernity and Beyond: the Trajectory of European Societies, 1945–2000* (London: Sage).

Therborn, G. (2000) 'Reconsidering Revolutions', *New Left Review,* II.

Thomas, C. (1985) *New States, Sovereignty and Intervention* (Basingstoke: Palgrave Macmillan).

Thomas, C. (1987) *In Search of Security – The Third World in International Relations.* (Boulder: Lynne Rienner).

Thomas, C. (2000) *Global Governance, Development and Human Security* (London: Pluto).

Thomas, C. and Weber, M. (1999) 'New Values and International Organizations: Balancing Trade and Environment in the North American Free Trade Agreement (NAFTA)', in Taylor, A. and Thomas, C. (eds), *Global Trade and Global Social Issues* (London: Routledge).

Thomas, C. and Weber, M. (2004) 'Politics of Global Health Governance: Whatever happened to "Health for All by the Year 2000"?', *Global Governance,* 10, 187–205.

Thorne, C.G. (1973) *The Limits of Foreign Policy: The West, the League, and the Far Eastern Crisis of 1931–1933* (New York: G.P. Putnam's Sons).

Tilly, C. (1975) 'Reflections on the History of European State Making', in Tilly, C. (ed.), *The Formation of National States in Western Europe* (Princeton: Princeton University Press).

Tilly, C. (1992) *Coercion, Capital and European States: AD 990 – 1992* (Cambridge: Wiley/Blackwell).

Trager, F.N. (1961) 'John Sydenham Furnivall, February 14, 1878–July 7, 1960: An Appreciation', in *The Governance of Modern Burma* (New York: Institute of Pacific Relations).

Tripp, C.A. (2000) *A History of Iraq* (Cambridge: Cambridge University Press).

UN (2007) 'United Nations Declaration on the Rights of Indigenous Peoples' (available at http://daccess-ddsny.un.org/doc/UNDOC/GEN/N06/512/07/PDF/N0651207.pdf?OpenElement).

US DoD (1995) *United States Security Strategy for the East Asia and Pacific Region.*

USAID (1984) *Private Enterprise Development* (United States Agency for International Development, Bureau for Program and Policy Coordination).

USAID (n.d.) *Agency Objectives.*

von Albertini, R. (1982a) *Decolonization the Administration and Future of the Colonies, 1919–1960* (New York: Holmes & Meier).

von Albertini, R. (1982b) *European Colonial Rule, 1880–1940: The Impact of the West on India, Southeast Asia, and Africa* (Westport :Greenwood).

von Hippel, K. (2000) *Democracy by Force: US Military Intervention in the Post-Cold War World* (Cambridge: Cambridge University Press).

Wade, R. (1996) 'Globalization and Its Limits: Reports of the Death of the National Economy Are Greatly Exaggerated', in Berger, S. and Dore, R. (eds), *National Diversity and Global Capitalism* (Ithaca: Cornell University Press).

Walker, M. (1995) 'Pentagon Trapped in Political Crossfire', *The Guardian Weekly*, July 16.

Walker, R.B.J. (1993) *Inside/Outside – International Relations as Political Theory* (Cambridge: Cambridge University Press).

Walker, R.B.J. (2002) 'International/Inequality', *International Studies Review*, 4, 7–24.

Wallerstein, I.M. (1999) 'The Rise of East Asia, or the World-System in the Twenty-First Century', in Wallerstein, I.M. (ed.), *The End of the World As We Know It: Social Science for the Twenty-First Century* (Minneapolis: University of Minnesota Press).

Weber, H. (2002) 'The Imposition of a Global Development Architecture: The Example of Microcredit', *Review of International Studies*, 28, 537–55.

Weber, H. (2004) 'The "New Economy" and Social Risk: Banking on the Poor?' *Review of International Political Economy*, 11, 256–386.

Weber, H. (2006) 'A Political Analysis of the PRSP Initiative: Social Struggles and the Organization of Persistent Relations of Inequality', *Globalizations*, 3, 187–206.

Weber, H. (2007) 'A Political Analysis of the Formal Comparative Method: Historicizing the Globalization and Development Debate', *Globalizations*, 4, 559–72.

Weber, H. (2010) 'The Politics of Global Social Relations: Organising "Everyday Lived Experiences" of Development and Destitution', *Australian Journal of International Affairs*, 64, 105–22.

Weber, M. (2005) 'Alter-Globalization and Social Movements: Towards Understanding Transnational Politicization', in Hayden, P. and El-Ojeili, C. (eds) *Confronting Globalization: Humanity, Justice, and the Renewal of Politics* (New York: Palgrave Macmillan).

Weber, M. (2007) 'The Concept of Solidarity in the Study of World Politics –Towards a Critical Theoretic Understanding', *Review of International Studies*, 33(4): 693–713.

Weber, M. (2009) 'Understanding and Analysing Social Movements and Alternative Globalization', in Hayden, P. (ed.), *The Ashgate Research Companion to Ethics and International Relations* (Farnham: Ashgate).

Weber, S., Barma, N., Kroenig, M. and Ratner, E. (2007) 'How Globalization Went Bad', *Foreign Policy*.

Wedel, J.R. (1998) *Collision and Collusion: The Strange Case of Western Aid to Eastern Europe 1989–1998 (*New York: St Martin's Press).

Weiss, L. (1997) 'Globalization and the Myth of the Powerless State', *New Left Review,* I.

Weiss, L. (1998) T*he Myth of the Powerless State; Governing the Economy in a Global Era* (Cambridge: Polity).

Weiss, L. (1999) 'Managed Openness: Beyond Neoliberal Globalism', *New Left Review,* I.

Westad, O.A. (2000) 'A "New", "International" History of the Cold War?', *Diplomatic History,* 24.

Whitehead, L. (1984) *Debt, Diversification, and Dependency: Latin America's Changing International Political Relations* Latin American Program (Washington, DC: Wilson Center).

Williams, M. (1994) *International Economic Organisation and the Third World* (Hemel Hempstead: Harvester Wheatsheaf).

Winichakul, T. (1994) *Siam Mapped: A History of the Geo-Body of a Nation* (Honolulu: University of Hawaii Press).

Wolf-Phillips, L. (1987) 'Why "Third World"? Origin, Definition and Usage', *Third World Quarterly,* 9, 1311–27.

Woo, J.-E. (1991) *Race to the Swift: State and Finance in Korean Industrialization* (New York: Columbia University Press).

Woo-Cumings, M. (1998) 'National Security and the Rise of the Developmental State in South Korea and Taiwan', in Rowen, H.S. (ed.), *Behind East Asian Growth: The Political and Social Foundations of Prosperity* (London: Routledge).

Worsley, P. (1979) 'How Many Worlds', *Third World Quarterly,* 1.

Yew, L.K. (2000) *From Third World to First: The Singapore Story: 1965–2000* (New York: HarperCollins).

# Index

## 184   *Index*